COMPUTER SCIENCE, TECHNOLOGY AND APPLICATIONS

ARTIFICIAL INTELLIGENCE

WORK, MACHINES AND HUMAN INTERACTION

Computer Science, Technology and Applications

Additional books and e-books in this series can be found on Nova's website under the Series tab.

COMPUTER SCIENCE, TECHNOLOGY AND APPLICATIONS

ARTIFICIAL INTELLIGENCE

WORK, MACHINES AND HUMAN INTERACTION

TONYA RANDOLPH
EDITOR

snova
New York

Library of Congress Cataloging-in-Publication Data

ISBN: 978-1-68507-313-8

Published by Nova Science Publishers, Inc. † New York

CONTENTS

PREFACE

Today, many Americans are concerned about the impact that artificial intelligence and machine learning will have on jobs. This book examines the impact of these factors on the workforce, including issues related to worker displacement, retraining of the current workforce, and developing a skilled technical workforce of the future that can thrive in an economy in which AI increasingly plays a role.

Chapter 1 - On Tuesday, September 24, 2019 at 4:00 p.m., the Subcommittee on Research and Technology of the Committee on Science, Space, and Technology will hold a hearing to examine the impact of machine learning and artificial intelligence on the workforce, including issues related to worker displacement, retraining of the current workforce, and developing a skilled technical workforce of the future that can thrive in an economy in which AI increasingly plays a role. The Subcommittee will also explore the disparate impacts on different industry sectors and different populations, as well as issues of safety, privacy, and security relevant to the human-technology interface.

Chapter 2 - This is an edited, reformatted and augmented version of The Hearing before the Committee on the Budget House of Representatives, Publication No. 116–30, dated September 10, 2020.

In: Artificial Intelligence
Editor: Tonya Randolph
ISBN: 978-1-68507-313-8

Chapter 1

ARTIFICIAL INTELLIGENCE AND THE FUTURE OF WORK*

Committee on Science, Space, and Technology

U.S. HOUSE OF REPRESENTATIVES SUBCOMMITTEE ON RESEARCH AND TECHNOLOGY COMMITTEE ON SCIENCE, SPACE, AND TECHNOLOGY HEARING CHARTER

Artificial Intelligence and the Future of Work
Tuesday, September 24, 2019
4:00 p.m.
2318 Rayburn House Office Building

* This is an edited, reformatted and augmented version of the Hearing Before the Subcommittee on Research and Technology Committee on Science, Space, and Technology, House of Representatives, Publication No. 116–48, Dated September 24, 2019.

PURPOSE

On Tuesday, September 24, 2019 at 4:00 p.m., the Subcommittee on Research and Technology of the Committee on Science, Space, and Technology will hold a hearing to examine the impact of machine learning and artificial intelligence on the workforce, including issues related to worker displacement, retraining of the current workforce, and developing a skilled technical workforce of the future that can thrive in an economy in which AI increasingly plays a role. The Subcommittee will also explore the disparate impacts on different industry sectors and different populations, as well as issues of safety, privacy, and security relevant to the human-technology interface.

WITNESSES

- Dr. Arthur Lupia; Assistant Director, Directorate for Social, Behavioral and Economic Sciences; National Science Foundation
- Dr. Erik Brynjolfsson; Schussel Family Professor of Management Science and Director, The MIT Initiative on the Digital Economy; Massachusetts Institute of Technology
- Ms. Rebekah Kowalski; Vice President, Manufacturing Services; Manpower Group
- Dr. Sue Ellspermann; President; Ivy Tech Community College

OVERARCHING QUESTIONS

- How will advances in artificial intelligence (AI) technologies, which includes machine learning (ML), affect work today and in the future? How are the potential workforce impacts of AI different from previous eras of technological advances?

- Will increased use of AI technologies exacerbate existing economic inequalities? If so, how, and what policies or practices may mitigate these impacts?
- What needs exist for retraining the current workforce to be successful in an economy with increased use of AI systems? How can educational institutions adapt their curriculum to prepare the future workforce?
- What are the key research questions to improve understanding of AI impacts on the workforce and to inform evidence-based policies and practices to support a well-trained workforce and minimize unintended consequences?

BACKGROUND

Previous Technological Disruptions

Today, many Americans are concerned about the impact robots and computers will have on jobs. A recent survey conducted by the Pew Research Center found that 65% of respondents think that robots and computers will definitely or probably take over many jobs currently performed by humans. Additionally, only 25% of respondents believe there would be new, better-paying jobs and only 43% believe that the economy would be more efficient if robots and computers were able to perform much of the work currently done by humans.[1] A 2017 Pew Research Center survey found that most Americans (64%) believe it is likely that people will have a hard time finding things to do with their lives.[2]

Major changes brought about by advances in technology and the fears that accompany them are not unique to the fears surrounding advances in

[1] https://www.pewresearch.org/global/2018/09/13/in-advanced-and-emerging-economies-alike-worries-about-job-automation/.

[2] https://www.pewinternet.org/2017/10/04/americans-attitudes-toward-a-future-in-which-robots-and-computers-can-do-many- human-jobs/.

AI technologies. An early example of anxiety related to technological advancement dates to the 19th century. The Luddite movement was born out of a fear among some British textile workers that they would be replaced by machines. In another example, advances in manufacturing allowed for production in greater volumes and with interchangeable parts, greatly reducing the amount of work for skilled artisans such as blacksmiths.[3]

Developments in AI

Rapid advances in computing power and the availability of large data sets have made AI systems increasingly efficient and accurate at tasks such as object and speech recognition, and data analysis. AI systems are also being used to aid in weather predictions[4] and medical diagnoses.[5] Much of the advances in these AI systems stem from advances in machine learning (ML), a type of algorithmic model that "learns" from patterns in input data – often but not always labeled training data - and applies that "knowledge" of such patterns to analyze new data. This self- improvement happens continuously as new data is fed into the system. Machine learning is currently used for numerous applications including photo tagging[6] and email spam filters.[7] A particular subset of machine learning algorithms called deep neural networks (DNNs) have been particularly responsible for increases in the accuracy, speed and applicability of ML systems.

Despite recent progress, however, humans are still more effective than computers at a wide array of tasks, particularly those that involve creativity, human connection or physical dexterity.[8]

---

[3] https://www.britannica.com/technology/interchangeable-parts.
[4] https://spacenews.com/ai-for-earth-observation-and-numerical-weather-prediction/.
[5] https://medicalxpress.com/news/2019-05-artificial-intelligence-lung-cancer-radiologists.html.
[6] https://hbr.org/2016/11/what-artificial-intelligence-can-and-cant-do-right-now.
[7] https://www.sciencedirect.com/science/article/pii/S2405844018353404.
[8] https://www.nap.edu/catalog/24649/information-technology-and-the-us-workforce-where-are-we-and.

Workforce Impacts of Machine Learning and Artificial Intelligence

Today, most economists characterize jobs as a collection of individual tasks. In general, all or most of these tasks are performed by the worker, and some subset of tasks are done by technology. Technological advances primarily affect these tasks in three ways. The first of these is substitution. A technology can be substituted for certain tasks that were previously performed by a person. One example of this involves automated teller machines (ATMs). ATMs substituted for bank tellers at performing the specific task of withdrawing cash but did not substitute for the entire occupation.[9]

The second way in which technology can affect tasks is to complement the worker. Continuing with the ATM example, ATMs complemented bank employees by freeing up the time they previously spent distributing cash, allowing them to spend more time on customer service and assisting with individual financial issues, tasks that cannot be performed by an ATM.[10]

Finally, technological advances can create new jobs. ATMs decreased the cost of operating a bank and allowed bank employees to spend more time focusing on customer needs. In turn, this led to an increase in the number of bank branches in the U.S. and in more people being hired to work in banks.[11] Technological advances can also create jobs that previously didn't exist; the invention of MRI imaging, for instance, created the need for MRI technicians, a previously nonexistent occupation.[12]

A recent report released by the Brookings Institution found that artificial intelligence and machine learning systems will have some effect on almost all tasks and occupations, though the nature and degree of impact

---

[9] https://papers.ssrn.com/sol3/papers.cfm?abstract_id=2690435.
[10] https://www.pnas.org/content/116/14/6531
[11] https://papers.ssrn.com/sol3/papers.cfm?abstract_id=2690435.
[12] .https://www.nap.edu/catalog/24649/information-technology-and-the-us-workforce-where-are-we-and.

will vary.[13] The strengths of current AI systems include classification and prediction, tasks that are repeatable, that do not need an explanation for how a decision was made, tasks for which a certain amount of error is acceptable and tasks that do not require a high amount of mobility or dexterity.[14] These systems may predominantly affect some of the low-wage, low-skill jobs with repetitive tasks.[15] One such occupation is customer service, with many companies now using AI-powered chatbots to interact with customers who have questions.[16]

Some high-wage, high-skill jobs could also be affected by AI systems. One prominent example of a high-skill, high-wage field where AI systems could increasingly play a role is medicine.[17] Radiology is one of the fields in which AI systems potentially have the greatest utility, given their efficiency in pattern recognition.[18] AI systems can be "trained" using x-ray and MRI images that are known to contain certain pathologies and then used by radiologists to scan new images to help detect those pathologies.[19] Another potential application that takes advantage of the strengths of machine learning is scanning documents to classify them or determine their relevance to a specific project. This could be used by any number of professionals including lawyers[20] or law enforcement professionals.

There are a number of factors that will determine how AI systems affect tasks and jobs and these factors are measured differently in different reports. A 2018 report from The Brookings Institution estimates that approximately 25% of U.S. employment will face high exposure to automation (defined as at least 70% of tasks being automatable) in the

---

13 https://www.brookings.edu/wp-content/uploads/2019/01/2019.01_BrookingsMetro_Auto ma tion-AIReport_Muro-Maxim- Whiton-FINAL-version.pdf.

14 https://science.sciencemag.org/content/358/6370/1530.

15 https://www.brookings.edu/wp-content/uploads/2019/01/2019.01_BrookingsMetro_Automa tion-AI_Report_Muro-Maxim-Whiton-FINAL-version.pdf.

16 https://www.salesforce.com/products/service-cloud/best-practices/how-ai-changed-customer-service/#.

17 https://www.ahajournals.org/doi/full/10.1161/circulationaha.115.001593.

18 https://www.sciencedirect.com/science/article/abs/pii/S1361841512000333.

19 https://medicalxpress.com/news/2019-05-artificial-intelligence-lung-cancer-radiologists. Ht ml.

20 https://www.forbes.com/sites/bernardmarr/2018/05/23/how-ai-and-machine-learning-are-tra nsforming-law-firms-and-the- legal-sector/#3f83acc432c3.

coming decades.[21] A 2017 study from the McKinsey Global Institute uses a slightly different metric and says that approximately half of current work tasks could be automated with current technology.[22] It is also difficult to predict what new jobs will be created by increased use of AI systems without knowing how sophisticated a technology will become or what industries it could enable.

An example of this can be seen in autonomous vehicles. While one report indicates that the introduction of autonomous vehicles (AV) could directly eliminate 1.3 to 2.3 million jobs in the next 30 years,[23] it is possible that the introduction of autonomous vehicles will produce more jobs than they eliminate both directly related to AV production and maintenance or in related fields such as infrastructure or city planning. However, it is difficult if not impossible to forecast these effects because it is unknown how quickly the technology will develop or how sophisticated it will become.[24]

Disparate Impacts Across Race/Ethnicity and Income

Because of existing structural inequalities and the related demographic distributions across different job categories, there are concerns about AI exacerbating existing racial and ethnic inequalities. Underrepresented minorities are predicted to face greater impacts from automation than white or Asian populations. A 2018 report by The Brookings Institution assessed that on average, 47 and 44 percent of tasks currently performed by Hispanic and black workers, respectively, have the potential to be

---

[21] https://www.brookings.edu/wp-content/uploads/2019/01/2019.01_BrookingsMetro_Automation-AI_Report_Muro-Maxim- Whiton-FINAL-version.pdf.

[22] https://www.mckinsey.com/~/media/mckinsey/featured%20insights/Digital% 20Disruption/Harnessing%20automation%20for%20a%20future%20that%20works/MGI-A-future-that-works-Full-report.ashx.

[23] https://avworkforce.secureenergy.org/wp-content/uploads/2018/06/Groshen-et-al-Report-June-2018-1.pdf.

[24] https://www.nap.edu/catalog/24649/information-technology-and-the-us-workforce-whereare-we-and.

automated, compared with 40 and 39 percent for white and Asian populations.[25]

In addition to fears that robots and computers will displace workers, Americans are concerned about the impact this displacement will have on wage inequality. In a 2018 Pew Research Center survey, 76% of respondents said they believe inequality will be worse than it is today as a result of job automation.[26] Between 1980 and 2017 real earnings rose among adults with college and post-college degrees while they fell for adults without a college degree.[27] A 2017 report by the National Academies of Science, Engineering and Medicine notes that "New computerized technologies do appear to have contributed to increased income inequality and are likely to continue to do so as long as they replace skills and tasks historically associated with low-wage or middle-wage occupations."[28] Given these effects, it is not surprising that people are apprehensive about the potential effects of AI systems on inequality.

Developing a Skilled Technical Workforce

Experts believe AI systems will not eliminate the need for skilled technical workers. Rather, these systems will change the tasks these workers perform and the skills they need to perform them. Predicting what these new tasks and occupations will consist of is difficult, but experts predict there will be a need for workers who can maintain AI systems and workers who can safely work alongside AI-enabled technologies.

---

[25] https://www.brookings.edu/wp-content/uploads/2019/01/2019.01_Brookings Metro_Automation-AI_Report_Muro-Maxim- Whiton-FINAL-version.pdf.

[26] https://www.pewresearch.org/global/2018/09/13/in-advanced-and-emerging-economies-alike-worries-about-job-automation/.

[27] https://workofthefuture.mit.edu/sites/default/files/2019-09/WorkoftheFuture_Report_ Shaping_Technology_and_Institutions.pdf.

[28] https://www.nap.edu/catalog/24649/information-technology-and-the-us-workforce-where-are-we-and.

A recent report by the National Academies of Sciences, Engineering and Medicine noted that by 2022, there may be a shortage of almost 3.4 million skilled technical workers.[29] The same report notes that "The demand for a skilled technical workforce is changing so rapidly that workers, employers, educators, policy makers and civic organizations need to be highly flexible and forward looking."[30]

Issues of Safety, Privacy and Security

AI systems have the potential to introduce several challenges pertaining to safety, privacy, and security. As robots powered by AI systems are increasingly integrated into workplaces, workers need to be able to work alongside those robots safely and to have confidence in the robot's movements and ability to detect people. The use of collaborative robots, which are designed to work alongside humans, will also require companies to rethink their approach to the safety of their workers. Numerous companies today use AI systems to monitor and analyze their workers. These systems can incorporate cameras and other sensors that watch what workers do or analyze their email and meeting habits. The companies may be gathering these data not in the name of surveillance, but in the name of efficiency and even in the name of worker happiness (e.g., creating workspaces more responsive to worker needs). However, the privacy issues associated with these systems are vast and it can be unclear what rights workers have regarding AI monitoring. The increasing use of AI systems in the workplace also presents security concerns. As with any computer system, there is a risk that the AI systems could be corrupted in a way that potentially harms workers.

---

[29] https://www.nap.edu/catalog/23472/building-americas-skilled-technical-workforce.

[30] https://www.nap.edu/catalog/23472/building-americas-skilled-technical-workforce.

Role of the Federal Government

There are a number of Federal efforts focused on the workforce issues presented by advances in AI. In 2016, NSF Director France Córdova unveiled the 10 Big Ideas for Future NSF Investments that are "meant to define a set of cutting-edge research agendas and processes that are uniquely suited for NSF's broad portfolio of investments, and will require collaborations with industry, private foundations, other agencies, science academies and societies, and universities."[31] One of the 10 Big Ideas is the "Future of Work at the Human-Technology Frontier" which features four research themes: building the human-technology partnership, augmenting human performance, illuminating the socio-technological landscape, and fostering lifelong learning.[32] The Big Idea is also the focus of a Convergence Accelerator track; the track is funded at $30 million in the FY 2020 budget proposal with the intention to raise $20 million from external partnerships.

The 2019 Executive Order on Maintaining American Leadership in Artificial Intelligence directs the National Science and Technology Council Select Committee on Artificial Intelligence to provide recommendations to the NSTC Committee on STEM Education "regarding AI-related educational and workforce development considerations that focus on American citizens."[33] The Select Committee will also provide technical expertise to the National Council for the American Worker on "matters regarding AI and the American workforce."[34] The 2019 "National Artificial Intelligence Research and Development Strategic Plan" contains a strategy titled "Develop Effective Methods for Human-AI Collaboration" and a strategy titled "Understand and Address the Ethical, Legal, and Societal Implications of AI."[35] "The

---

[31] https://www.nsf.gov/about/congress/reports/nsf_big_ideas.pdf.

[32] https://www.nsf.gov/news/special_reports/big_ideas/human_tech.jsp.

[33] https://www.whitehouse.gov/presidential-actions/executive-order-maintaining-american-leadership-artificial-intelligence/.

[34] https://www.whitehouse.gov/presidential-actions/executive-order-maintaining-american-leadership-artificial-intelligence/.

[35] https://www.nitrd.gov/pubs/National-AI-RD-Strategy-2019.pdf.

Networking & Information Technology Research and Development Program Supplement to the President's FY2020 Budget" also details a key program titled "Promote safe and effective methods for human-AI collaboration" and one titled "Develop methods for designing AI systems that align with ethical, legal and societal goals."[36]

Chairwoman STEVENS. This hearing will come to order. Without objection, the Chair is authorized to declare recess at any time. Good afternoon. Welcome, and thank you to our witnesses for joining us here today. We are all looking forward to your testimony. Thank you also for your flexibility with the later start this afternoon. I'd like to take a moment to offer my deepest sympathies to Majority Whip Clyburn on the passing of his beloved wife, Emily. My thoughts are with him and his family during this time of sorrow.

We are here today to examine the role of artificial intelligence in shaping the work of the future. Recent developments in machine learning algorithms, combined with increasing computing power and data generation, have enabled rapid advances in the accuracy, efficiency, and applicability of artificial intelligence (AI) systems. AI systems have already begun to change the nature of work and the workforce. They are being used in manufacturing processes, medical care, and customer service.

As we talk—and we will talk about this—as we talk about job loss that will occur as advanced technology increasingly affects all occupations and wage levels, companies in my district in south- eastern Michigan are also telling me how much trouble they are having trying to fill the jobs they have available. A 2017 study by the McKinsey Global Institute found that approximately half of all work activities could be automated by technologies that are already available today, so we need to start having the discussion at a broader level about how available jobs will transform, rather than disappear, as specific tasks are taken over by AI systems, and

---

[36] https://www.whitehouse.gov/wp-content/uploads/2019/09/FY2020-NITRD-AI-RD-Budget-September-2019.pdf?utm_campaign=the_algorithm.unpaid.engagement&utm_source=hs_email&utm_medium=email&utm_content=76813461&_hsenc=p2ANqtz-9YwlzM0xzEZXjAp9IJ9TDAORRDSDf0IYgS3XXyApa81aE6sjWrwk4YzCe_bhLX-UPfbbvEUMVDpvOuLLjU69oK8HOj9cBEfUFIz3lak83mNfCXFrs&_hsmi=76813461.

the workers take on new job roles. The advances enabled by artificial intelligence also have the potential to create new kinds of jobs, and in doing so, elevate the standard of living and quality of life for many.

Sixty-five percent of children entering elementary school today, in the year 2019, will ultimately end up working in completely new job types that currently do not exist. As the integration of these technologies transform work and create new jobs, there will be significant need to ensure we are training workers to succeed at all levels, from the factory floor worker to the radiologist. The key is ensuring that the gains from AI systems are shared by all Americans, increasing the quality of life for everyone. As we discussed at a hearing in this Committee in June, if our Nation leads in the responsible development of AI, we can help set the standards and norms the rest of the world will follow. That applies equally to the use of AI in the workplace.

We are holding this hearing today to discuss what we do know, and also explore what we do not know, and the compelling topic of the future of work has certainly compelled many. Research studies, companies who are organizing and orienting their organizational development, academic institutions, and this very body, are compelled to act. As AI-powered robots become more common, the question we ask is, how do we ensure worker safety alongside these robots? Will artificial intelligence be routinely used to monitor workers, as some companies do today? How do we balance privacy rights with the potential productivity benefits and worker benefits these analyses could provide? How do we keep this data secure, and prevent its malicious use? And finally, how do we get a better understanding of the macroeconomics and labor outlook so that the government, companies, colleges, universities, and workers can all plan for this transition? It's the question hanging above us in this 21st century age. These are just some of the questions the researchers are pursuing.

So I am greatly looking forward to today's hearing, because we are compelled to act, to explore, to develop good policy, to stand up for the value of work, what knowledge and tools, researchers, companies, and workers need going forward, and how Federal science agencies, such as the NSF (National Science Foundation), are helping to lead the way.

Before I recognize Dr. Marshall for an opening statement. Wait, hold on 1 second. We're pausing on an opening statement. OK. Before we move on for opening statements, what I'd like to do at this time is to present for the record a letter from Kelly Services in support of this hearing, and I would also like to submit the executive summary from the 2018 report written by the great Mark Muro, and his team from The Brookings Institution, titled "Automation and Artificial Intelligence: How Machines Are Affecting People and Places," a great read that's recommended by many.

[The prepared statement of Chairwoman Stevens follows:]

Good afternoon, welcome and thank you to our witnesses for joining us here today, I'm looking forward to hearing your testimony. Thank you for your flexibility with the late start today. I'd like to take a moment to offer my deepest sympathies to Majority Whip Clyburn on the passing of his wife; my thoughts are with him and his family during this time of sorrow.

We are here today to examine the role of artificial intelligence in shaping the work of the future. Recent developments in machine learning algorithms, combined with increasing computing power and data generation, have enabled rapid advances in the accuracy, efficiency and applicability of artificial intelligence systems.

AI systems have already begun to change the nature of work and the workforce. They are being used in manufacturing processes, medical care, and customer service.

As we talk about the job loss that will occur as advanced technology increasingly affects all occupations and wage levels, companies in my district are telling me about how much trouble they are having trying to fill the jobs they have available. A 2017 study by the McKinsey Global Institute found that approximately half of all work activities could be automated by technologies that are already available today. We need to start having the discussion at a broader level about how the types of jobs available will change rather than disappear, as specific tasks are taken over by AI systems and the workers take on new tasks.

The advances enabled by artificial intelligence also have the potential to create new kinds of jobs, and in doing so, elevate the standard of living and quality of life for many. 65% of children entering elementary school today will ultimately end up working in completely new job types that currently do not exist.

As the integration of these technologies changes jobs and creates new jobs, there will be a significant need to ensure we are training workers to succeed at all levels, from the factory floor worker to the radiologist. The key is ensuring that the gains from AI systems are shared by all Americans, increasing the quality of life for everyone. As we discussed at a hearing in this Committee in June, if our Nation leads in the responsible development of AI, we can help set the standards and norms the rest of the world will follow. That applies equally to the use of AI in the workplace. We are holding this hearing today to discuss what we do know, but the fact is there is a lot we still do not know. As AI-powered robots become more common, how do we ensure worker safety alongside these robots? Will artificial intelligence be routinely used to monitor workers, as some companies do today? How do we balance privacy rights with the potential productivity benefits and worker benefits these analyses could provide? How can we keep this data secure and prevent its malicious use? And finally, how do we get a better understanding of the macroeconomics and labor outlook so that the government, companies, colleges and universities, andworkers can all plan for the transition? These are just some of the many questions researchers are pursuing.

I look forward to hearing from today's distinguished panel who will help us understand what we do know now, what knowledge and tools researchers, companies, and workers need going forward, and how Federal science agencies such as NSF are helping to lead the way.

Chairwoman STEVENS. So at this time I would like to introduce our witnesses. Our first witness is Dr. Arthur Lupia. Dr. Lupia is the Assistant Director of the Directorate for Social, Behavioral, and Economic Sciences at the National Science Foundation. He also serves as the Hal R. Varian Collegiate Professor of Political Science at the University of Michigan. Delighted to have you here on behalf of the University of Michigan, as well as the NSF, Dr. Lupia, and you also serve as the co-Chair of the Office and Science and Technology Policy's Subcommittee on Open Science. Dr. Lupia's research focuses on processes, principles, and factors that guide decisionmaking and learning. He earned his bachelor's degree in economics from the University of Rochester, and his social science Ph.D. from the California Institute of Technology, Caltech.

Our next witness is Dr. Erik Brynjolfsson. Dr. Brynjolfsson is the Schussel Family Professor of Management Science and Director of the MIT Initiative on the Digital Economy. His research focuses on the effects of information technologies on business strategy, productivity and performance, digital commerce, and intangible assets. He is the author and co-author of several books, including "The Second Machine Age: Work, Progress, and Prosperity in a Time of Brilliant Technologies." We applaud you for this milestone work that you have published, sir. We are delighted to have you here at this hearing, and we also note that you received your bachelor's and master's degrees in applied mathematics and decision sciences from Harvard University, and a PhD from MIT in managerial economics.

Our third witness is Ms. Rebekah Kowalski. Ms. Kowalski is the Vice President of Manpower Manufacturing, a role she has held since January 2019 throughout her long and remarkable career at ManpowerGroup. Her current portfolio focuses on developing solutions that help organizations and leaders deal with the implications of the shortage of skilled workers, and the evolution of roles and skills. She previously led the team that worked with MXD, a digital manufacturing institute, to identify how roles and skills will evolve as manufacturing changes with the increasing introduction of digital technologies, a truly profound work of primary research that has helped many companies orient and prepare for the future of work. Ms. Kowalski received her B.A. in English from the University of Wisconsin-Parkside.

Our final witness, Dr. Sue Ellspermann, is the President of Ivy Tech Community College of Indiana. Prior to her role at Ivy Tech, Dr. Ellspermann was Indiana's 50th Lieutenant Governor, from 2013 to March 2016. As Vice Chair of the Indiana Career Council, she led efforts to align the State's education and workforce development system to meet the needs of employers, a continued focus for her as President of Ivy Tech. She certainly focuses on the cross-cutting collaboration that is so needed with our training centers and our employers. And Dr. Ellspermann earned her bachelor's of science in industrial engineering from Purdue University, and herUniversity of Louisville. Absolutely fabulous.

As our witnesses should know, you will each have 5 minutes for your spoken testimony, and your written testimony will be included in the record for the hearing. When all of you have completed your spoken testimony, we will begin with questions. Members will have 5 minutes to question the panel. And at this time, Dr. Lupia, we'd like to start with your 5-minute testimony. Thank you.

TESTIMONY OF DR. ARTHUR LUPIA, ASSISTANT DIRECTOR, DIRECTORATE FOR SOCIAL, BEHAVIORAL AND ECONOMIC SCIENCES, NATIONAL SCIENCE FOUNDATION

Dr. LUPIA. Thank you. Good afternoon, Chairwoman Stevens, Representative Marshall, and Members of the Subcommittee. My name is Dr. Arthur Lupia. I am the Assistant Director of the Social, Behavioral, and Economic Sciences Directorate at the National Science Foundation. It is a pleasure to be with you this afternoon to discuss how NSF is helping our fellow citizens prepare for the future of work.

Work is a vital and dynamic element of our society. Work powers our offices and our factories. It supports our communities, and our Nation. And as we can all see, work is changing. We know that AI and related technologies can increase national competitiveness by making businesses, governments, and social organizations more competitive and more effective. These technologies can also create many new careers. If these technologies are applied with sufficient foresight, they can create new opportunities for workers, and improve quality of life for communities across the country. How can we achieve a future where technological change benefits as many people as possible? At the National Science Foundation, we believe that achieving this future requires working together. Our Future of Work at the Human Technology Frontier Program treats future work, future technology, and future workplaces as deeply integrated and intertwined elements of our Nation's work- based ecosystem. In NSF's Future of Work approach, we collect data on worker experiences to inform social and behavioral research on workers and workplaces. This research, in turn, can guide technological development. Work like this can reveal new ways to empower workers, and increase productivity.

Studying workers, workplaces, and technology together are the key to creating benefits that everyone can realize, and pioneering research of this kind is already underway. On the screen is one of the projects NSF has recently supported. This is a human being in an exoskeleton. Today's exoskeletons help human beings transport very large objects, and navigate impossible situations. But this project is about tomorrow's exoskeletons. The device that you see here is not just an exoskeleton of the body. It's an exoskeleton of the mind. This exoskeleton of tomorrow provides information to the worker through an augmented reality system. The system empowers the worker to process information, and make better decisions, with unprecedented speed. This type of technology is awesome, and it'll have impacts far beyond factory floors. Today, for example, the Veterans' Administration is one of the Nation's leading users of exoskeletons. Tomorrow's exoskeletons will open new opportunities for our veterans. NSF's Future of Work Program supports this technology by incentivizing developers, AI experts, and workplace specialists to collaborate. Working together, researchers and developers can increase performance, decrease injury, expand access, and improve quality of life in ways that just would not be possible if any of these groups worked alone. That's what NSF can do. To date, NSF's Future of Work Big Idea supports projects in a wide range of work contexts, including health care, power grids, farming, learning, scientific research, transportation, emergency response, and, of course, manufacturing.

NSF not only supports fundamental research in these areas, but also supports efforts to bring these big ideas to market. For example, NSF recently unveiled new Future of Work awards from its Convergence Accelerator. NSF's Convergence Accelerator is designed to fund technology-based partnerships that simultaneously advance national priorities and create new opportunities for American workers. For example, a project based at the University of Michigan is examining how to combine research in AI, data science, and industrial psychology to find better ways to link workers with innovative new training and educational opportunities that will help them not only contribute, but thrive, and build amazing careers in their new workplaces. This is an exciting time for our country, and, like you, NSF is grateful to see our Nation's brightest minds collaborating on the fundamental research that will transform our workplaces, empower our workforce, and provide tremendous new sources of innovation for our Nation. So thank you for having this hearing today, and for the opportunity to testify. I'm happy to answer any questions you may have. [The prepared statement of Dr. Lupia follows:]

Dr. Arthur Lupia Assistant Director for Social, Behavioral and Economic Sciences National Science Foundation, Before the Subcommittee on Research and Technology Committee on Science, Space and Technology United States House of Representatives on "Artificial Intelligence and The Future of Work" September 24, 2019

Introduction

Chairwoman Stevens, Ranking Member Baird, and members of the subcommittee, it is a privilege to be with you today to discuss how the National Science Foundation (NSF) is positioning the United States to continue our strong leadership in the development of new technologies and to also respond to the challenges and opportunities those new technologies present for the future of jobs and work.

Established by the National Science Foundation Act of 1950 (P.L. 81-507), NSF is an independent Federal agency whose mission is "to promote the progress of science; to advance the national health, prosperity, and welfare; to secure the national defense; and for other purposes." NSF is unique in carrying out its mission by supporting fundamental research across all fields of science, technology, engineering and mathematics (STEM) and all levels of STEM education. NSF is also committed to the development of a future-focused science and engineering workforce that draws on the talents of all Americans. NSF accounts for approximately 25 percent of the total Federal budget for basic research conducted at U.S. colleges and universities and has been vital to many discoveries that impact our daily lives and drive the economy. NSF is and will continue to be a respected steward of taxpayer dollars, operating with integrity, openness, and transparency.

A vibrant scientific workforce and breakthrough discoveries enabled in part by NSF investments sustain, accelerate, and transform America's globally preeminent innovation ecosystem. A long- term vision, belief in the promise of fundamental research, and commitment to pursuing risky, yet potentially extraordinary discoveries are the hallmarks of NSF. NSF's investments empower discoverers to ask the questions and develop the technologies that lead to the next big breakthroughs.

NSF Leadership in Artificial Intelligence Research

The landscape of jobs and work is changing at unprecedented speed, enabled by advances in computer and information science and engineering, including data analytics, artificial intelligence (AI), and robotics, together with new conceptions of work and workplaces. This scientific and technological revolution presents a historical opportunity to the Nation through the creation of new industries and occupations, enhanced productivity and quality of life, and the potential for more people to participate in the workforce. However, these changes also bring challenges, such as the possibility of jobs lost to automation and increased demand for workers with higher skills. Other equally important challenges include new security threats, potential for algorithmic biases, and workplace policies and practices that have not kept up with rapid changes in the nature of work.

NSF has a long and rich history of supporting transformative research in AI, machine learning, robotics and data science. NSF also plays an important role in both measuring the STEM workforce through the National Center for Science and Engineering Statistics, as well as growing it through investing in human capital. NSF leadership is helping to drive and coordinate AI research and development efforts across the federal government. The NSF Director co-chairs the National Science and Technology Council's (NSTC) Select Committee on AI, which advises the White House on interagency AI Research and Development (R&D) priorities and establishes structures to improve government planning and coordination. In addition, the NSF Assistant Director for Computer & Information Science & Engineering co-chairs the NSTC Machine Learning and AI Subcommittee and also co-chairs the NSTC Networking and Information Technology Research and Development Subcommittee, both of which serve to coordinate federal R&D investments in AI as well as other related information technology areas. For example, NSF was a key contributor to the National Artificial Intelligence Research and Development Strategic Plan: 2019 Update published in June of this year.

NSF also invests significant resources, nearly $450 million in Fiscal Year 2019, in fundamental research, workforce development, and advanced, scalable computing resources that collectively advance AI. Indeed, many of the transformative uses of AI that we are witnessing today are founded in Federal government investments in fundamental AI research that reach back over decades. For example, NSF-funded researchers began working on what is now known as collaborative filtering, pairing AI research with the growth of the Internet in the 1990s. This work fuels the recommender engines on popular websites like Netflix and Amazon and propel a significant proportion of e-commerce activity.

NSF has also launched several special-emphasis programs through various public-private partnerships. The NSF Program on Fairness in Artificial Intelligence in Collaboration with Amazon, will explore building trustworthy AI systems that are readily accepted and deployed to tackle grand challenges facing society. Specific topics of interest include transparency, explainability, accountability, bias, mitigation strategies, validation, and inclusivity. NSF has also joined with the Partnership on AI to understand the social challenges arising from AI technology and enable scientific contributions to overcome them. Within the Federal government, NSF andthe Defense Advanced Research Projects Agency have teamed up to explore high-performance, energy-efficient hardware and machine learning architectures that can learn from a continuous stream of new data in real time.

Building the foundations of tomorrow's AI innovations will require new interdisciplinary collaborations, resources, and strategic visions — principles that NSF has championed in its support of fundamental AI research. NSF's ability to bring together numerous fields—including computer and information science and engineering, along with cognitive science and psychology, economics and game theory, knowledge of the physical world, engineering and control theory, ethics, linguistics, mathematics, philosophy—gives the agency a unique role in expanding the frontiers of AI and addressing the challenges of the future.

The Future of Work at the Human Technology Frontier (FW-HTF)

In 2016, the National Science Foundation unveiled a set of "Big Ideas," 10 bold, long-term ideas that identify areas for future investment at the frontiers of science and engineering. The Big Ideas represent opportunities to position our Nation at the cutting edge of global science and engineering leadership by bringing together diverse disciplinary perspectives to support convergence research.

The Future of Work at the Human-Technology Frontier (FW-HTF) Big Idea is one mechanism by which NSF is responding to the challenges and opportunities for the future of jobs and work. The overarching vision is to support convergent research to understand and develop the human-technology partnership, design new technologies to augment human performance, illuminate the emerging socio-technological landscape, understand the risks and benefits of new technologies, understand and influence the impact of artificial intelligence on workers and work, and foster lifelong and pervasive learning.

Specifically, the FW-HTF Big Idea will advance our understanding of how technology and people interact, distribute tasks, cooperate, and complement each other in different specific work contexts. Researchers will advance the knowledge base related to worker education and training and formal and informal learning to enable all potential workers to adapt to changing work environments. We will also advance our understanding of the links between the future of work at the human- technology frontier and the surrounding society, including the intended potential of new technologies and the unintended consequences for workers and the well-being of society.

Achieving these goals requires integration and convergence of disciplines across computer science, engineering, learning sciences, research on education and workforce training, and social, behavioral, and economic sciences. A convergent perspective is essential to understand and shape long-term social and economic drivers, so that advanced technology can empower individuals and strengthen the social fabric. A convergent perspective also informs our Nation about how to develop education and re-skilling opportunities that can confer technology's benefits to all citizens.

In FY 2019, NSF began making the first awards under the FW-HTF Big Idea. One such award at the University of Michigan is investigating how humans and robots work together in construction environments. Despite recent advances in robot functionality, many fundamental questions in human-robot interaction remain unanswered. Another award supports a collaboration among Purdue University, Indiana University and the Massachusetts Institute of Technology to develop simulations that can help manufacturers design factories where workers thrive.

NSF is also funding research in learning technologies that prepare learners for new opportunities ahead. Our Cyberlearning for Work at the

Human-Technology Frontier program examines new ways to help learners of all ages gain the STEM skills that will give them new opportunities in tomorrow's workplaces. As an example, researchers at the University of Washington are working on improving the educational tools available to learners of all ages who are studying coding. By leveraging recent advances in computer science and machine learning, the project will create a new online learning technology that automatically generates more personalized practice content for learners with different backgrounds. These activities can create critical tools to support the gender, racial, ethnic, regional and intellectual diversity of our computing workforce.

The Convergence Accelerator

The NSF Convergence Accelerator is designed to identify areas of research where investment in convergent approaches – those bringing together people from across disciplines, united to solve problems – has the potential to rapidly translate to high-benefit results and advance ideas from concept to deliverables. The Convergence Accelerator complements NSF's basic research support by creating dynamic partnerships that can include stakeholders from industry, foundations, government, nonprofits and other sectors.

On September 10th, NSF announced the first awards through its Convergence Accelerator pilot. Forty-three awards totaling $39 million will support projects across the country that will find new ways to leverage advances from across the sciences and engineering to enhance the lives of American workers. Roughly half those awards are focused on the Future of Work and will address subjects such as predictive AI tools and the educational technologies needed for adult learning.

The Convergence Accelerator awards span a wide range of industries, populations, and partnerships. One award to the University of Central Florida will combine the most recent advances in deep learning, semi-structured interviews, surveys, and work-life journal data analysis in building a hybrid framework to predict the multi-dimensional impact of AI on future jobs in the human resources industry.

These 43 awards are just the first step in funding through the Convergence Accelerator. Over the next six months, teams of researchers will participate in an "Innovation Curriculum" that will help them improve their initial ideas, augment their teams through new partnerships, improve communications, and deliver groundbreaking new advances.

The Role of Social Science Research

Understanding the human and social aspects of changing workplaces and technologies give us the opportunity to use these technologies to improve the quality of work and quality of life for all Americans. From neurons to neighborhoods, and from farms to factories, social and behavioral scientists offer a distinct and valuable form of service to help us understand the human component of the changing nature of work.

In recent years, NSF's Social, Behavioral, and Economic Sciences (SBE) Directorate has led NSF's Future of Work effort and supported related research. A few examples include:

- Researchers at Carnegie-Mellon University in Pittsburgh are examining the effects of current and emerging technologies on labor outcomes with a precision that will provide meaningful insights for training programs. This work can help worker education and reskilling programs serve more people more effectively in less time.
- Vanderbilt University's Center for Autism and Innovation is working to improve opportunity and quality of life for people with neuro diverse conditions such as autism, ADHD, and dyslexia by investigating approaches to enhance retention, engagement, and productivity in STEM jobs, and specifically to harness unique capabilities accommodate for individual needs.
- Investigators at Michigan State University are examining the impact of widespread automated vehicle adoption on ride-hailing and truck hauling. Being able to predict changes will allow us to better prepare and retrain drivers, helping both industry and American workers.

- A team at the University of California-Irvine is using real time assessment to develop fair and accurate AI systems that will guide interventions to improve team cohesion, performance, workload, and collaboration and reduce interruptions, to help teams of the future work smarter, better, and happier

Concepts such as lifelong learning and values-based design are key elements of these efforts. Both concepts encourage researchers and entrepreneurs to consider the social consequences of technological change in early developmental stages – rather than after unintended consequences occur. Looking forward, social and behavioral scientists are working with their fellow scientists, engineers, and innovators from across the country to empower America's workers and help America's next generation of job creators better manage the challenges and opportunities of the future of work.

Conclusion

The discoveries and innovations funded by NSF have a long record of improving lives and meeting national needs. With the support of this Committee and the Congress, NSF will continue to invest in the fundamental research and the talented people who improve our daily lives and transform our future. As we look to the Future of Work, we are committed to supporting interdisciplinary research through the Big Ideas, the Convergence Accelerator and our core research programs that bring together all fields of science to ensure that our workers, researchers, students, innovators and industries are best positioned to take advantage of the major technological advancements we see today and will see in the future.

Thank you for the opportunity to testify today and for your continued support of NSF. I will be pleased to answer any questions you may have.

National Science Foundation Dr. Arthur Lupia is Assistant Director of the National Science Foundation. In that capacity, he serves as head of the National Science Foundation (NSF) Directorate for Social, Behavioral, and Economic Sciences (SBE). He also serves the Hal R. Varian Collegiate Professor of Political Science at the University of Michigan and as co-chair of the Office of Science and Technology Policy's Subcommittee on Open Science. Prior to arriving at NSF, he served as Chairperson of the Board for the Center for Open Science, as chair of the National Academies Roundtable on the Communication and Use of Social and Behavioral Sciences, and as a leader of many scientific advisory boards.

Dr. Lupia's research and related public work examines processes, principles, and factors that guide decision-making and learning. His efforts clarify how people make decisions, and choose what to believe, when they lack information or face adverse circumstances. Lupia draws from mixes of mathematics, statistics, neuroscience, economics, psychology and other scientific disciplines to advance these topics. His work on civic competence, information processing, how voters learn and science communication has influenced scholarly practice, public policy, and classroom teaching in many countries.

Dr. Lupia has been a John Simon Guggenheim Fellow, a Andrew Carnegie Fellow, and is a recipient of the National Academy of Sciences Award for Initiatives in Research. He earned his bachelor's degree in economics at the University of Rochester and his social science PhD at the California Institute of Technology.

Chairwoman STEVENS. Dr. Brynjolfsson? Yes.

TESTIMONY OF DR. ERIK BRYNJOLFSSON, SCHUSSEL FAMILY PROFESSOR OF MANAGEMENT SCIENCE AND DIRECTOR, THE MIT INITIATIVE ON THE DIGITAL ECONOMY, MASSACHUSETTS INSTITUTE OF TECHNOLOGY

Dr. BRYNJOLFSSON. Good afternoon, Chairwoman Stevens, Representative Marshall, and Members of the Committee. Thank you so much for inviting me to share some of the research my team and I have been doing. Addressing the opportunities created by AI is one of the most important challenges for government in the coming decade. Thanks to AI, some weird and wonderful things are beginning to happen. Cars are learning to drive themselves. Machines can now recognize your friends' faces. When you see people walking down the street talking on their phones, you don't know if they're talking to another human or to a machine, and expecting the machine to answer. Just last week Siri tried to join into a conversation I was having about interest rates.

However, it's also critical to understand that we are very far from what we call artificial general intelligence, the kind of AI that spans the full range of human intelligence. While machine learning is now superhuman in many tasks that involve mapping a particular set of inputs into outputs, humans outperform machines in most other cognitive tasks. Therefore, we are not facing the imminent end of work, but we are facing a major restructuring of work. In research that I've been doing with my colleagues, we find that few, if any, occupations will be fully automated by this new wave of technologies, but at the same time, few, if any, will be unaffected. Instead, most will be transformed. For instance, the job of a typical radiologist consists of 27 distinct tasks. While machine learning has made impressive advances in some of them, like reading medical images, it is of little use in most of the other tasks, like counseling patients.

So massive unemployment is not the challenge of our era. Instead, we face challenges in two other areas. One is delivering productivity growth, and the other is reducing inequality. To date, despite impressive improvements in AI, productivity growth has actually slowed down. Between 1995 and 2004 it averaged 2.8 percent per year, but since 2005 productivity has been just 1.3 percent per year. That's less than half the growth rate previously. So why is that? Well, the bottleneck is actually not the technology, but rather the lack of complementary process innovations, workforce reskilling, and business dynamism.

The second challenge is inequality. There's no economic law that says that everyone will benefit from technological advances. As the economic pie grows, it's possible for some people to be left behind, even as others benefit disproportionately. Indeed, over the past several decades the benefits of economic growth have been very unequal. Not only has the median income barely grown since the late 1990s, but other social indicators have actually worsened. For the first time in history, average life expectancy of Americans has begun to fall, driven by worse mortality of less educated Americans. It's no coincidence that these are exactly the Americans who haven't shared in our economic growth.

So my policy recommendations can be grouped into five key areas. The first one is to reinvent education. We need to recommit ourselves to investment in education. It's a field that the U.S. has once led the world. We also need to reinvent it so that we focus more on the kinds of skills that machines cannot match. These include creativity and interpersonal skills.

Second, we need to rebalance capital and labor. As noted in a recent research report by the MIT Work of the Future Initiative, our tax code and other policies are heavily skewed toward helping capital, rather than labor. We need a more-level playing field, particularly as AI starts to affect more and more of the labor force. This means taxing capital at comparable rates, encouraging investments in human capital, just as we do for physical capital, and updating corporate governance to recognize workers as stakeholders alongside stockholders. We can also expand the Earned Income Tax Credit to boost incomes for the working poor, and use revenues from things like carbon taxes to lower taxes on work.

Third, we need to invest in U.S. technological leadership. U.S. leadership in AI and other technologies is at serious risk because we have cut Federal investment in R&D (research and development), even as other nations have boosted theirs. Federal science agencies, like the NSF, working with our leading universities and private industry, have a central role in maintaining and extending America's science and technology leadership in AI and other areas. Fourth, we need to welcome high skill immigrants. A vastly disproportionate number of America's leaders in science and business are immigrants, or the children of immigrants. When I ask my students at MIT what was the most important message I should convey to you here in Washington regarding AI policy, they unanimously advised me to push for less restrictive immigration policies. And fifth, we need to work hard to support entrepreneurship. Boosting entrepreneurship can help reverse the stagnation of wages for the bottom half of the income distribution, particularly those who have been most adverse affected by automation. Among the policies that can help with this is decoupling healthcare from employment, reforming occupational licensing, and direct investments in teaching and entrepreneurship, and boosting new business formation.

With the right policies, AI can be harnessed to make the next decade the best decade in U.S. history.

[The prepared statement of Dr. Brynjolfsson follows:]

Artificial Intelligence and the Future of Work Congressional Testimony of Erik Brynjolfsson, September 24, 2019

Good afternoon, Chairwoman Johnson, Ranking Member Lucas, Chairwoman Stevens, Ranking Member Baird, and members of the Committee. Thank you for giving me this opportunity to summarize and share some of my research on the implications of AI for the economy. Addressing the opportunities created by AI is one of the most important challenges for the government, for business and for individuals over the coming decade. I'm gratified that this Committee is taking this challenge seriously. While I primarily focus on my own research for this testimony, I will also draw on work by my team at MIT IDE, work by the MIT Work of the Future initiative, the AI Index, many other researchers. These are my own views. I am not speaking for anyone else.

1776 was a remarkable year. The United States declared its independence, creating a new kind of nation. Adam Smith wrote the Wealth of Nations, laying the foundations for free enterprise, and James Watt introduced a superior steam engine, igniting the industrial revolution. Our nation, and the world, are immensely freer and wealthier than our ancestors because of these three milestones and the subsequent changes they set in motion.

Today, we are also at a crossroads of history. The people in this room will help us choose the path forward. I will begin my testimony by summarizing some key changes in the underlying technologies, then discuss the implications for work, productivity and the broader economy, and conclude with five policy recommendations.

The biggest drivers of economic growth are advances in technology, specifically general purpose technologies like the steam engine, electricity and computers. These technologies not only have important direct effects, but also enable myriad complementary innovations in technology, business processes and economic organization. The most important general purpose technology of our era is AI. Indeed, it may be the most general of all general purpose technologies because if we can create intelligent machines, we can use that intelligence to solve many other problems.

The most important advances in AI have been in the area called machine learning called deep neural networks or deep learning. Because of insights by researchers like Geoffrey Hinton, Yann LeCun and Yoshua Bengio, these techniques enable machines to learn from data dramatically more effectively than ever before. For instance, in 2010, the best algorithms could recognize and label images on the large Imagenet dataset with barely 70% accuracy.

Today, using deep learning techniques, they are about 98% accurate, surpassing human level performance on the same dataset. Similarly, deep learning techniques enable voice recognition systems to understand spoken language well-enough to respond to simple questions or instructions. While they are far from perfect, we are in the midst of the remarkable 10-year period of history where we went from machines not understanding human speech, to machines and humans routinely talking to each other in natural language. Machines now outperform humans in a wide variety of tasks that only humans could do before, from choosing which ads to show when we read an article on the web, to recommending who to hire or lend money to, to reading our medical images and diagnosing our diseases.

The recent advances in machine learning are breath-taking and important. However, it is critical to understand that we are very far from artificial general intelligence that is, the kind of AI than spans the full range of human intelligence. Machines learning is now superhuman in many tasks that involving mapping a set of inputs into a set of outputs (e.g., images -> labels, voice recordings -> transcripts; clickstream data -> advertising recommendations; medical data -> diagnoses) but humans outperform machines in most other tasks and we will almost surely continue to do so for decades.

In particular, humans have a big edge in tasks involving creativity, interpersonal skills and emotional intelligence, and physical dexterity. This means we are not in danger of mass unemployment anytime soon. There is no shortage of work that needs to be done in our society that only humans can do. In work I've been doing with Tom Mitchell and Daniel Rock, we've mapped out, in some cases literally, where machine learning technologies will have the biggest impacts. The typical occupation consists of 20-30 distinct task, some of which are much easier for machine learning systems to do than others. Our research shows that few, if any, occupations will be fully automated by the new wave of technologies. At the same time, few, if any, will be unaffected. Instead, most will be transformed. For instance, the job of a typical radiologist consists of 26 distinct tasks, from reading medical images, to consulting with other physicians and experts, to advising and counselling patients. While machine learning has made impressive advances in reading medical images, it is of little use in most of the other tasks done by radiologists. We have used our techniques to predict which occupations will be most affected, as well as which industries, which geographic regions and even which individual firms.

Our research tells us that we face two urgent economic challenges: a lack of productivity growth and too much inequality.

Productivity is what determines the wealth of nations, the success of companies and the living standards of individuals. While advances in technology are the catalyst of productivity growth, that growth is not realized unless and until a cascade of complementary innovations are implemented. For instance, when American factories first electrified, there was negligible productivity growth for the first 30 years. It was only after the first generation of managers retired and a new generation replaced the old "group drive" organization of machinery, which was optimized for steam engines, with the new "unit drive" approach that enable assembly lines that we saw a doubling of productivity. Today, despite impressive improvements in AI, not to mention many other technologies, productivity growth has actually slowed down, from an average of over 2.4% per year between 1995-2005 to less than 1.3% per year since then.

The bottleneck is not the technology – though faster advances certainly wouldn't hurt – but rather a lack of complementary process innovation, workforce reskilling and business dynamism. Simply plugging in new technologies without changing business organization and workforce skills is like paving the cow paths. It leaves the real benefits largely untapped.

However, by making complementary investments, we can speed up productivity growth. In this way, the economic pie will be bigger, giving us trillions of dollars of additional resources to address challenges in healthcare, the environment, poverty, national security and overall economic well-being.

While productivity is important, it isn't everything. There is no economic law that says that everyone will benefit from technological advances or productivity growth. As the economic pie grows, it is possible for some people to be left behind, even as others benefit disproportionately. For the first two centuries since 1776, that was not the case. Most Americans benefitted as we created an economic system that generated shared prosperity. But over the past several decades, the benefits of economic growth have been much more unequal. Not only has median income barely grown since the late 1990s, but other social indictors, have worsened. Deaths from despair, namely suicide, drug addiction and suicide, are skyrocketing, particularly among Americans with a high school education or less. And for the first time in history, average life expectance of Americans has begun to fall, again driving by worse mortality of less educated Americans. It's no coincidence that these are exactly the Americans who haven't shared in our economic growth, as technologies automate many of the tasks they once did. As a society, we haven't helped them develop the new skills needed to thrive in an increasingly technological economy, or updated our organizations to put their skills to effective use.

What does the future hold? That depends almost entirely on our choices, including the choices made in Congress.

My policy recommendations can be grouped into five key areas.

Reinvent Education

This is not the first time America has faced a challenge from powerful new general purpose technologies. In the early 1800s, nearly 90% of Americans worked in agriculture, by the end of that century it was only

42%. The former farmers didn't simply become unemployed. Instead they were redeployed. They went into manufacturing and services, driving productivity and growth. A big reason that transition was successful was that America led the world in education, first via primary schools and later high schools. This created not only world-leading prosperity, but also one of most equal societies on the planet, with extensive upward mobility.

Today, we need a similar commitment to education. It won't be enough to simply invest more in human capital, although we should surely do that. We must also reinvent education to focus on the types of skills that machines can't match. As noted above, these include creativity (in science, the arts, entrepreneurship and beyond) as well as interpersonal skills (leadership, teamwork, persuasion, caring, coaching, etc.). The skills needed are not just hard skills, like software coding and STEM, but also the softer skills, from the arts, to social work, to entrepreneurship. My experience is that both hard skills and soft skills can be nurtured by the right environment and curricula.

This transformation can and must be done not only in K-12 schools, but also through an expanded commitment to vocational education, our colleges and universities, graduate education and life-long learning. Online education is also part of the solution, not simply via MOOCs, but also via embracing the "experiment and test" philosophy that enables so many technology firms to rapidly iterate and improve their offerings. The same philosophy needs to be brought to education.

Rebalance Capital and Labor

As noted in the recent report by the MIT Work of the Future initiative, of which I'm a member, our tax code and other policies are heavily skewed toward capital at the expense of labor. As the share of GDP that goes to labor continues to fall, we must create a more level playing field, particularly as AI starts to affect more and more of the labor force. This means taxing capital and labor at comparable rates, encouraging investments in human capital just as we do for physical capital, and updating corporate governance to recognized workers as stakeholders alongside stockholders. We can also expand the earned income tax credit to boost incomes for the working poor and use revenues from carbon taxes and other Pigouvian taxes to lower taxes on work and create a carbon dividend.

Invest in US Technology Leadership

The US has long been a leader not just in AI, but in a broad swath of technologies. That technological leadership is at serious risk because even as we have cut federal investment in R&D, other nations have boosted theirs. Data from the AI Index, where I serve on the steering committee, documents a host of metrics that show the falling share of research being done in the US. Federal science agencies, working with our leading universities and private industry, have a central role in maintaining and extending America's science and technology leadership in AI. In particular, my MIT colleagues Jon Gruber and Simon Johnson have put forth a compelling plan for Jumpstarting America that not only extends our pre-eminence but also shares the benefits from innovation more widely.

Welcome High Skill Immigrants

A vastly disproportionate of America's leaders in science and business are immigrants or the children of immigrants. This reflect the fact that the US has long been a magnet for talent and a place where that talent could flourish. Sadly, that strength is being severely undercut by our recent immigration policies. When I asked my students at MIT what was the most important message I should being to Washington regarding AI policy, they unanimously advised me to push for less restrictive immigration policies. Every international student I spoke to, whether undergraduate, graduate or post-doc, as well as most of my foreign-born faculty colleagues, had harrowing stories to tell of difficulties they have add with our immigration and visa process. These have prevented them from attending conferences, participating in research projects and in far too many cases, led them to move to Canada, Europe, India, China or other nations to continue their research, rather than the US. A more welcoming immigration policy, especially for top talent, would not only be a huge boost for the US, but also good for the world, since it would make it easier for the best minds to work together.

Support Entrepreneurship

While stories of technology-driven entrepreneurship are common in the media, the data tell a different story: as documented by John Haltiwanger, Steven Davis and many others, new business formation is down, fewer people are working in young firms, economic and geographic mobility is down and almost every measure of business dynamism has declined over the past 20 years. This has hindered new technologies from being translated into new products and service that benefit the economy. Boosting entrepreneurship will help reverse the stagnation of wages for the bottom half of the income distribution, particularly those groups who have been most adversely affected by automation. This is not because everyone should become an entrepreneur or gig worker but because it’s the core function of entrepreneurs to invent the new goods, services, companies and jobs that supplant the previous types of work that are being automated. Among the policies that can help with this is a reform of occupational licensing, decoupling of healthcare from employment, and direct investments in teaching entrepreneurship and boosting new business formation.

Artificial Intelligence is the most transformative technology of our era. It has begun to affect many specific tasks, but its biggest impacts are still ahead. AI creates enormous opportunities for boosting productivity. But the key to unlocking these benefits is not merely more or better technology investment, but also investment in the intangible complements, including new skills, new organizational processes and new business models. As powerful and pervasive as AI will be, we are not facing the imminent end of work or mass unemployment. Instead, we are witnessing a growing inequality and disruption as many tasks, disproportionately those done by lower wage workers, are affected by the technology.

With the right policies, we can harness the power of AI. With the right policies, particularly in reinventing education, rebalancing capital and labor, investing in US technological leadership, welcoming immigrants and boosting entrepreneurship we can create an economy that creates not only prosperity but shared prosperity. With the right polices, the next decade can be the best decade in US history since 1776.

References

[1] Acemoglu, D. & Autor, D. (2011) Skills, tasks and technologies: Implications for employment and earnings. In *Handbook of Labor Economics*, Volume 4b.

[2] Acemoglu, D. & Restrepo, P. (2019). Automation and New Tasks: How Technology Displaces and Reinstates Labor. *Journal of Economic Perspectives*, 33(2), 3–30. doi:10.1257/jep.33.2.3.

[3] Autor, D., & Salomons, A. (2017, June). Does productivity growth threaten employment? *In ECB Forum on Central Banking*, Sintra, Portugal (pp. 26-28).

[4] Autor, David, H. (2019, May). Work of the Past, Work of the Future. In *AEA Papers and Proceedings* (Vol. 109, pp. 1-32).

[5] Brynjolfsson, E. & McAfee, A. (2008). Investing in the IT that makes a competitive difference. *Harvard Business Review*, 86(7), 98–107.

[6] Brynjolfsson, E. & McAfee, A. (2014). *The second machine age: work, progress, and prosperity in a time of brilliant technologies.* First edition. New York: W.W. Norton & Company.

[7] Brynjolfsson, E. & McAfee, A. (2015) Will Humans go the way of horses? Labor in the Second Machine Age. *Foreign Affairs*, 94(4), 8–14.

[8] Brynjolfsson, E. & McAfee, A. (2017). The business of artificial intelligence: What it can—and cannot—do for your organization. *Harvard Business Review Big Idea Digital Articles*. July 3–11.

[9] Brynjolfsson, E. & Mitchell, T. (2017). National Academies of Sciences, Engineering and Medicine. *Information Technology and the U.S. Workforce: Where Are We and Where Do We Go From Here?* Washington, DC: The National Academies Press. doi: 10.17226/24649.

[10] Brynjolfsson, E., & Mitchell, T. (2017). What can machine learning do? Workforce implications. *Science*, 358(6370), 1530–1534. doi: 10.1126/science.aap8062.

[11] Brynjolfsson, E., Eggers, F., & Collis (Gannanameni), A. (2019). Using massive online choice experiments to measure changes in well-being. *Proceedings of the National Academy of Sciences* 116(15), 7250-7255. doi: 10.1073/pnas.1815663116.

[12] Brynjolfsson, E., Rock, D., & Syverson, C. (2019) The Productivity J-Curve: How Intangibles Complement General Purpose Technologies, *American Economic Journal: Macro (forthcoming).*

[13] Brynjolfsson, E., Rock, D., & Syverson, C. (2019). Artifical intelligence and the modern productivity paradox: A clash of expectations and statistics. In A. Agrawal, J. Gans, & A. Goldfarb (Eds.) The economics of artificial intelligence: An agenda (pp.23–57). *National Bureau of Economic Research Conference Report.* University of Chicago Press.

[14] Brynjolfsson, Erik, Tom Mitchell, and Daniel Rock. 2018. "What Can Machines Learn, and What Does It Mean for Occupations and the Economy?" *AEA Papers and Proceedings*, 108: 43-47.

[15] D. Autor, D. A. Mindell, & E. B. Reynolds (2019). *The work of the future: Shaping technology and institutions.* Cambridge, MA: Massachusetts Institute of Technology Industrial Performance Center.

[16] E., McAfee, A., & Spence, M. (2014). New World Order: Labor, Capital, and Ideas in the Power Law Economy. *Foreign Affairs,* 93(4), 44–53. http://www.jstor.org/stable/24483556.

[17] Mitchell, T., & Brynjolfsson, E. (2017). Track how technology is transforming work. *Nature,* 544(7650), 290–292. doi: 10.1038/544290a.

[18] Russakovsky, O., Deng, J., Su, H., Krause, J., Satheesh, S., Ma, S., ... & Berg, A. C. (2015). Imagenet large scale visual recognition challenge. *International journal of computer vision,* 115(3), 211-252.

TESTIMONY OF REBEKAH KOWALSKI, VICE PRESIDENT, MANUFACTURING SERVICES, MANPOWERGROUP

Ms. KOWALSKI. Chairwoman Stevens, Ranking Member Dr. Baird, and Representative Marshall, on behalf of ManpowerGroup, thanks for the invitation to speak today on such an incredibly important topic. ManpowerGroup is the world leader in innovative workforce solutions. Every day we connect more than 600,000 people to work around the world in a wide range of skills and industries. One of our most predominant industry sectors is the manufacturing sector, and I oversee our manufacturing solutions practice. I've worked with a lot of companies as they are struggling to deal with the twin challenge of finding enough rightly skilled talent, and figuring out how they're going to navigate the bright new future that digital offers.

Manufacturers are reporting talent shortages as they struggle to find the right blend of technical and soft skills. Our perspective is that AI, machine learning, and other digital technologies produce new jobs that require new skills. Some of those we can't even imagine yet.

Our research shows that over 90 percent of employers expect to be impacted by digitization over the next 2 years. Eighty-seven percent of them plan to maintain or increase head count. Four percent say they don't know. And yes, there is a small number, 9 percent of them that say that they anticipate a reduction. Fully 75 percent say this is going to require new skills, skills that we do not currently have in our workforce, and skills that we can't actually even anticipate.

In 2017 we released a study with MXD, which was formerly known as the Digital, Manufacturing, and Design Innovation Institute, on how digital technologies, including AI and machine learning, would impact manufacturing jobs. The study was accomplished in partnership with academia and industry, and identified 165 new or significantly evolved roles. Today the majority of manufacturing roles are in the general entry level population, by count. That is— those are roles like picker/packer, assembler, operator, helper, laborer. And the manufacturing sector, the backdrop here, is that we are going to produce 3.5 million new jobs over the next decade, while at the same time 2.7 manufacturing workers are set to retire. Many of the new jobs will be in these more specialized areas, like technicians, testers, analysts, specialists, and that's a significant shift for us.

We have the following concerns. First, employers are uncertain about how digitization will impact roles and skills, and over what period of time. Second, the ability of employers of all sizes to invest in upscaling falls far short of what is required to produce the workforce they need, both from a time and resource perspective. Third, the talent shortage impacts all types of talent, from entry level to leadership, meaning employers have to determine the best way to allocate precious dollars. That disproportionately impacts small and mid-sized manufacturers.

There are several obstacles to being resourceful around talent attraction and upscaling. One, it's difficult for organizations to predict workforce needs more than a year in advance. Strategic work force planning does not have as long of a horizon as it needs. Without enough exact match talent, we need to shift to hiring on potential and learnability, but H.R. (human resources) systems and processes are still geared toward finding an exact match. Third, job descriptions need to be less stationary, and more evolutionary, so that individuals can actually anticipate the need for ongoing learning and adaptation. And four, organizations lack sufficient funding for workforce training.

An example of improved training processes is what we do with Rockwell Automation in our Academy of Advanced Manufacturing, where we take veterans and we put them through a 12-week embedded program, and we graduate them as Certified Automation Technicians. They walk away with a job that, on average, is double what they were making when they came in, and the employer walks away with the talent that they need. With 12 million manufacturing workers in the U.S., we need those kinds of nimble programs, many, many more of them, in order to ensure that people have a path to sustainable prosperity, and we need to start now. Don't count the humans out.

Talent is, in fact, the most renewable resource we have on the planet. It is ready to learn, adapt, and thrive in new environments, and we need to work collectively now across educators, employers, and individuals to become proactive builders of talent to develop a workforce with the skills employers and individuals need to remain competitive, both now and in the future.

Thank you again to the Subcommittee for the opportunity to share my testimony.

[The prepared statement of Ms. Kowalski follows:]

PREPARED STATEMENT OF REBEKAH KOWALSKI, VICE PRESIDENT, MANPOWER MANUFACTURING U.S. HOUSE OF REPRESENTATIVES COMMITTEE ON SCIENCE, SPACE, AND TECHNOLOGY, SUBCOMMITTEE ON RESEARCH AND TECHNOLOGY HEARING ON "ARTIFICIAL INTELLIGENCE AND THE FUTURE OF WORK" SEPTEMBER 24, 2019

Chairwoman Stevens, Ranking member Baird, and members of the Subcommittee -

On behalf of ManpowerGroup, thank you for the invitation to speak today on the impact of machine learning and artificial intelligence on the workforce.

ManpowerGroup is a world leader in innovative workforce solutions. Every day, we connect more than 600,000 people to meaningful work across a wide range of skills and industries. We are a $21 billion company that operates in 80 countries with nearly 30,000 employees.

Context of the Manufacturing Labor Market

In 2017, we released a study with MxD (formerly the Digital Manufacturing Design & Innovation Institute "DMDII") on how digital technologies, including Artificial Intelligence and Machine Learning would impact manufacturing jobs. The study identified 165 roles that would either be new or evolved.[37]

This evolution of roles is impacting all sectors as artificial intelligence, robotics, machine learning, and automation hasten innovation cycles creating new products and services. See Figure 1 below for an example of

[37] ttps://www.uilabs.org/innovation-platforms/manufacturing/taxonomy/ and h ttps://workforce-resources.manpowergroup.com/home/the-future-factory.

the roles that are evolving or emerging as these technologies are applied to the traditional sectors of Healthcare, FinTech, and Manufacturing:

New jobs and skill requirements are emerging at the same time as employers are having almost unprecedented difficulty in getting access to talent.

A hot jobs market with 107 consecutive months of job growth, 3.7% unemployment rate, and population growth that has hit an 80-year low are all key contributors. Our latest quarter of the*ManpowerGroup Employment Outlook Survey* shows a strong hiring intent across all sectors.[38] The bottom line is that today, there is < 1 person for each open job, including individuals who are on the sidelines and unemployed. And with the highest quit rate since 2001, the squeeze on employers is getting tighter. The future outlook is not much brighter. In Manufacturing specifically, the sector is set to produce 3.5 million new jobs over the next decade, but 2.5 million are on pace to retire, leaving US manufacturers with a 6 million shortfall in available talent for jobs that are evolving rapidly – a double squeeze.[39]

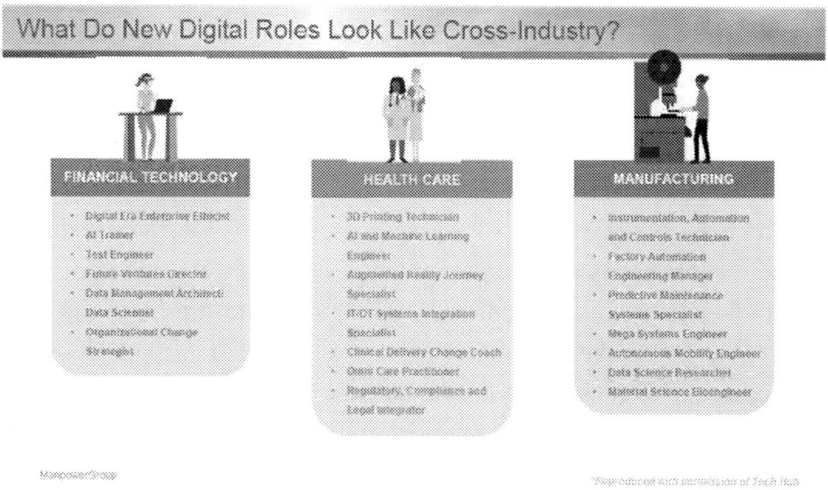

Figure 1. What Do New Digital Roles Look Like Cross-Industry?

[38] https://manpowergroup.us/meos/public/pdf/employment-outlook-forecast.pdf.
[39] https://manpowergroup.us/meos/public/pdf/employment-outlook-forecast.pdf.

ManpowerGroup's annual Talent Shortage Survey measures the difficulty employers are having in hiring talent. In 2018, 46% of US employers reported difficulty in finding the talent they were looking for, this is compared to 14% just 8 years prior.[40] Of the Top 10 toughest jobs to fill, 3 are particularly relevant to Manufacturing: Skilled Trades leads the list at #1; Technicians are at #7; and Production & Machine Operators are at #10.[41] Employers say the top three reasons they have difficulty in finding talent:

- 26% said lack of applicants
- 21% said lack of experience
- 14% said applicants lack required hard skills (technical competencies)[42]

ManpowerGroup's Recruitment Difficulty Index aggregates across all sectors and roles. We believe the double squeeze of available workforce and rapid evolution of roles & skills is reflected in the difficulty we are having in recruiting individuals for our thousands of customers across the U.S. Figure 2 shows the 'heat map' comparing recruiting difficulty in 2012 to 2019. As you can see, the market context for preparing the workforce for rapidly evolving roles & skills is one of scarcity. This climate will require employers to be resourceful and creative in evaluating and selecting talent. We advocate for hiring on potential (vs. 'exact match' of skills and experience), and then investing in upskilling and reskilling that talent to take them into the future. There is simply no 'fresh' resource of talent coming into the US either through an increase in population or significant populations of untapped potential. Digital technologies will certainly help close the gap, but it will also create new jobs and opportunities for which we are fundamentally unprepared.

---

[40] https://go.manpowergroup.com/talent-shortage-2018#shortagebycountry.
[41] https://go.manpowergroup.com/talent-shortage-2018#shortagebycountry.
[42] https://go.manpowergroup.com/talent-shortage-2018#shortagebycountry.

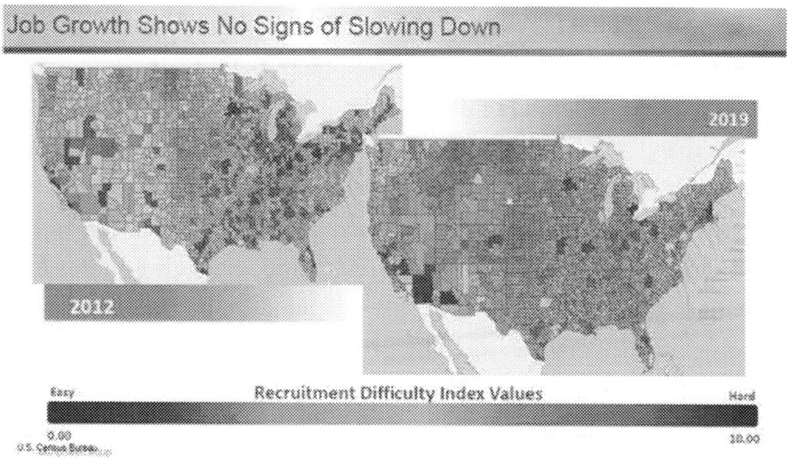

Figure 2. Job Growth Shows No Signs of Slowing Down.

Impacts of AI and Machine Learning on Manufacturing Workforce

ManpowerGroup's perspective is that the Digital Era will rush in new jobs that require new skills. Our research shows that 90%+ of employers expect to be impacted by digitization in the next two years, 75% believe that this will require new skills in their workforce. 87% of employers plan to increase or maintain headcount as these new technologies evolve their products and services, 4% are unsure of the impact and only 9% plan to decrease their workforce.

In the Manufacturing sector, the majority of roles are in the general, entry level production workforce that consists of roles such as picker/packer, assembler, operator, and helper/laborer. Our research with DMDII shows that as US manufacturing transitions to an increasingly digital model there will be an increase in higher skilled roles such as: analyst, specialist, tester and technician. It could take 1-2 years to train the skilled manufacturing workforce for roles of the future, and much longer to train the unskilled population. (For additional detail on this, please review pages 49-52 of the DMDII & ManpowerGroup Report, The Digital

Workforce Succession in Manufacturing). Individuals will move from the direct operation of tasks to using technology to facilitate those tasks, and in some cases, operating bundled technology to complete many more operations than they could if they were completing the tasks manually.

The speed at which evolved roles and skills are required is highly dependent on the speed of the uptake of technology inside of organizations. Figure 3 shows the general progression of technological generations in the Manufacturing sector. There is no crystal ball on timing, as organizations make the decision to make capital investments in new technology based on what they believe their return on investment (ROI) will be and over what timeline it will be achieved. This ROI can be measured in terms of increased productivity (faster time to market, lowered costs, etc), an evolved product offering that opens up new consumer markets and thus drives up revenue growth, or a complete reinvention of their playing field, and many points in between. See Figure 4 for a breakdown of what percentage of roles in manufacturing organizations are shifting, evolving and being redefined. 28% of evolving roles are on the production floor. Many organizations are on the sidelines, waiting to jump in as the price of technology drops, others are first adopters, and many more are operating legacy technologies in one plant and the newest, cutting-edge technologies at another. In general, those production facilities tied to food and pharma or a Tier 1 defense contractor, will tend to take up new technologies faster than, say, a small manufacturer who makes cutting tools and is a Tier 4 or 5 supplier. That said, a tipping point will be reached in terms of the percent of labor tied to manual and transactional tasks and the percentage of workers with the skills to operate and cooperate with the newest digital technologies. That tipping point will likely come sooner than the pace at which we are preparing our workforce.

This last point out is born out in some key data. Figure 5 shows the shift in both percentage of jobs and skills that employers are requiring as they increasingly digitize their operations, including an increased uptake in automation and AI technologies.

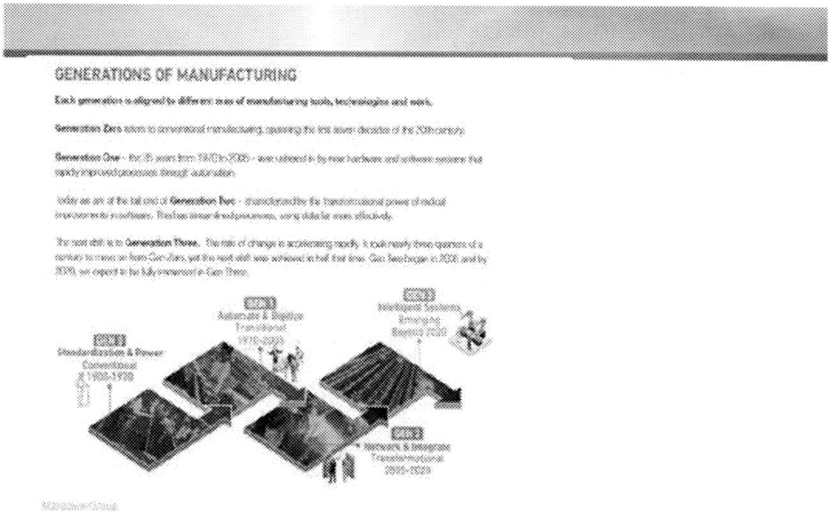

Figure 3. Generations of Manufacturing.

Figure 6 shows the increased investment that employers are making in training their employees. Much of this investment is driven by employers' understanding that the skills required to do jobs today are not the ones that will be required with tomorrow's technology. That said, based on our conversations with employers, ManpowerGroup has the following concerns:

- *First*: employers are uncertain about how digitization will impact roles and skills and over what time. As mentioned earlier, 75% of employers believe that digitization will require an evolution in skills, but they are less clear on the specifics of that evolution.
- *Second*: we hear regularly from employers across the spectrum of enterprise size that their ability to invest in upskilling falls short of what is required to produce the workforce they will need over time. Put simply, they need either more money or more time. Increasingly, the lack of skilled workforce is impeding their ability to invest in new technologies. A 2017 study by MAPI showed that for 60% of manufacturers surveyed, the number one impediment to investing in technology was a rightly skilled workforce.

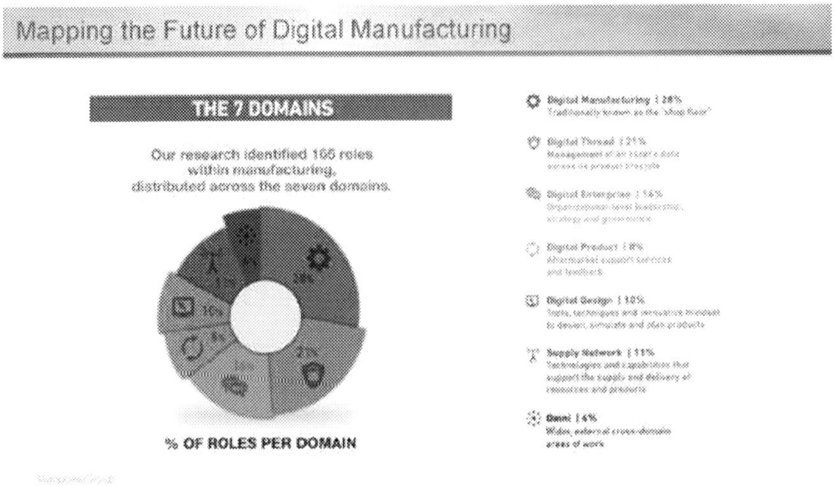

Figure 4. Mapping the Future of Digital Manufacturing.

- *Third*: the talent shortage is impacting employers across all types of talent: the transactional, entry-level talent on the production floor today; the transitional talent that will bridge their legacy and newly digital operations; and the transformational talent that will take them forward. This means that employers are having to determine the best way to allocate precious training and development dollars, what they will do themselves, and where they will need to invest in partnerships. This pain is felt across all sizes of employers, but there is a disproportional impact on the small and mid-size employers who not only have fewer resources, but also compete with large and mega-size employers who have established brands, richer benefits, and more varied career opportunities for employees.

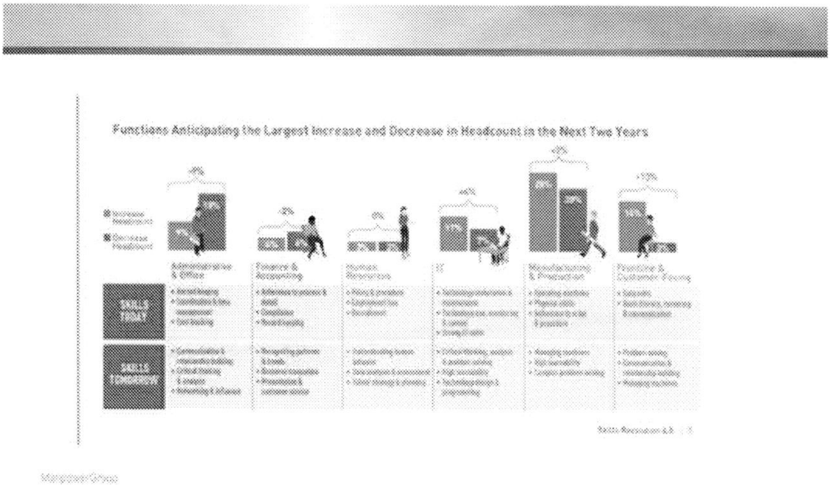

Figure 5. Functions Anticipating the Largest Increase and Decrease in Headcount in the Next Two Years.

Worker displacement is a risk in jobs that are heavily routinized (picker/packer, helper/laborer, and certain assembly and operator roles). The potential for displacement in terms of size and timing is, as indicated above, variable, but it is coming. It is helpful to think of this in terms of ladders and pipelines. Today, the bottom rung of the ladder in production is represented by the heavily routinized roles that require little in the way of qualifications to perform. As digital technologies are increasingly adopted, the bottom rung of the ladder is redefined. It is crucial that those individuals currently qualified for only entry-level work get on the ladder and move up with intent. It is also crucial that talent that cannot progress to certain new roles be pipelined into other roles that are created or redefined that may not be on the production floors.

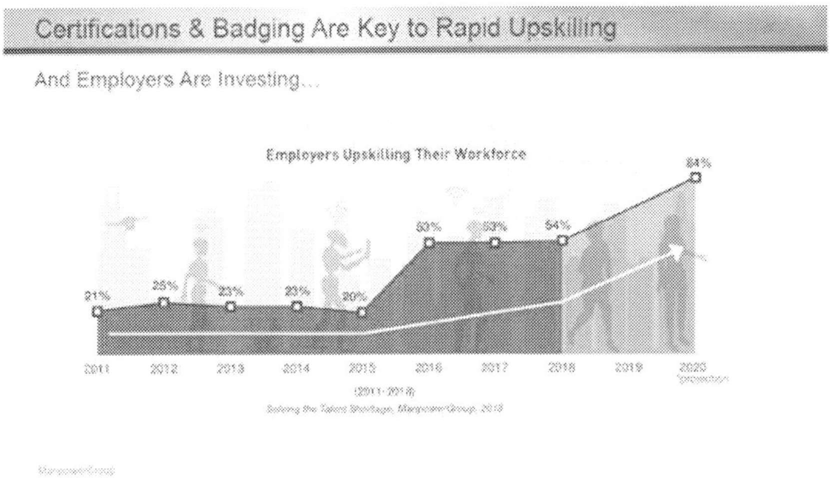

Figure 6. Certifications and Badging are Key to Rapid Upskilling.

Table 1.

Employees	Employers
• Improved worker safety through digital safeguards and predictive maintenance • Lower 'wear and tear' on workforce as robots take on repetitive motion and weight bearing tasks • Lowered barrier to workforce entry – examples: increased use of digital simulations for training and work process guidance • Enriched career paths that take individuals from entry level production to higher paying analyst, specialist, and technician roles or pipeline into newly created roles in other parts of the organization • More flexibility in how individuals work (at a distance, shift flexibility, etc.)	• Increased productivity • More rapid cycles of innovation improving overall US competitiveness in global manufacturing • Decreased waste as modeling evolves to increased use of digital twins for processes, products, services, and analytics for predicting behavior • Technology offsets some of the worker shortage, but this is offset by the need for talent to learn new skills to operate technologies in all domains of the modern manufacturing enterprise

Doing this will require organizations to be resourceful in terms of what is most important in hiring talent. From ManpowerGroup's perspective, the most important thing to measure for will be what we call Learnability, that is the ability to learn and acquire new skills and adapt to changing circumstances. This will help employers and employees weather ongoing cycles of adaptation with resilience.

New technology adoption will create many benefits for employees and employers, not limited to the above.

It is worth noting that ManpowerGroup also anticipates significant growth in the professional segment. See *Figure 7* for a representative listing of roles that we see emerging. We anticipate a continuing surge of cybersecurity related roles as "more digital" and "more data" becomes the mantra of modern manufacturing organization. The security of data moving across production floors and through the supply chain, not to mention how data is being used to drive new IP in the US or how assets that are tied to consumer safety and data are secured means an explosion in workforce tied to managing security at all levels and in all domains of manufacturing. ManpowerGroup's real-time analysis shows a shortage of 500,000 IT workers today.[43]

This shortage will compound very quickly as malicious attacks grow in both number and sophistication and goes beyond the IT domain into process and policy work, risk mitigation, data quality, and threat awareness. Additionally, we anticipate growth in the number of individuals who are responsible to train AI, determine strategic direction on product and process opportunities that emerge from the increased use of AI, provide guardrails and checkpoints on those strategies, and translate strategic direction into tactical execution. We also anticipate that in a more digital era, a premium will be placed on human connection, driving a surge in roles related to customer experience. These represent real opportunities for career path progression from all areas of the manufacturing organization.

---

[43] Data is ManpowerGroup Solutions proprietary analysis and the data is aggregated across multiple platforms including but not limited to ManpowerGroup's Recruitment Difficulty Index, ManpowerGroup Solutions TAPFIN IntelliReach platform, Gartner Talent Neuron and Bureau of Labor Statistics.

Figure 7. Manufacturing is Upskilling.

Unique Challenges for Small and Medium-Sized Manufacturer's

Most manufacturing firms in the United States are quite small. In 2016, there were 249,962 firms in the manufacturing sector, with all but 3,837 firms considered to be small (i.e., having fewer than 500 employees). In fact, three-quarters of these firms have fewer than 20 employees.[44] These organizations face unique challenges in the digital era, yet also have unique opportunity to benefit from it. Small and Medium-Sized Manufacturer's (SMM's) must invest in digital technologies that will help them grow and evolve their products and services that align with shifting market demand. They must invest in technology, however, any investment in tech is wasted if they aren't also investing in talent that have the skills to use it.

The double squeeze outlined earlier is also impacting SMM's. We hear regularly from SMM's that they are having difficulty in finding, hiring, training, re-training, and retaining talent.

---

[44] U.S. Census Bureau, Statistics of U.S. Businesses.

ManpowerGroup's 2018 Talent Shortage Survey reveals that small and mid-size companies have a bit of an edge. *Figure 8* shows that though micro and small companies across all sectors are having difficulty finding talent, the largest companies experience the highest level of difficulty.

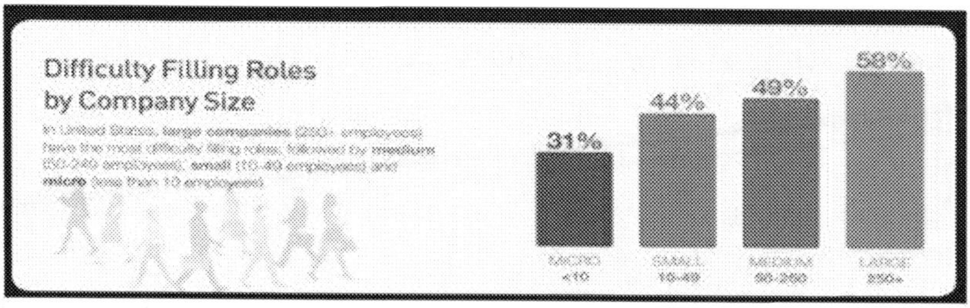

Figure 8. Difficulty Filling Roles by Company Size.

- Opportunity: Generally, SMM's have more flexibility to take risks and be creative when tapping under-leveraged populations as there are fewer and less complex processes and systems for them to navigate in the talent acquisition and retention process. They can also be more creative in creating career, equity stake and owner pathways.
- Challenge: Traditional career paths are limited relative to their larger peers and in many cases are competing with larger organizations with richer benefits packages with greater leverage in pay and incentive plans and more varied career opportunities. Many SMM's have felt the sting of investing in creative recruiting and training programs just to see the talent siphoned off by larger corporations. Though SMM's can be nimbler and more creative, they have fewer resources to invest in talent acquisition, and learning & development and more inherent risk if the bets they have made on building talent don't pay off.
- Distinct Challenge: SMM's have higher risk when it comes to cybersecurity as many of them do not have the resources to invest

> in specialized talent. In many cases, a single individual wears many hats (for example, an engineer doing the work of engineer, IT, and safety). As the costs associated with these risks escalate, there needs to be strong consideration around what talent pool SMM's can tap into to better secure the supply network.

SMM's will need to be incredibly resourceful in how they navigate acute talent shortages and evolving roles and skills in the digital era. The good news is that their size lowers barriers to creativity and agility; however, they will need more support from public and private entities such as the MEP network to guide their short- and long-term talent strategies and market their unique career opportunities. SMM's will need to seek out ways in their communities to work with each other and their customers to create talent channels to create effective change. Shared platforms - or coopetition - that maximize their investments on talent acquisition, learning & development, employee transportation, and talent sharing will be important especially as they increasingly consider non-traditional pools of talent that can help them out of their talent crisis.

Retraining and Professional Development of Current Workforce

With less than one person available for each job opening in the U.S. today[45] finding rightly skilled talent for the manufacturing workforce has never been more challenging. The manufacturing sector in the U.S. is estimated to produce up to 2 million new jobs over the next decade. At the same time, almost 2.7 million manufacturing workers are set to retire by 2025 (taking their knowledge and skills with them).[46]

---

[45] Bureau of Labor Statistics. September 2019, https://www.bls.gov/news.release/empsit.nr0.htm.

[46] Skills Gap and Future of Work Study, Deloitte Insights and The Manufacturing Institute, 2018.

Against the demographic backdrop outlined in the first section, we know new workers will not be enough to close the gap. Technological evolutions will be able to close some of the gap, but we must become far more resourceful in how we look at our current workforce and workforce re- training programs.

This is not just about worker training specific to production roles, but also the entire ecosystem of manufacturing as well as pipelining individuals into jobs where they have adjacent skills (as noted earlier, ManpowerGroup believes there will be growth in cyber, quality, customer service, analyst, specialist, and technician roles). There are several obstacles to ensuring mobility of talent inside of organizations:

- Strategic workforce planning – organizations struggle to balance the long-term and short-term of their workforce planning. It is difficult for them to predict needs more than one year into the future.
- Systems and processes – talent acquisition and management systems have been fine-tuned to assumptions around abundance. Systems and processes are geared toward getting the highest possible fit and systematically weeding out talent that is not an exact match. As hiring on potential becomes increasingly important, systems need to be re-programmed and re-trained (many are increasingly AI driven) and processes need to be re-thought.
    - Our analysis showed that in September 2019 there were over 500,000 open IT jobs in the U.S. – that's roughly the population of Minneapolis. Almost half of these jobs are for software engineers and a quarter are IT project managers. Employers are demanding more specific skills for these positions today than they did two years ago, such as expertise in Amazon Web Services rather than just Cloud. In two more years, it will be different again. This rapid evolution is having tremendous ripple effects on all industries, especially manufacturing. Therefore, processes that govern workforce

eligibility need to be revisited to determine if they are unnecessarily restrictive and artificially limiting the available talent pool. Similarly, talent management systems that support the existing population need to be re-set to make talent mobility options more transparent to hiring managers.

- Evolved job descriptions – job descriptions are created and often stay stagnant, long after technology has impacted the jobs and evolved the skills required to do them. Modern HR Information Systems do not currently allow for rapid evolution of job descriptions nor is there a general culture and mindset that supports continuous evolution of skills in an organization. This is predominantly because, from a historical perspective, evolution of tasks to create outputs was seen as something that needs to be aligned with pay rate increases. Today the tasks are the same, but they are done differently, which does not always require a revision in the compensation plan.
- Sufficient funding for worker training – Learning & Development organizations have been downsized and more worker training is being accomplished through partnerships and cooperative agreements. Organizations are in the tough position of determining which roles need training first and how to deliver it at speed and scale. Navigating funding options for worker training at the state and federal level is complex and the requirements from incentives for specific pools of talent, types, of training to measurements of success can be drastically different. In some instances, funding programs are aligned to outdated definitions (such as multi-year and 2,000- hour requirements on certain apprenticeships) and do not align with organizations' willingness to experiment and take risks. The net impact is that an organization's pilot program on worker training may be limited in its scale and benefit only a relatively small percentage of workers.

The critical blend for the workforce now and in the future is soft, technical, and digital skills as shown in Figures 9 and 10.

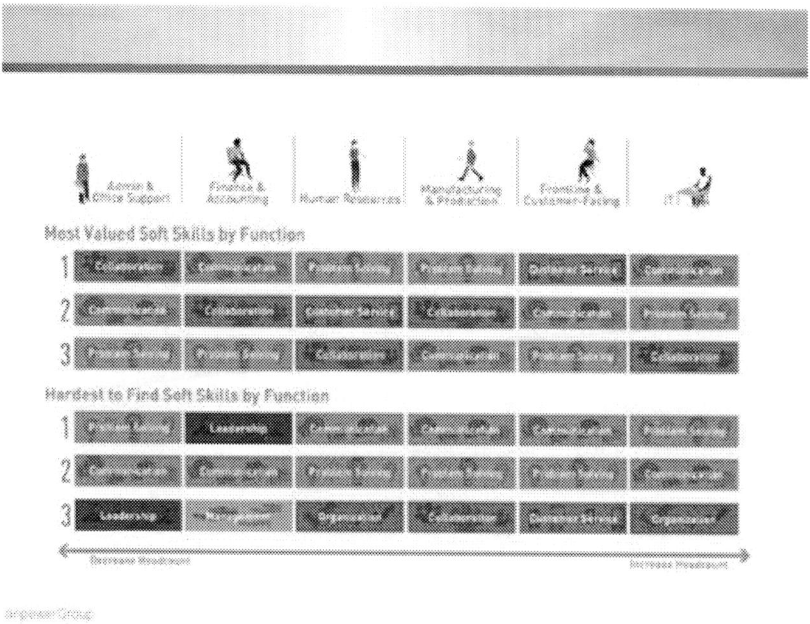

Figure 9. Most Valued Soft Skills by Function; Hardest to Find Soft Skills by Function.

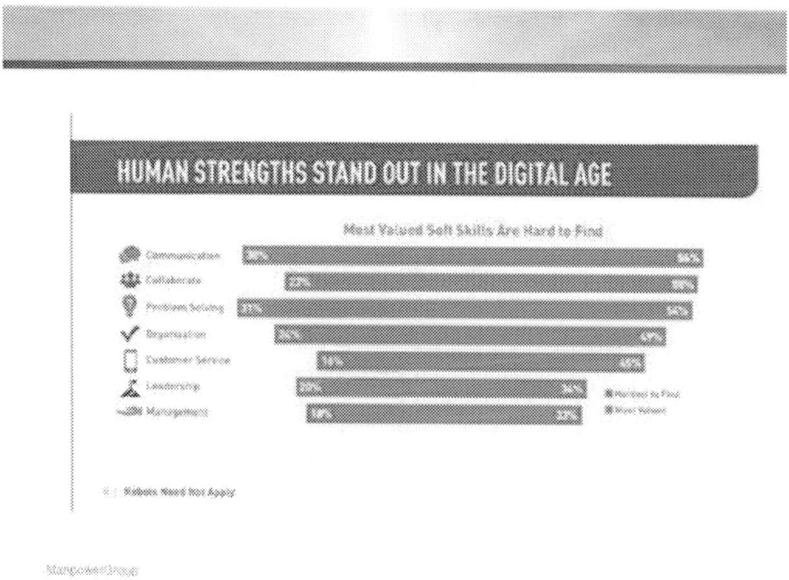

Figure 10. Human Strengths Stand Out in the Digital Age.

Improved Training & Recruitment to Develop Skilled Technical Workforce

While much of the training and recruitment needs are addressed above there are additional points to consider.

An example of improved training for a skilled technical workforce can be found in our work with Veterans. Veterans share many technical and soft skills that are critical in the digital economy, but often have difficulty representing their skills in terms employers understand. This is increasingly prevalent in high tech manufacturing jobs where electro-mechanical skills are at a premium and where large numbers of military personnel are working on industrial computer systems. We looked at skills adjacencies and the concept of learnability using in-depth assessments and identified veterans who'd benefit from the Academy of Advanced Manufacturing. In partnership with Rockwell Automation, we invested in an academy to upskill and reskill veterans for higher-paying, in-demand jobs within the digital manufacturing industry. The program continues to be a win-win. We're helping service men and women earn more – the majority of academy graduates have doubled; some even tripled their previous salaries - and stay employable for the long term while helping employers address their skills gap.

In recruiting, we need to be more resourceful in working with under-leveraged populations such as formerly incarcerated, limited eligibility (no HS diploma or GED), women, individuals with physical and cognitive disabilities. It would take 243,934 people with Disabilities to connect to jobs and match their respective unemployment rate to the 3.7% national rate. There are also over 400,000 military spouses in the U.S. and only half are participating in the labor market with double the national unemployment rate.[47] These represent excellent talent pools to tap into and digital technologies decrease the amount of time to train, onboard and provide ongoing reinforcement.

---

[47] Bureau of Labor Statistics. September 2019. https://www.bls.gov/jlt/.

We need to reimagine partnership between individuals, education and employers and become systems thinkers. Talent strategy has evolved from a historical high-growth, highly stable environment, where companies had time and resources to be builders of talent. Individuals joined organizations for life and stayed long enough to provide a strong return on investment.

Globalization brought shrinking margins and cost-cutting. Companies responded by labor cost reduction and just-in-time recruitment. Wages, once set by the enterprise, are now set by the market, and the bifurcation of the workforce began. Higher skilled people enjoyed pay increases, lower skilled people did not. Companies became consumers of talent and minimizers of overall labor costs.

Now, companies need to quickly adjust to what is happening in the marketplace to get a quicker return on investment and grow. Talent cycles are shorter, so people need to upskill in short bursts. Training has to impact more quickly and present a faster time to value. Even with low unemployment, wages are rising for people with in-demand skills.

To win in the digital age an effective talent strategy should have four parts: build, buy, borrow and bridge. See Figure 11. Build your talent pipeline by identifying future potential, driving a culture of learnability through the organization and providing accelerated training programs will be critical to success in the digital age.

Buy skills where necessary. Employers need to understand that candidates are consumers too; in order to attract and engage the best and brightest, HR needs to be a master marketer. We need to continue to evolve the narrative around manufacturing. The word manufacturing connotes 'dark, dirty, and dangerous.' Better messaging needs to align with words that attract talent: makers, maker spaces, innovation, high tech, etc. Manufacturing is where innovation and high tech go hand in hand.

Borrow from external talent sources. Organizations must learn to cultivate communities of workers inside and outside of the company.

Bridge people with adjacent skills from one role to another to complement existing skills. Leaders have a critical job to optimize the skills they have and find alternative pathways so those whose skills no longer fit can bridge to changing or emerging roles.

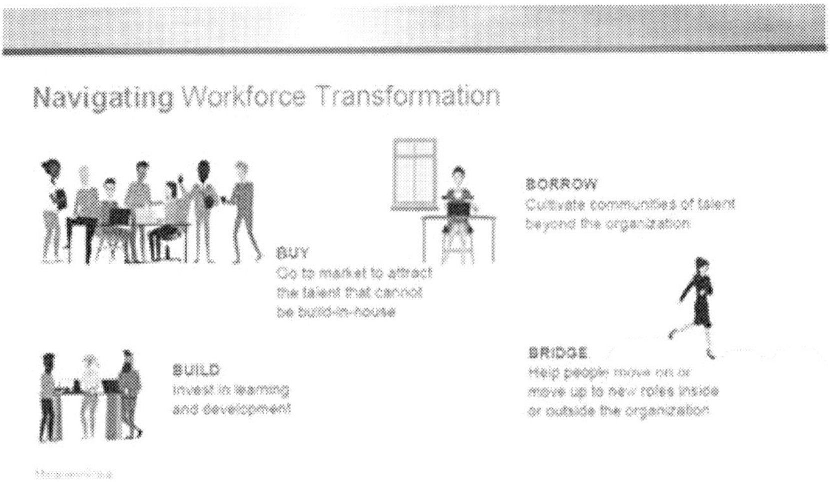

Figure 11. Navigating Workforce Transformation.

Conclusion

Digitization, automation and transformation are impacting every industry, disrupting skills and creating new jobs. Manufacturing is the vanguard, with new roles appearing as fast as others become obsolete.

Manufacturers are reporting growing talent shortages as they struggle to find the right blend of technical and soft skills to fill new positions. The catalyst for the early stages of this skills shift was automation – machine strength. Now sector wide transformation has been turbocharged by the Internet of Things, the digitally connected enterprise, the relentless expansion of data and Artificial Intelligence (AI) to handle the scope of the challenge – machine thinking.

The potential for manufacturing to transform industries and drive economic growth has never been greater, thanks to the rapid advancement of new technologies. Against the backdrop of an existing skills shortage and with skills needs evolving so rapidly, we can only reach this potential with new and evolving skills for the current and future workforce. Talent is the most renewable resource on our planet: ready to learn, adapt and thrive in new environments. Employers can no longer go to market to buy new skills when they want them. We need to all become builders of talent to develop a workforce with the skills employers and individuals need to remain competitive.

Rebekah Kowalski
Vice President, Manpower Manufacturing

Rebekah Kowalski was appointed Vice President of Manpower Manufacturing in January 2019. She leads a matrixed team of sales, marketing, delivery, service, and consulting professionals across Manpower's Enterprise (national) and Convenience (branch-based) teams to drive break-through growth in the sector in the US and Canada and to upskill Manpower's thousands of North American-based associates.

Rebekah's work focuses on developing solutions that help organizations and leaders deal with the implications of both the shortage of rightly skilled workers, and the evolution of roles and skills. Rebekah led the team that worked with MxD to identify how roles and skills will evolve as manufacturing transforms with the introduction of more digital technologies.

Previously, Rebekah served as Vice President, Client Workforce Solutions - ManpowerGroup, North America, driving business growth through cross-brand solution development that supported clients and their workforce by creating sustainable pipelines of future-focused talent through new models and partnerships.

Rebekah is a recognized expert in innovative workforce solutions in the Manufacturing sector. She co-created and leads with Rockwell Automation the design, development, and management of the Academy of Advanced Manufacturing, a partnership between ManpowerGroup and Rockwell Automation to develop future-focused talent.

Rebekah is passionate about education leading into a sustainable career and has served on both the Board of the Wisconsin Education Business Roundtable and the Executive Committee of Competitive Wisconsin. She is currently an active member of the University of Wisconsin System Business Council and the Advisory Board of i.c.stars, an immersive technology workforce training and placement program for promising young adults.

TESTIMONY OF DR. SUE ELLSPERMANN, PRESIDENT, IVY TECH COMMUNITY COLLEGE

Dr. ELLSPERMANN. Thank you, Chairwoman Stevens, Ranking Member Baird, welcome, and Representative Marshall. It's really a privilege to be here representing community colleges today, and Ivy Tech Community College specifically, as we talk through machine learning, artificial intelligence, and particularly how that's affecting community colleges, and how we're working with industry and businesses to establish an ecosystem to address the changing demands. I also will speak at the end about what the Federal Government could do to assist in this work.

So remember that community colleges are the most common type of U.S. College, with Ivy Tech being one of those, established in 1963 as a vocational/technical college, now the largest in the Nation Statewide system, singly accredited, with 150,000 students and 18 campuses, 40 locations. But think about our student, who is now—the traditional student is that community college-like student, who is part time. Average age is probably 27 years old, Pell eligible, and a quarter of those students have dependents, children, that is, and you can see more in our report.

But how will that impact us as we look at AI and machine learning? And what you heard from several of my colleagues here is that there will be some displacement, but with that displacement will become very good opportunities, and it's up to our community colleges to prepare those students, those employees, for the wide spectrum of industries and opportunities that are out there. So let me talk about just a few of the very concrete things that we've done, and I thank Ms. Kowalski for sharing some of those as well in the manufacturing space, but one that I'm sure she'd be interested in is the partnership that Ivy Tech's done with the Smart Automation Certification Alliance as they've developed the first certifications in industry 4.0, which we know will be factories of the future, and the kind of credentials we'll need in that very connected manufacturing environment.

But at the community college level, we work with many partners, for instance, Sales Force, through their Pathfinders Program to earn Sales Force developer and administrator certifications. We have many certificates in informatics and software development at the Associate level. We work with Apple in their iOS systems applications. We work with Cisco, as they overhaul their certifications, to embed those right into our IT programs. With Amazon Web Services, we are developing cloud computing certificates, and soon to be an Applied Associate in Cloud Computing. All of those are staying with those industries and particular businesses to make sure that we're providing our students with the kind of skills that they will need.

I'm going to speak to a partnership we have with industry, particularly our Achieve Your Degree Program, which is a redesign of the tuition reimbursement program, where industries actually pay for, at the end of that cycle, the tuition that that employee of theirs pursues, but we, concierge-style, come to the industry, that business, to enroll, to do financial aid eligibility, and then to ensure that the programs align with what the business has. In doing that, we've had a great partnership with our Indiana Chamber of Commerce, Statewide, more than 200 companies doing that. I'll just share one, with Cook Group in Bloomington, Indiana, where 500 of their employees are being skilled up, have already earned 100 credentials in the last 3 years.

Now, in design, we put everything, from an economist standpoint, into quadrants to make sure that the highest demand areas with the smallest supply of employees are being built up into those particular quadrants. We'll describe those quadrants more in our full report, but in doing that, we make sure that we are putting our focused energy in the high-demand areas, that we're shrinking problems that need to shrink, and that we are seeking equilibrium in this highly changing environment. And it's working. In IT we, just last year, increased our completions by 75 percent in a single year, and we see that across our programs.

I'm going to spend my last moments talking about what we could do with some Federal support. You know, employers hate to have to pay Unemployment Insurance (UI) into that trust fund. Several years ago, most of our States were in a deficit. We were in Indiana. Congressman Baird remembers that. Today we are at $900 million in the black. Those funds could be deployed toward this work re-scaling earlier than when that person is displaced, but when you decide on that technology, and we're hopeful that there will be some willingness of this Congress to look at making that available to a State and a community college system to experiment with how we could deploy a portion of those UI funds in these ways. We look for all kinds of support in reducing regulation so that we can change at the speed of the technologies that we're working with to ensure that all of our workers have those opportunities. And with that, I'll just thank you for the opportunity for appearing before the Subcommittee, and the opportunity to share the work of Ivy Tech Community College.

[The prepared statement of Dr. Ellspermann follows:]

Written Statement of Dr. Sue Ellspermann, PhD, Ivy Tech Community College of Indiana Before the Research and Technology Subcommittee of the Committee on Science, Space, and Technology Hearing Title: Artificial Intelligence and the Future of Work United States House of Representatives September 24, 2019

Chairwoman Stevens, Ranking Member Baird, and Members of the Subcommittee, thank you for the opportunity to appear before you today to represent Ivy Tech Community College of Indiana and share with you the work that we, and other community colleges across the country, are doing to develop a skilled technical workforce of the future.

Today, I will discuss how machine learning and artificial intelligence are affecting how community colleges and vocational schools educate and train the workforce; how Ivy Tech Community College is working with industry, government, and academia to establish an ecosystem to address the changing demands for the skilled technical workforce; how Ivy Tech is using its Career Coaching and Employer Connections program to assist students in developing a career plan for the jobs of the future; and how the Federal government can work with community colleges and vocational schools to address future research and education needs.

Community colleges are the most common type of U.S. two-year colleges, and they offer millions of students a better way to reach their goals, whether their goal is to get a good career in a shorter period of time, or to get a better, more affordable start to a bachelor's degree by transferring credits on to a four-year school.

For its part, Ivy Tech was founded in 1963 as Indiana Vocational Technical College. Back then, we focused primarily on technical and vocational education. Now, we are Indiana's only community college, a statewide entity with 18 campuses and more than 40 locations. We are accredited by the Higher Learning Commission and offer programs in advanced manufacturing, engineering, and applied science; information technology; nursing and health sciences; business, logistics, and supply chain; public affairs and social sciences; and arts, sciences, and education. Additionally, we offer more than 100 transfer programs with in-state and out-of-state schools and provide students with hands-on experience in some of the state's most advanced technologies and training facilities. While we are the largest singly-accredited statewide community college system in the nation, we shape our curriculum with the needs of local communities in mind and keep higher education accessible for those communities' residents, which results in over 97% of our graduates staying in Indiana.

Our students typically attend on a part-time basis, and the average age of our students is 27 years old. Half of our students are Pell-Eligible and 24% have dependents.

Table 2.

Ivy Tech Student Demographics	
White	73%
Black/ African-American	11%
Hispanic/ Latino	4%
Multiracial	4%
Asian	2%
Other / Not Available	5%

How Machine Learning and Artificial Intelligence Are Affecting How Community Colleges and Vocational Schools Educate and Train the Workforce

Most conversations about the impacts of artificial intelligence (AI) and machine learning in the workplace end with one word: displacement. It is true. Research by The Center for Technology at Brookings states that 14% to 54% of jobs will be eliminated due to automation over the next 20 years. In addition, more than half of CEO's suggest they will be reducing jobs while only 16% plan on increasing jobs. Low-skilled workers in industries such as manufacturing, logistics, and customer service call centers will indeed be displaced, but that does not mean they will be unemployed or unemployable. According to Forbes, where the evolution of technology threatens jobs, it also creates new jobs. Because community colleges were created to be responsive to workforce and student needs in particular communities, AI and machine learning challenge community college and vocational school leaders to prepare a wide spectrum of students for industries that are changing faster than higher education has been able to move in the past. As such, community colleges are forming new partnerships with businesses to provide employers with exactly what they need out of their employees by developing new certifications and nimble programs to address the demand and changes that will inevitably arise from the implementation of AI and machine learning. At the community college level, programs of study have become more flexible in delivery methods by adding more online coursework and through restructuring traditional timing of course work through accelerated programs and shorter course offerings like eight-week courses.

How Ivy Tech Community College is working with industry, government and academia to establish an ecosystem to address the changing demands for the skilled technical workforce;

Ivy Tech is addressing the changing demands for the skilled technical workforce in many ways by partnering with industry leaders to develop flexible degrees that are interdisciplinary in nature, changing our delivery models for class offerings and receipt of payments to best meet student and employer needs, and establishing a comprehensive data-driven program and workforce demand review process to ensure we are keeping our fingers on the pulse of changes in our communities.

Partnerships with industry leaders enable Ivy Tech to address the changing demands. For example, the College has partnered with the Smart Automation Certification Alliance (SACA), other community colleges, and businesses across the country to develop certifications demonstrating competencies in Industry 4.0 skills. We are embedding those certifications in our current programs and training faculty to teach the content. These credentials can be stand alone in the form of digital credentials.

The College's partnership with Salesforce, called Pathfinder, provides students with technical and business skills training to earn a Salesforce Developer or Administrator certification. This qualifies them to fill more than 300,000 positions at Salesforce partner employers. In 2020, the School will introduce two certificates into the Informatics and Software Development associate degree programs allowing the certifications to crosswalk into new College credit-bearing certificates. We have partnered with Apple to build its Swift curriculum – the program language for development of the iOS applications – into our software development degrees, enabling students to earn certifications and giving them access to Apple partner employers. Ivy Tech is also working closely with Cisco as they overhaul their certifications, which will also be embedded within our

School of IT programs. The rising amount of data via the Internet of Things (IoT) requires technical solutions to both manage data and perform data analytics – data stored in the cloud. Via a partnership with Amazon Web Services, the School of Information Technology has created a framework for the creation of "Emerging Technology" certificates, including a Cloud Computing certificate with courses from the Amazon Web Academy. Ivy Tech foresees the creation of an Associate of Applied Science in Cloud Computing as well.

Through each of these partnerships, the College acknowledges that the future of education is through life-long learning that allows students to advance in their careers while they continue to earn valuable credentials that build on one another.

We know that in the future we will need to develop new degrees that support careers not in existence today. The model we have now will allow us to develop those quickly and align them with the needs of our employers in all areas of the state.

The College is also working to address demands by changing our delivery models for class offerings and receipt of payments to best meet student and employer needs. One change is through eight-week course format offerings, which allow students to focus on fewer courses at a time and to complete their degrees more rapidly. National data showed that eight-week course offerings support increased student success over the traditional 16-week sessions, and the results at Ivy Tech have been similar. We have found that our course success rates are higher and drop rates lower for students in 8-week courses than in traditional 16-week courses, and this is especially good for students who are working while attending school, allowing us to address the requirements of employers who continue to have business needs while wanting to encourage employee development.

Additionally, Ivy Tech has created an accelerated Cyber Academy in partnership with the Indiana National Guard at the Muscatatuck Urban Training Complex, the Department of Defense's largest urban training center. Students earn a Cyber Security/Information Assurance Associate of Applied Science degree in an 11-month, 60 credit hour program, which includes flexibility to modify up to 20 percent of the course curriculum to meet emerging military requirements and needs for cyber-military occupational specialties.

Most notably is our Achieve Your Degree (AYD) program, a proven construct for collaboration between Ivy Tech and employers marketed through the Indiana Chamber of Commerce to offer employees the opportunity to earn a community college education at minimal cost aligned with employer professional development goals and business outcomes.

All degree programs and pathways are approved by the employer with the intention of supporting internal professional development and training opportunities to reduce turnover, foster loyalty and career advancement within the company. These employer approved program offerings include stackable credentials, cohort course offerings, individual academic plans aligned with employer professional development, and dedicated Ivy Tech courses.

Through AYD, the College identifies financial aid, if available, and uses tuition deferral, coupled with a company's tuition reimbursement policies, which serves to eliminate or greatly minimize student upfront costs. This is achieved through the use of tuition deferral, in-state tuition, scholarships, and gap funding by employers or community organizations.

Bloomington, Indiana-based Cook Group is one of 200 College partners in this effort and has been one of the biggest with nearly 500 Cook employees enrolled and 100 credentials earned within the last three years. Through Cook's agreement, participants can earn a certificate stackable through associate degree in seven programs including biotechnology, business administration, hospitality, and various computing and informatics tracks aligned to their business needs.

To ensure the College remains focused on the occupational demands in each area, in 2017, the College began classifying programs into one of four quadrants, developing campus-level and statewide metrics to measure annual progress toward the goal of producing graduates in high-demand fields, meeting the current and future needs of Indiana employers.

Those classification are as follows:

- Growing: High-Demand from Employers/Low Supply Completions (Quad 1)
- Capped: High-Demand from Employers/Limited-Enrollment Completions (Quad 2)
- Shrinking: Low-Demand from Employers/High Supply Completions (Quad 3)
- Equilibrium: Demand/Supply Equilibrium (Quad 4)

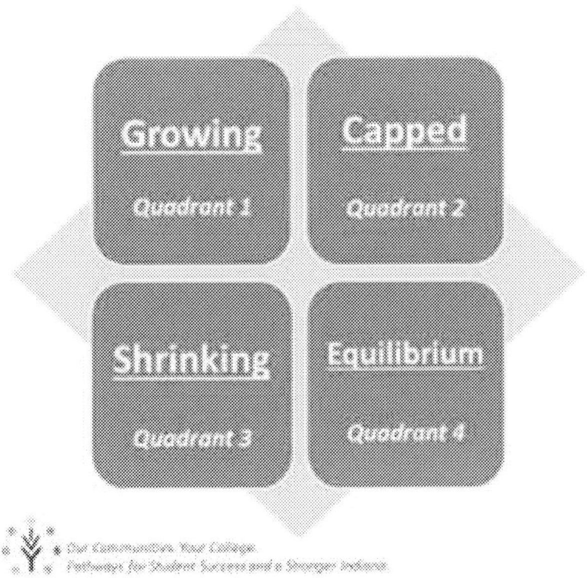

Figure 12.

Ivy Tech campuses analyze local supply and demand data annually as part of their program review process, which guides decisions to grow or suspend programs. The program review process requires campuses to evaluate program offerings that do not meet enrollment and completion thresholds, taking market demand into consideration. Examples of programs suspended based on market demand data and employer feedback include: Criminal Justice and General Studies programs in South Bend and Anderson. Suspending programs that are not aligned to local demand allows campuses to reallocate faculty and resources to grow high-demand programs. For example, several campuses added faculty to the Supply Chain Management program, and every campus now has Information Technology programs aligned to their employer needs. Supply Chain enrollment grew 21.8% from fall 2017 to fall 2018, and this growth will accelerate due to the addition of faculty and active marketing and recruiting.

Ivy Tech's School of Information Technology focused on the continued growth of IT programs, reflective of the ever-increasing demand for IT talent statewide. Due to the strong marketability of skills attained by Ivy Tech students as well as the local, state, and national demand within the Information Technology sector, the number of course enrollments in IT classes increased by 21.1% from spring 2017 to spring 2018. Moreover, the highest percentage increase in completions for the entire college came from the School of Information Technology over both recent one-year and two-year periods at 74.8% and 162.4%, respectively.

Responding to Indiana's tremendous demand for registered nurses and licensed practical nurses, Ivy Tech's School of Nursing optimized faculty loading, hired additional faculty where needed, more efficiently utilized campus resources, and took advantage of state legislation that allows the College to hire faculty with Bachelor of Science credentials who are currently pursuing a Master's degree or Nurse Educator certificate. These efforts resulted in increased enrollment in nursing programs, with 2,946 students enrolled in Associate of Science and Practical Nursing programs at 18 campuses in fall 2018. The school graduated 1,564 students from the Associate of Science and Practical Nursing programs in the 2017-18 academic year, with an on-time completion rate of 83%. Campuses continue to work toward the expansion of nursing programs, including building or re-modeling in Muncie and Kokomo. Parkview Health in Fort Wayne entered into a shared staff/faculty memorandum of understanding (MOU) with the College that allows a Parkview nurse to work as a full-time Ivy Tech faculty member for two years at the College's Fort Wayne campus. Ball Memorial Hospital in Muncie signed a MOU allowing for a "Dedicated Education Unit" that allows one unit of the hospital to be solely dedicated to Ivy Tech nursing students. All will allow for increased enrollment as long as the number of nursing and health sciences faculty also increases.

The College now integrates analyses of workforce supply and demand data into considerations of physical plant investments, equipment funding, and personnel decisions. In the area of physical plant investment, each campus is now required to tie labor market supply and demand analysis to their capital project requests. That analysis serves to illustrate current and future needs of employers in the service area. This results in renovations and other changes to campus facilities being tied directly to determinants such as the needs to grow, sustain, minimize, or eliminate programs. Coupled with this approach around capital projects and physical plant, all requests related to equipment, including annual Perkins Grants requests, are required by the College to be tied directly to the supply and demand analysis.

Overall, this strategic approach of leveraging supply and demand data has created more robust discussions for campus, employers, community, state, and College systems office leaders around the importance of thoughtfully utilizing scarce resources and their appropriate allocation.

How Ivy Tech Is Using Its Career Coaching and Employer Connections Program to Assist Students in Developing a Career Plan for the Jobs of the Future

Over the past year, the College has worked to integrate career outcomes as a vital part of a student's academic journey from application through employment. The college's new Office of Career Coaching & Employer Connections (CCEC) will engage with students early, often, and proactively to provide career support and track completion of indicators. At the beginning of their Ivy Tech experience, students will utilize career exploration and clarity tools as well as labor market data to select a program aligned with their interests, skill sets, and desired wage and employment goals. As students make more informed choices about their fields of study, they will switch programs less frequently and be more likely to choose a higher wage, high-demand career path. Students will develop a Career Action Plan (CAP), completing tasks strategically designed to lead to work-and-learn experiences, which in turn will make students twice as likely to secure employment. The CAP includes resume development, ongoing interview preparation, regular engagement with employers, and employability skill development. Employers will have defined points of contact to assist them in navigating the engagement and recruitment processes to connect with students, developing work-and-learn experiences, and securing talent.

Ivy Tech's new approach to career services emphasizes career readiness practices alongside academics throughout the duration of the student experience. Implementation of these strategies will result in a clear and meaningful pathway for students to and through Ivy Tech that equips them with the knowledge and skills needed to thrive in the workforce. Skilled graduates will leave Ivy Tech prepared to attain meaningful careers, which will ultimately enhance the Hoosier workforce and economy and strengthen communities across the state. Further, Ivy Tech's goal is for students to report earnings at or above Indiana's median wage by one year post-graduation. CCEC will measure its success in achieving meaningful employment outcomes through rigorous data collection. Students will share their post-graduation status, including job placement and wages, through Ivy Tech's First Destination survey. Ivy Tech will validate data utilizing its existing partnership with the State of Indiana Department of Revenue and the Department of Workforce Development.

Recommendations for how the Federal government can work with community colleges and vocational schools to address future research and education needs.

Going forward industry and government need to work together to identify those workers whose jobs will be eliminated and begin skilling up immediately. One way to do this is to rethink federal unemployment insurance (UI) allowing employers to deploy a portion of the funds they are required to pay towards skilling up employees they know will be displaced by technology within the next two years. Indiana currently has a nearly $900 million surplus in UI and 50,000 open jobs that require a post-secondary credential. Federal regulations currently determine the number of days' notice employers must give to employees, so changes would need to be made to incentivize employers to give more advance notice, their ability to deploy UI funds towards upskilling, and enable employees to retrain before losing their job. Those jobs identified as more at-risk of being lost due to automation and digitization could receive a higher level of priority, and employees in those jobs, if given additional time, could spend a portion of the day on their existing job and portion of their day attending classes or training at a community college. While it is important to have funds to address needs during a recession, allowing a willing state and community college to serve as an experimental site would leverage the lowest cost training for individuals who will be most affected and reduce the amount of UI deployed as these individuals remain employed. The impact of unemployment is far more than loss of a paycheck; it has psychological, family, and financial impacts. Solutions that proactively upskill individuals whose jobs will be replaced with technology should be a top priority of the federal government.

The federal government can also work with community colleges to modify regulations that hamper schools' ability to be nimble and meet business needs. Many regulations, while intended to protect against harm, do not serve the intended purpose and slow down approval processes needed to ensure that programs are financial aid eligible, and, on the student side, create additional obstacles for students. Programmatic reviews that are required for a simple name or course change can take months to receive approval, and students enrolling in short-term courses are still not eligible for financial aid because of program length. Additionally, student financial aid verification requirements result in lost aid to students who need it most.

States also need continued support of funding opportunities to support faculty training and equipment upgrades. Because technology so rapidly changes, it is important that students can train on current equipment. Use of virtual reality trainers can help some, but support of models like apprenticeships in nontraditional industries can advance work-based learning that is essential in developing the skills and experience employers require. Technology is constantly evolving and skills formerly required only by technicians and engineers like design, data analytics, and innovation are increasingly required by more entry-level positions.

Finally, the federal government can work in tandem with community colleges to reach underrepresented groups to encourage the attainment of post-secondary credentials in high wage technology intensive careers. Many of these potential students need wrap-around services like child care, transportation, healthcare, food, and even addiction services to successfully complete the credential that could help them improve their lives. Forward-thinking partnerships between community colleges and the federal government to develop holistic programs can help meet and anticipate the demand for skilled workers in an ever more AI, digitized, automated workplace.

Thank you again for the opportunity to appear before this Subcommittee and share the work of Ivy Tech Community College. I applaud and appreciate your leadership and service to our country.

ACHIEVE YOUR DEGREE™
IVY TECH COMMUNITY COLLEGE

INDIANA CHAMBER

Ivy Tech Community College and the Indiana Chamber are pleased to offer Chamber members a unique and innovative solution to meet current and future workforce needs. Achieve Your Degree allows employees the opportunity to earn a credential through a combination of online and on-campus coursework and defer the tuition payment until the end of the semester. Chamber members enrolled in the Achieve Your Degree program are eligible for a 5% rebate on paid employee tuition.

What Are the Benefits to My Organization?

The talent currently housed in your organization will be cultivated and developed; this talent will then become more involved in the community and will stay company-loyal due to your support.

You are responsible for anything the student's financial aid package does not cover, but Ivy Tech will help you design a tuition-reimbursement policy to cover these costs. The tuition payments for students will also be deferred until the end of the semester, ensuring students take advantage of financial aid opportunities. All employees will receive in-state tuition.

How Does the Application Process Work?

Ivy Tech staff will come on-site to assist employees with online applications for both the College and financial aid.

What Support Is Available to My Employees?

Ivy Tech offers individualized advising, financial aid, admissions assistance, and tutoring to assist employees with their courses and help foster success. Ivy Prep, a program designed to develop skills to best prepare your employees for college math and English, is also available.

What Support Is Available to Me?

Ivy Tech will provide you with all necessary collateral needed to advertise the program, as well as a point person to help coordinate everything for your employees.

Next Steps

1) Complete the Memorandum of Understanding
2) Work with Ivy Tech to determine a date for an on-site information and enrollment session
3) Determine your point person for the Achieve Your Degree program
4) Identify academic programs to fund
5) Market Achieve Your Degree program to your employees

Benefits of Achieve Your Degree as a Member of the Indiana Chamber

Your Organization

- Chamber members enrolled in the Achieve Your Degree program are eligible for a 5% rebate on paid employee tuition
- State funding through Next Level Jobs grant opportunities
- Ivy Tech will help design a custom program tailored to your company's employees

Your Employees

- Many class options, both in-person and online, available at multiple locations across Indiana
- Multiple start dates throughout the year
- Classes in 16-week and 8-week formats
- Expanded skillsets to become more valuable employees

Learn more at indianachamber.com/achieve

Dr. Sue Ellspermann has more than 30 years of experience in higher education, economic and workforce development, and public service.

In May 2016, Dr. Ellspermann was selected to serve as President of Ivy Tech Community College of Indiana, its first female president.

In January 2018, Ivy Tech launched its new five-year Strategic Plan, "Our Communities. Your College. Pathways for Student Success and a Stronger Indiana." The plan's vision is for Ivy Tech students to earn 50,000 high-quality certifications, certificates, and degrees per year aligned with workforce needs. The plan aligns with Indiana's goal to equip 60 percent of the workforce with a high-value, post-secondary degree or credential by 2025. Through achievement of this goal, the College will help increase Hoosier per capita income and support the transformation of the state's advanced industries economy. The plan development covered 18 months, including a restructure of the College, comprehensive fact finding conducted internally and externally, including thousands of faculty, staff, students and statewide stakeholders.

Dr. Ellspermann most recently served as Indiana's 50th Lieutenant Governor from 2013 until March of 2016. As the vice chair of the Indiana Career Council she led efforts to align Indiana's education and workforce development system to meet the needs of employers which is her continued focus at Ivy Tech. Her public service began in 2010 when she was elected as the State Representative for District 74.

Ellspermann formerly served as the founding Director of the Center of Applied Research and Economic Development at the University of Southern Indiana and also owned and operated Ellspermann and Associates, Inc., an independent consulting firm licensed in the training and facilitation of Simplex Creative Problem Solving.

Early in her career she spent time with Frito-Lay and Michelin Tire Corporation. Ellspermann holds a Ph.D. and M.S. from the University of Louisville in Industrial Engineering and a B.S. from Purdue University also in Industrial Engineering.

She is married to James Mehling, a former high school principal. She has a blended family of four daughters, three sons-in-law, two grandsons and two granddaughters.

Chairwoman STEVENS. Well, thank you all, and at this time the Chair would like to recognize Ranking Member Dr. Baird for his opening remarks. Thank you.

Mr. BAIRD. Thank you, Madam Chairwoman. I apologize for being late, but I do admire you for going on without me. Thank you.

Chairwoman STEVENS. We're a team, you know.

Mr. BAIRD. So I appreciate this opportunity. I appreciate you waiting on me, and I'd like to make this opening statement, and thank you for holding this "Artificial Intelligence and the Future of Work" Committee hearing. Since the term AI was introduced in the 1950s, we have made some huge advances in the field, and thanks to critical investments by government and industry, universities and the United States, in leading global AI research and development.

Today AI systems have been deployed in every sector of the U.S. economy. These technologies have already delivered significant benefits for the U.S. economic prosperity, for the environmental stewardship, and the national security. AI has long been a subject of interest of the House Science Committee, and we have held several important and productive hearings on this topic. In the past we have discussed how to define AI, the science of AI technologies, and the needs for standards to address ethics and potential bias. Now, this afternoon, we will examine AI from the prospective of the American worker.

In order to remain a leader in AI, I believe we must prepare our workforce for the next generation of opportunities in this technology, and for our future, defined by a lifelong learning experience. In order to grow our economy, I also believe we must acknowledge and understand how AI is changing, and will continue to change, the jobs and lives of hardworking Americans. This is a large scale effort that is going to require cooperation between industry that was already mentioned here, industry, academia, and the Federal agencies, so I'm pleased to see that the Trump Administration is making this issue a priority, and recently established the National Science Council for the American Worker and the American Workforce Policy Advisory Board. American industry has responded well to the Administration's initiatives. Over 300 companies and organizations have pledged to study and expand education, training, re-skilling opportunities for American workers to gain AI-relevant skills.

We also need to re-think how we educate future workers, and re-skill the workers of today, all the way from K through 12 schools to the community colleges, the vocational schools, and the 4-year universities. Some leaders in the U.S. education system are already finding innovative ways to develop a highly skilled AI workforce, one of the future. We have heard about some of those efforts from my friend, Dr. Sue Ellspermann, President of the Ivy Tech Community College system in our home State of Indiana. Sue, so glad to have you here today. At Ivy Tech, Dr. Ellspermann works to address the changing demands of employers in the Hoosier State by providing strategic support and career planning for students at community colleges and vocational schools, and working closely with local industry. I look forward to hearing more about her im portant work in our community, and how it will be applied across the country.

Over the next few months, this Committee will be working toward bipartisan legislation to support a national strategy on artificial intelligence. The challenges we must address are how industry, academia, and the government can work together on AI challenges, including today's critical workforce questions, and what role the Federal Government should play in supporting industry as it drives innovation. I want to thank our accomplished panel of witnesses for their testimony today, and I appreciate the opportunity to hear how this Committee and the Federal Government can support innovation and education to ensure a bright future for America's workers, our students, and maintain our leadership in AI. So thank you.

[The prepared statement of Mr. Baird follows:]

Chairwoman Stevens, thank you for holding today's hearing on "Artificial intelligence (AI) and the Future of Work."

Since the term AI was first coined in the 1950s, we have made huge advances in the field. And thanks to critical investments by government, industry, and universities, the United States is leading in global AI Research & Development.

Today, AI systems have been deployed in every sector of the U.S. economy. These technologies have already delivered significant benefits for U.S. economic prosperity, environmental stewardship, and national security.

AI has long been a subject of interest for the House Science Committee and we have held several important and productive hearings on this topic.

In the past, we have discussed how to define AI, the science of AI technologies, and the needs for standards to address ethics and potential bias.

Now, this afternoon, we will examine AI from the perspective of the American worker.

In order to remain a leader in AI, I believe we must prepare our workforce for next generation opportunities in this technology and for a future defined by lifelong learning.

In order to grow our economy, I also believe we must acknowledge and understand how AI is changing and will continue to change the jobs and lives of hardworking Americans.

This is a large-scale effort that is going to require cooperation between industry, academia and federal agencies.

So I am pleased to see that The Trump Administration is making this issue a priority and recently established the National Council for the American Worker and the American Workforce Policy Advisory Board.

American industry has responded well to the Administration's initiatives. Over 300 companies and organizations have pledged to study and expand education, training, and reskilling opportunities for American workers to gain AI-relevant skills.

We also need to rethink how we educate future workers and reskill the works of today, all the way from K-12 schools to community colleges and vocational schools, to 4-year universities.

Some leaders in the U.S. education system are already finding innovative ways to develop a highly-skilled AI workforce of the future.

We will learn more about some of those efforts from one of our witnesses today, my good friend, Dr. Sue Ellspermann, President of the Ivy Tech Community College system in our home state of Indiana.

At Ivy Tech, Dr. Ellspermann works to address the changing demands of employers in the Hoosier State by providing strategic support and career planning for students at community colleges and vocational schools and working closely with local industry.

I look forward to hearing more about her important work in our community, and how it can be applied across the country.

Over the next few months, this Committee will be working towards bipartisan legislation to support a national strategy on Artificial Intelligence.

The challenges we must address are how industry, academia, and the government can work together on AI challenges, including today's critical workforce questions, and what role the federal government should play in supporting industry as it drives innovation. I want to thank our accomplished panel of witnesses for their testimony today.

I look forward to hearing how we can support innovation and education, to ensure a bright future for America's workers and students and maintain our leadership in AI.

Chairman STEVENS. If there are Members who wish to submit additional opening statements, your statements will be added to the record at this point.

[The prepared statement of Chairwoman Johnson follows:]

Thank you, Chairwoman Stevens and Ranking Member Baird, for holding this hearing. I would also like to welcome this esteemed panel of witnesses and thank each of you for accommodating the rescheduling of today's hearing. We are here today to discuss an urgent challenge facing the country. Artificial intelligence is a rapidly advancing, sophisticated technology that promises to transform the way we live and work.

As Chairwoman, I take seriously the responsibility entrusted to this Committee to support the nation's research and innovation enterprise for the benefit of society. We are increasingly feeling pressure from our global competitors, particularly in the case of AI. As countries like the United Kingdom, Germany, and China invest heavily in this technology, there is a strong sense of urgency to race headlong toward technological maturity and widespread adoption.

I want to urge caution. We must take the time to draw upon lessons learned from past technological disruptions, assess the opportunities and potential risks, and implement a coordinated national strategy to ensure the benefits of AI are enjoyed by everyone. We are here to explore one of the primary concerns associated with AI - its potential impact on the workforce. Many Americans are understandably worried that AI-driven automation and robots will make their jobs obsolete.

Research has a critical role to play in informing how AI is integrated into the American workforce. Research can help employers understand the benefits and risks of this technology. Just because it seems like a task can be performed by an AI system, does not mean it can or should be, at least not without a human still in the loop. Research can also improve our understanding of the human-technology relationship. This can inform decisions regarding how best to integrate AI into the workflow so it can both complement and enhance the value of the worker. Research can advance the development of effective practices for retraining the current workforce and for ensuring workers have the flexibility to be lifelong learners. Research can provide students and those pursuing a career change with a clear under- standing of emerging industries and occupations, so they can chart an education path best suited to their goals.

Artificial intelligence holds immense promise to spur economic growth and make our lives easier. We are at a critical point in the development of this technology, and we must ensure we have the research knowledge base necessary to maximize these benefits for everyone.

I look forward to today's testimony and discussion and I yield back.

Chairwoman STEVENS. Fabulous. At this time we're going to begin the 5-minutes of questioning, and the Chair will recognize herself for 5 minutes.

Dr. Lupia, in your testimony, you discuss a recent award made to the University of Michigan to support research on how humans and robots are working together in construction environments, and you stated that, despite recent advances in robot functionality, many fundamental questions in robot interaction remain unanswered. Do you mind elaborating on that a little bit further, and also, could you touch on some of the major social science research questions regarding human/robot interaction, and where we need to go from here?

Dr. LUPIA. Thank you for that question. As discussed in the opening statements, there are things right now that AI and robots can do that humans can't do, but there are many things that humans can do that robots can't do. And when we're thinking about the workplace of the future, particularly its impact on workers and workplaces, you know, there are these fundamental questionsabout what the two groups know now, and what can we expect them to know in the future, to empower workers.

So I think about farms, for example, right? So I grew up on a farm, and so, when I was a kid, people milked cows. And, if you've ever done that, it's not the most fun thing. But now they have robots that can milk cows, so if you think about how—just—a farm that's pretty simple, there are things that people can do that robots can't do, and things that robots can do that people can't do. And so, through a number of grants, we're trying to help factories, farmers, offices, and so forth think through, "How do you make workplaces more efficient?" "How do you make them more effective, with this set of evolving skills?"

Some of it requires trust, right? So if we're going to automate a manufacturing process, the worker has to trust the robot, or the machine. And trust is a great thing, unless the robot's about to do the wrong thing. And so you've always got to have an override capacity. What we're trying to do at NSF is bring large groups of people together to understand, at a pretty fundamental level, when is the trust relationship going to work, when is it going to fail, and as robots get better at things, how does that change how we should organize the workplace? So that's the fundamental question.

It takes understanding humans, because if you press the override button at the wrong time, you can disrupt the process. If you wait too long, unintended consequences can happen. So understanding the human/robot interaction is really critical to all of the progress we want, from manufacturing, to farms, to offices of the future.

Chairwoman STEVENS. To be successful. And, Ms. Kowalski, you might have given us the line of the day, which is don't count the humans out. And you also, in your testimony, discussed the rapid change in skills being sought by employers. And, you know, in terms of how we think about job descriptions to account for this rapidly changing marketplace for skills, and also promote a mindset of supportive, continuous skill development, how do we do it all? How do we bring that together?

Ms. KOWALSKI. So I think there's a few things. One is just determining that this is what we have to do, right? It's a decision that we have to make, that we cannot allow the workforce to stay still, that there is no grassy plateau on which we'll all be able to stretch out when transformation is done. It will be an unending climb, and evolution and adaptation, which we're very good at as human beings, right? But the way that we approached education and employment was we educated to the job. People came into an exact match environment, and then they made progressions up the ladder based on merit. We haven't seen something come in that acts so rapidly.

Think about automation, and the—it was about 15 years playing out in the last cycle. We're talking about something that's going to play out, by this research, in 3 to 5 years that's unfolding now. And it will get faster, and the peaks and troughs will get steeper, and so how we get people attenuated to that shift, that starts all the way back in K–12, and moves all the way through—and in employment. And the hardest thing is going to be taking the people that are currently employed and helping them understand they haven't done anything wrong. They are hardworking, they've been doing a great job, and these are the new set of skills that they have to assimilate, and there has to be a new contract, right? And that contract is one of you put in for continuous adaptation and evolution, we'll be right there to meet you with the resources.

You know when we were good at doing that? Was in the 1950s and 1960s, when we hired on potential. We built whole companies hiring on potential for jobs we didn't even know what they were going to look like, and people got used to making the progression, and having a partnership with employment and educators in order to do that. And it's going to take a system to do it.

Chairwoman STEVENS. Well, I am just at time, so—you can tell we're in a rich topic area. So I'm going to yield back the remainder of my time, and I am going to recognize Dr. Baird for 5 minutes of questioning. You've got this, Dr. Baird.

Mr. BAIRD. Thank you, Madam Chair. And, Dr. Ellspermann, I'm sure that you recognized I was probably going to start with you.

Dr. ELLSPERMANN. Thank you.

Mr. BAIRD. The thing that, and I know you spent a lot of time in this area, and thinking about it, but the needs of the industry today, compared to the future, and this technology that we're discussing today, is changing so fast because of quantum computing, and that sort of thing. So I guess, in other words, how do you feel, or how do you see Ivy Tech balancing that need for today, and then in the future? Kind of give us some feel what you think that might look——

Dr. ELLSPERMANN. Very good. So, actually, 3 years ago, the General Assembly in Indiana understood how important it would be that we would be work-forced aligned as a system, and actually required that, in addition to having a provost I have a Chief Work- force Officer, which makes sure this alignment happened.

So I alluded in my comments to this way that we classify all of our programs, because we know it's a moving target, we know that there is BLS (Bureau of Labor Statistics), and Emsi, and other good data out there, economically, to project the future. We know that broadly, but it's not accurate at the local level, so we take that, and we let the local industry work with us to look at what's coming, what is the real demand, and then we size our programs on every campus, every program, to be that right size.

And that's where our quadrants, that quadrant one of—quadrant one is where we focus. It is those high-demand, low-supply, not enough students to fill that work, and making sure we're building those programs. We have limited enrollment programs that we have to push on. We have programs that have to shrink so that they are the right size, or maybe discontinue, and then finally equilibrium. That work is working. It is working across our State. We can take the local data to understand that maybe the economic data is not quite accurate to what the local needs are, and we could shore up, and we could shrink, and we do that in a very rapid way. What becomes challenging is the support at the Federal level to get those kind of programs, when you need new programs stood up, to quickly stand those up in 3 to 6 months so that an employer gets the kind of skill set that they need. And so we look to any support we can get with our U.S. DOE (Department of Education) to quickly approve programs. But, as I shared, looking at new ways to anticipate, when we know these changes are coming, and we know there's a higher demand, how do we identify that employee at risk early, even if it is just a year, or a year and a half in advance? We can then begin skilling before that individual is out of a job, unemployed, which is, for many, much more than just about being out of a job. It is psychological impact. It is a feeling that a trust has been broken with that employer, so how do we proactively work with them?

And whether we use Unemployment Insurance as a part of that trigger, we need to change that mindset to create that contract again between employer and employee. And I believe the community colleges, at least Ivy Tech, is working very hard to get there, but I know we will be the front lines for most of employers as they look to scale up their employees, and it's our job to be as rapid as we can.

Mr. BAIRD. Thank you. Dr. Lupia, I'm glad to hear you came from a farm, and I couldn't help but say—several of you mentioned the importance of the human factor. I think you mentioned that. But I just want you to know that those old cows have a vested interest in how well these—but anyway, I thought maybe you might want to elaborate—I've been fascinated by NSF's convergence accelerators since Director C′ ordova spoke about them in this Committee in May. Would you mind elaborating on how this new approach to research will improve our understanding of the future of work, and enhance the lives of American workers?

Dr. LUPIA. Absolutely, sir. Thank you for asking that question. The convergence accelerators really build on the traditional NSF approach. So in NSF, we fund all of science, but the idea with the Convergence Accelerators is, from the beginning, you bring in other partners, people in the room, who, if great ideas emerge, they can bring them to market. So the Convergence Accelerators have really been an exciting way to think about how to take amazing collaborations and bring them to market.

So I'll give you one example, because we just started funding these things. One has to do with re-skilling the workforce, and it is funded, coincidentally, at Purdue University, and it focuses on apprenticeships. So both of my grandparents were in the trades, and the way that you've learned a trade for 100 years is through an apprenticeship. So that takes a number of months, and you follow somebody around, and you learn the trade. But for a small company it's really expensive to take one of your workers and have them do an apprenticeship for 6 months. So one of the Convergence Accelerators is a project built around using technology to do apprenticeships at scale.

So imagine we could take what a master plumber knows, or a master technician, or someone who runs a computer, and we can follow them around, and then create scalable, low-cost ways to distribute this information to everybody. And one of the ways you can do that is through having simulations. So instead of one person shadowing the expert, you can build a simulation where 50 people can have a virtual reality experience of shadowing the expert. And so it has a lot of the benefits of the traditional apprenticeship, and of course you still need the one-to-one contact, but this is a way to really make that happen at scale. And, again, if you're a small company, if you can go to a community college, or somewhere else, and get this type of training, it's a real game changer.

So the idea here is apprenticeship, lower costs, improve speed and reliability, minimize errors, and this is something that the Converge Accelerator, I think, can really do to help companies across the country.

Mr. BAIRD. Thank you.

Chairwoman STEVENS. At this time the Chair would like to recognize Dr. Marshall for 5 minutes of questioning.

Mr. MARSHALL. All right. Thank you, Chairwoman. Dr. Ellspermann, I'm a community college graduate, my wife, community college graduate, huge fans of my community colleges. The technical colleges can quickly pivot to the job needs of my community, and I think that's where the rubber meets the road. How do you measure success? What are you measuring to say, we're being successful in our technical college that you run?

Dr. ELLSPERMANN. We measure success the way most Americans do, by wages. We actually measure the wages of our graduates 1 year out to see what they're making. Our goal is that 80 percent of all of our graduates will make above median wage 1 year after completion. We're at 45 percent today, we were at 38 percent 2 years ago, and we're marching our way—but we think that is one fair way to do that. In addition, too, we also hold ourselves accountable to those four quadrants. We want 80 percent of our programs to be in equilibrium, meaning we're roughly producing the number of graduates needed for our community.

Mr. MARSHALL. And are you measuring their debt when they're leaving too?

Dr. ELLSPERMANN. We have minimal, you know, community college debt is kind of the best kind of debt. It's, like, under $10,000. It's the way to do college. But we do measure debt, and we do measure what those students have, and always are looking for ways to continue to reduce that.

Mr. MARSHALL. I'm not sure how long you've been at Ivy Tech, but what are you doing differently today than 1 year ago, than 3 years ago, or 5 years ago?

Dr. ELLSPERMANN. We have reinvented how we're delivering. So we've gone from traditional 16-week courses to 8-week courses because, guess what, adults do better in that format. There's higher pass rates, lower drop rates. We've just redesigned our online education. We're one of the largest online educators in the country. We know we have to do that better because, guess what, single moms need to be able to take courses online, and they have to be as good as the face-to-face delivery. So in that redesign, we are looking at all of the way we do our work to align better to industry, and to deliver in the best way for our students. And there's much more to do, Congressman.

Mr. MARSHALL. So certainly, as an obstetrician, you're hitting on exactly who I'm thinking of, that single mom who maybe could get her auntie, or her sister, to come in and help with the kids for 6 weeks or 8 weeks, but it's hard to get them to commit to 18 weeks. One of the things that we're certainly looking at is using Pell Grants in a non-traditional situation, what you're describing. Hopefully we can make some progress there at some point in time.

Dr. ELLSPERMANN. Thank you.

Mr. MARSHALL. So we have the NSF person here, Dr. Lupia, as well. What would you tell him? How could NSF work better with community colleges and technical colleges? What ideas out there are outside the box that you wish we could get better engaged with NSF?

Dr. ELLSPERMANN. I would say certainly in helping us to adopt that technology early. We are not funded at the levels of research institutions, as you might guess, so keeping our labs up to date with that front-edge technology at the same time industry's getting it, not a generation later. We really need to have it early. Certainly Perkins helps on that front, but that cycle of rapid change is so much quicker than it was generations ago that we have to be able to refresh our equipment every year, two, or three, which there's probably a partnership to be built there.

Mr. MARSHALL. OK. Dr. Lupia, any return thoughts, or comments?

Dr. LUPIA. We are so grateful for the work that your organization does, and part of our Future of Work Project is really to try and make this information and these collaborations happen a lot earlier. So the scientific approach is, there's a relationship between jobs and skills. Most jobs take a whole bunch of skills, and as jobs evolve, some of the skills that we have now will still be relevant, but there will be these other new skills that you can use.

So we are working with government, industry, and a whole range of researchers to try and project, "How are skills and jobs likely to evolve?" If we can figure that out, and put that into data bases, and match it to jobs as they're evolving, then our partners can make that data available to everyone—because that's the idea, right? We have projects in several States—Georgia, West Virginia now—where we're collecting data from them, and then trying to push out real-time and usable data about how jobs are likely to change. This can produce really great efficiencies, because now we can tell community colleges and others these are the skills that employers need now, these are the skills they're likely to need 6 months from now, 12 months from now, 24 months from now.

And with that type of data you not only get these efficiencies, now you have this possibility someone can go to a college and not just get the next job, but be able to be given the skills that can help them build a career, that can take the next two or three steps in their life. So we want to be a tailwind to them, and very supportive.

Mr. MARSHALL. Sounds good. I'm going to start my Community College Caucus here someday. I need to do that. Thank you so much for being here, and I yield back.

Chairwoman STEVENS. Great, thank you. And at this time we're going to begin a second round of questions.

Dr. Brynjolfsson, as you've kind of defined the two urgent economic challenges around lack of productivity growth and too much inequality, and then gave us a list of pretty cogent and solid recommendations on how to address those, do you mind weighing in a little bit around some of the ethical considerations that come up on this topic, and how those either might be urgent right now, or might become more urgent as we move forward?

Dr. BRYNJOLFSSON. Absolutely. I think those are some of the most urgent challenges. They're a little outside some of the economics, but some of them also have an economic implication as well. Machine learning systems have been remarkable at helping us make all sorts of decisions, but one of the things we've also discovered is that they're only as good as the data that go into them, and oftentimes machine learning systems that are trained on decisions that humans made end up perpetuating, or even amplifying, the biases that we often have. So when it comes to hiring, or making credit loan decisions, or who gets parole, if the humans who are making those decisions have a set of biases, those are going to be captured by the systems and repeated. So there have been a number of academic studies that—these are one of the challenges.

There's both a challenge and an opportunity there. Part of the challenge with machine learning systems, particularly when they're using deep neural net technology, is that it is difficult to understand what's going on inside the black box. They capture data, sometimes from thousands or millions of examples, and they spew out a recommendation, and it's hard to know exactly why, and that makes it challenging to second guess it and say, wait a minute, this may not be right.

But the opportunity is that we can use techniques like one called a Turing Box, where you have repeated sets of inputs, with different characteristics going in, and sets of outputs coming out, and you start learning what kinds of biases the machine may have inadvertently picked up, and you can correct those in a way that may actually, ultimately, I think, be easier to correct than our own human biases. Because, after all, it's not like humans are perfect either.

So I wouldn't necessarily rule out using machine learning systems for some of these challenges, even when they are imperfect, but we should put very high on the agenda better understanding of some of the ethical and other biases that they can create.

Chairwoman STEVENS. And, Ms. Kowalski, coming out of your taxonomy that you helped to lead with MXD, do you mind just chiming in on some of the job roles that you identified that might be pertinent to some of the points that Dr. Brynjolfsson just talked about?

Ms. KOWALSKI. Yes. It's a great question. There are five that I think really, really pop out of the work. One is what we call the digital era enterprise ethicist, and that's a conceptual title, of course, no one puts that out there, but it was, you know, an individual success profile of a role of who gets to make those decisions. Who makes the call? Who says how far is too far?

Traditionally these decisions have been kind of bandied about, maybe IT owns this, or Risk owns it, or Legal owns it. Well, now, the way organizations are built in the digital era, it does not land neatly in one of those silos, it spreads across. And so where the buck stops actually is in a place where no one ever imagined it. And so there are—you made a comment earlier about how processes haven't caught up, so that's decisionmaking processes, that's organizational structures. It's a recognition that there's distributed decisionmaking more and more now in organizations, and we still have an end-of-year code-of-conduct compliance, you know, mindnumbing 2-hours of training that we take that don't actually get to can you identify the decisionmaking framework that your organization uses for developing new products, solutions, or making decisions around human beings? That's a fundamental issue that has to be dealt with now.

A couple other things, in terms of just roles that you're going to see popping up, obviously an organization only has one ethicist like that, but does have to establish the framework that supports it, but some of those specialist roles, like the machine learning specialist, the collaborative robotic specialist, the autonomous mobility engineer, right, how do you make sure that, you know, people of different ethnicities are recognized by that autonomous vehicle, right? How do you make sure that your H.R. systems are wired not to filter people out, but actually to bring people in, based on potential? So those are some of those roles that we see coming up across all organizations, and obviously a few of those are quite specific to the manufacturing sector. And it's important that we figure these out, because what I see right now is a lot of organizations just trying to spread that responsibility out without actually recognizing that those need to be defined disciplines.

Chairwoman STEVENS. As we talk about technical talent, and the push for the hard-skilled trades, and the work that we see out of our community colleges, and the push for people to go into apprenticeship, and other training programs, we still feel the need to train for analog, but also embrace the soft skill digital. And I'm slightly over time, but with just the remainder that I'm going to steal here, I'd love for each of you to just comment on this shift here, and the balance of the soft with the hardnosed technical skills that are still required in many jobs. And, Dr. Ellspermann, if you want to start, we'd certainly——

Dr. ELLSPERMANN. I'd be happy to. We recognized 3 years ago that we weren't doing enough to prepare students to be successful in the workforce: Number one, making the right decisions in the careers, being prepared for the world of work, because not every student anymore comes to us already with some prior work experience, and that they would be successful so—building that in, so we are in the midst of rolling out what we call our Career Coaching and Employer Connections, which ensures every student, when they begin with us, begins building a career action plan, which includes work and learn experiences in industry to build some of that kind of real-world work.

We build in, certainly, soft skills throughout the curriculum, but those skills are learned best on the job, making sure every student has that experience before they get out there. But it is an early and often experience, meeting with employers being out there, interviewing, understanding what's expected. And we know there's a lot to be done that we've never been really asked to do in the past, but is required by our industry, and know that that's a part of the future.

Ms. KOWALSKI. So I'll pick up on this theme of moving from analog to digital roles. So, if you were to look at the research that we have, you'd see that 28 percent of those 165 new or highly evolved roles are sitting on the production floor, and what we estimatedwas about 1 to 2 years of building up that talent that would prepare them to take on progressively more digital roles.

Because at the heart of it, the shift is really from doing things physically, physical operations, to accomplishing those operations through systems and technology. So you see a lot more skills like quantitative, tech-assisted, optimization-focused, integrative, mobile, virtual, and remote. That wasn't in the lexicon, really, 5 years ago, even 3 years ago. You know, organizations that were starting to talk about it were the OEMs (original equipment manufacturers), for instance, that participated in this study. Now it's spreading throughout the supply network, and we have quite a task in front of us to gear people up, because right now they'll have to bridge from those more tactical analog roles into the transitional. So organizations have to keep a foot planted firmly where they are now, and reach for the future.

Dr. BRYNJOLFSSON. Thank you for that question. I think this is a very important issue, about the balance between hard and soft skills. I teach at the Massachusetts Institute of Technology, so certainly I have an appreciation for the importance and value of hard skills. There are a number of technical capabilities that our workforce is lacking and that we need to supplement. In some cases, they can be compensated very highly. But I also want to stress that soft skills are increasingly the ones that are less automatable, and therefore more humans will be needed to do those softer skills. They often have a longer span of relevance and usefulness.

In the science article that I included as background, we created a framework for which tasks are suitable for machine learning. And, indeed, the ones that were less likely to be automated were many of the softer skills, involving creativity and interpersonal skills, persuasion, caring, coaching, leadership, and teamwork. These are things that are very important in the workforce, and I also think that there are opportunities to teach them, not just on the job, but by reinventing and reorganizing our educational curriculum.

And a research agenda to better understand the kinds of skills that are needed going forward, I think, would be a useful supplement to be able to map our strategies, both in education and workforce training, going forward.

Dr. LUPIA. I'd just like to state a principle and an example. One of the overarching principles for this problem is the idea of values-based design. So when you build a new technology, oftentimes we're thinking about the products, and we're not thinking about the people. And so you don't think about the people, and the workers, and the consumers, until the end of the process, when the unintended consequences and the inefficiencies are already built in. A lot of our recent misadventures with Big Tech, I think, are an example of not thinking about the people at the beginning.

So now, when we think about the future workforce, with values-based design, we're thinking about the people in the workplace, and how they're going to interact. If you think about that—starting at time one, when you start to build the code, when you start to write the algorithms and so forth, there are all kinds of efficiencies that you can realize later on. And one of the efficiencies, with respect to the workforce, is personalized practice. Because once we think about how the new technology, and the new workplaces aregoing to affect people, now we can start to understand the set of skills that are going to be needed, and we can start to design personalized education so that people can learn efficiently the skills that they will need in this new place. But if you start with values at the beginning, you get to those outcomes.

And in the point of practices, NSF is already trying to help support this through its Advanced Technological Education Program, or ATE. There are hundreds of community colleges and 48 ATE centers around the country that are really preparing students for STEM (science, technology, engineering, and mathematics) and the skilled technical workforce. We've got 17 million Americans in the skilled technical workforce now that are in the workflow.

They're building the machines, and maintaining the computers, and so forth, and the ATE Program is really meant to encourage and improve the training of science and engineering technicians at both undergraduate and secondary levels. So the things we're doing right now are things like ATE, but the future benefit really comes from thinking through, you know, what are the human impacts of technology?

Chairwoman STEVENS. Thank you. And I'm lucky that my colleague likes me, because I spent some of that liking capital going slightly over, but it was really to hear from all of you, and to have your expertise. So, at this time, I'd like to recognize my good friend, Dr. Jim Baird, for 5 minutes of questions.

Mr. BAIRD. Thank you, Madam Chair, and my question now is going to be directed at all of you, at some point here. But, you know, online, you know, I have grandchildren that can use these faster than they could talk, almost, and so my question relates to that, in a way. We're using online courses for both formal and informal education, and so I guess the question is this: Do we have any research that tells us what online courses, and how to make those effective? And then also, how do online courses, and what you're doing—and AI relate to STEM education? We're carrying a bill about the STEM careers, and so on. So I'm going to start with—at your left, my right, and move that way, go ahead. Thank you.

Dr. ELLSPERMANN. Congressman Baird, let me just say that I think we realize that online education is here to stay. It's not going to take over all of education. It's not the best way for all of education. It's not the preferred learning style for many. But we know, as I shared earlier with that single mom, she's got to have that opportunity to learn. So we have to—as educators, it's our responsibility to improve it constantly. It's come through many iterations. It'll go through many more, but it'll also be hybrid, and augmented, and many things that, as technologies we're talking about here today, ever greater enables us to make that online experience more real, more virtual, more—in the way that that learner wants to learn it.

But I think we understand, as community colleges, we have to lean in, and it's not an either/or, it's an and, it's a both, and we need to continue to evolve. So we study, we know we have a gap between our face-to-face and our online learning. It's double digit right now, which is not acceptable, so our goal is to eliminate that gap. That will be one measure of quality, but we will continue to look for ways to make that experience better for the online learner.

Ms. KOWALSKI. So I would agree with my co-panelist here that it is a both/and. We have a number of occupations that employers won't accept a fully virtual experience for, so they require some sort of hands-on. I'm not going to let you touch an aircraft wing unless you have actually touched an aircraft wing before you come into my hangar, thankfully, right. And yet the promise of this is pretty profound.

So if you think back to the statistics that I shared earlier, in terms of the gap that we have facing us in manufacturing right now, the only way to close it is to become incredibly resourceful about who we bring in from the sidelines. Women are certainly one untapped resource, but what about people with physical and cognitive disabilities? Some of the greatest advancements made in digital technologies actually allows them to participate. The exoskeleton Dr. Lupia shared before is a marvelous example of how we can bring people in who, before this, have never even imagined actually having the ability to participate in workforce.

Strictly in online education, and kind of what we think of as the standard, this is part of how ManpowerGroup is helping our associates upskill. We're offering all of our associates access to free education so that they can move up, with this idea. And just to validate what you were saying earlier, 6 to 8 weeks, that's the ability of an individual who's working full time, sometimes two jobs, and raising kids. So it opens up more opportunity than we've ever seen before, but it's not going to be the only way that we can educate, because there are some things fundamentally that require hands-on.

Dr. BRYNJOLFSSON. Thank you for that question, Dr. Baird. At MIT we've been doing a lot with online education for quite a while. One of the first big courses that we did was an online circuits design course. A couple hundred thousand people took it. Anant Agarwal organized it. One of those students was actually in Mongolia, and got a perfect score on it. It turned out to be a 17-year- old boy, and it was someone who wouldn't have been reached otherwise if there weren't this kind of technology. MIT went ahead and admitted him to the regular program, and it was somebody we probably wouldn't have found otherwise.

We have put all of our regular courses online through the Open Courseware for free. People can just access and read them. In fact, you can see my syllabi, and see my lecture notes, and problem sets. There's also an online system called edX. It's a consortium of universities—it started with MITX, then Harvard and others joined— that coordinates course materials to have them in a little more structured way so that you go through a curriculum. And these are what we call MOOCs, massive online courseware. I think there was an early wave of hype and excitement about them, you know, taking over, and doing all sorts of things. It worked very well in some areas, like the Circuits Course. It didn't work so well in others.

It's certainly not a silver bullet, but I think there are four things that we've learned. One is that, for many applications, you can get enormous scale, and much lower cost, than we could've previously. Second, one of the unexpected benefits was an ability to personalize. People learn at different rates, and there's different media that work better for other people, and you can have things extremely customized, and even personalized, and we're learning how to do that better. Third, it often makes sense to do a hybrid system, where you have people meet in person, particularly for some of the softer skills we were talking about. We often combine where people physically get together, know their classmates, do things together, then work separately online, then come back together, which is actually how a lot of workforce works as well, after all.

And then last, but not least, in fact, probably most importantly, I think that the biggest lesson is that there is no one best way of doing online education. What we need to do is continually experiment and test. The success of a lot of tech companies has been this approach of A/B testing, constantly trying a new product, seeing if it works with different subsets of people, and we've very much taken that to heart with our online course offerings, and companies like Coursera, Udacity, have been very successful in trying things. And sometimes they work, sometimes they don't, but it's an attitude of experiment testing. So your question was spot on, what is the research showing what is working, and what isn't working? And there's a whole set of things that have failed miserably, another set of things that have succeeded. But I think we're still in very early days, and the digital approach allows you to gather data at a scale, and cost, and speed that just can't be matched in other ways.

Dr. LUPIA. Well, thank you for asking that question. At NSF there's a foundation-wide effort to really support basic research on how to develop, evaluate, and improve online learning structures. One common way of doing it is you collect a lot of information about the types of things people need to know, you correlate that with information about the types of tasks that they may be asked to do, you integrate that with information about curricula, and how people are doing in learning environments, and you take all that data together, and then you can really evaluate not just what does somebody remember after they take a test, but what can they do 6 months later? So there's all kinds of projects like that being funded at NSF, from trucking to farms and there's even one for veterans. So the idea is, you know, how do you structure curricula to help veterans who want to get into STEM pipelines, because veterans have special abilities, and sometimes special challenges.

I guess the biggest headline, in terms of what we've been doing recently, is—about a year ago the Boeing Company gave $10 million to NSF to try and really boost activity in this field. And, within the last few weeks, we have announced five new awards to study open source learning platforms to try and train and re-skill workers at a larger scale, and these were just announced. It's going to be done at the University of Southern California, Purdue, Northeastern, Colorado School of Mines, and Oregon State University. They're all getting a couple million dollars to test some really big ideas they have in different ways. So it's, like—what is it, "coopetition," or something? They're doing it in different ways, but they're all going to be able to learn from each other.

And I think this is, you know, our approach is to fund a lot of different innovations in the hope that some of them figure out something really innovative that can be spread all over the country.

Mr. BAIRD. Well, thank every one of you, and thank you, Madam Chair, for letting us have that amount of time.

Chairwoman STEVENS. Well, before we bring this hearing to a close, it is evident that we are having a hearing with giants, in terms of the expertise of our witnesses here today. And it was not shared, but the new Dems have a Future of Work Taskforce that Congressman Bill Foster chairs, and I'm a part of. Some of our colleagues who do not sit on the House Science Committee, we will be sharing with them this testimony here today, all of your testimony, and the questions.

And certainly we find ourselves in a profound, and exciting, and sometimes perplexing moment, and so your expert testimony will guide our Committee going forward, and help us to embrace some of these challenges, turn them into opportunities, and continue to push forward in a measured and data-driven way, and in a way that really respects where our economy is heading, and can head, and how we push to continue to support the workforce of the future.

So thank you all so much for coming to Washington today, or taking some time to come to the Science Committee to join us for today's hearing. This record will remain open for 2 weeks for additional statements from Members, and for additional questions that the Committee may ask of the witnesses, and of which we are expecting. So, at this time, our witnesses are excused, and this hearing is now adjourned.

[Whereupon, at 5:22 p.m., the Subcommittee was adjourned.]

APPENDIX I: ANSWERS TO POST-HEARING QUESTIONS

Responses by Dr. Arthur Lupia

HOUSE COMMITTEE ON SCIENCE, SPACE, AND TECHNOLOGY
SUBCOMMITTEE ON RESEARCH AND TECHNOLOGY

Questions for the Record to:
Dr. Arthur Lupia
Assistant Director, Directorate for Social, Behavioral and Economic Sciences
National Science Foundation
Submitted by Congressman Daniel Lipinski

1. I introduced the Growing Artificial Intelligence Through Research, or GrAITR, Act because I am concerned about the current state of AI R&D and education here in the US. My bill dedicates additional resources to AI research and education and requires interagency coordination through an interagency committee, to help ensure that America maintains its lead on technology development and our workforce develops skills necessary to effectively develop and utilize AI.

   Dr. Lupia, you described in your testimony how NSF is driving coordination with other research and development efforts across the federal government, including co-chairing NSTC subcommittees of relevance. How would NSF and the broader federal research community benefit from legislative mandate on interagency AI coordination?

   My bill also would direct the NSF to establish Multidisciplinary Centers for AI Research and Education. These centers should promote interdisciplinary AI research as well as support long-term and short-term workforce development in AI. At least one Center must have the primary purpose of integrating AI into K-12 education. Dr. Lupia, how could centers like this compliment NSF's ongoing work in building our future workforce pipeline?

   Answer: As noted in my written statement, NSF leadership is helping to drive and coordinate AI research R&D efforts across the federal government. Through active participation on, including co-chairing of, various NSTC subcommittees and working groups of relevance to AI research, education, and workforce development, NSF is engaging with other federal agencies to help ensure America maintains its lead in artificial intelligence. These interagency efforts are crucial to a coordinated and strategically sound path forward with respect to federal funding for all aspects of AI. In addition, NSF funds workshops that inform the broader federal research community's priorities, which subsequently inform funding priorities at NSF.

   NSF supports a variety of centers programs that contribute to the Foundation's mission and vision. Centers exploit opportunities in science, engineering, and technology in which the complexity of the research program or the resources needed to solve the problem require the advantages of scope, scale, duration, equipment, facilities, and students. Centers are a principal means by which NSF fosters interdisciplinary research. Earlier this month, NSF issued a solicitation for National AI Research Institutes, which aims to support multi-disciplinary, multi-institutional projects on foundational and translational aspects of AI beginning in FY 2020. Each National AI Research Institute project would receive up to $20 million over five years. One of the thematic areas emphasized in the FY 2020 funding opportunity is AI-augmented learning. The National AI Research Institutes program is joint between NSF and several other federal agencies – a concrete result of the coordination described above.

APPENDIX II: ADDITIONAL MATERIAL FOR THE RECORD

Letter Submitted By Representative Haley Stevens

KELLY SERVICES

September 24, 2019

The Honorable Haley Stevens
Chair
Research and Technology Subcommittee
House Science, Space, and Technology Committee
U.S. House of Representatives
Washington, DC

Dear Representative Stevens:

I was delighted to learn that Research and Technology Subcommittee of the House Science, Space, and Technology Committee is holding a hearing on "Artificial Intelligence and the Future of Work". As you know, Kelly Services embraces our role in connecting people to work in ways that enrich their lives. Our core mission balances automation based economic growth and transformation with workforce needs. We strongly believe that employment for those who may face disadvantages from many circumstances, including automation, is fundamental to quality of life and dignity.

There is a great need to learn and further explore the implications of automation on people, and possible updates needed to public policy. We urge Congress to collect information, hold hearings, and engage to develop an integrated approach to policy that will support both our nation's economic growth and leadership in artificial intelligence. As our economy modernizes our nation's leaders will need to gather information to ensure technology, economic, tax, education, and labor policy supports the American economy and its workforce.

I would like to note that the Work Opportunity Tax Credit (WOTC) is a policy (albeit not a policy under the House Science Committee jurisdiction) that provides incentives and resources to ensure training and employment of those who are disadvantaged. With a minor update, like those made in the past to address specific workforce disadvantages, WOTC could be a tax incentive used for worker retraining when technology or automation leads to upskilled positions and needs. Kelly Services has extensive experience and success with WOTC (see attachment) as an incentive that allows the company to develop and invest in the systems and recruitment required to employ those who are on the sidelines and not currently working, certainly upskill training could be another use for this credit.

Again, thank you so much for your work in raising awareness and focus on the impact of artificial intelligence on the workforce. Please do not hesitate to contact me if you have any questions or need any further information.

Sincerely,

Matt Harvill /S/

Matt Harvill
Vice President, Operations Shared Services Center

WOTC: Attachment

WOTC is a cost-effective tool to encourage the hiring of disadvantaged workers with low skills and other barriers to employment.

- First enacted as of October 1, 1996 as part of comprehensive welfare reform.
- The credit encourages employers to incur the additional costs of hiring and training individuals who may have never been in or succeeded in the workforce (TANF, SNAP, Unemployed Veterans, Long Term Unemployed, etc.)
- Overtime, Congress has changed categories of individuals who may qualify as WOTC eligible when employed.
- Extensive analysis of WOTC over time demonstrates it leads to long term employment of individuals who were not formerly in the work force AND it saves money by reducing federal and state government -assistance payments

WOTC by the Numbers

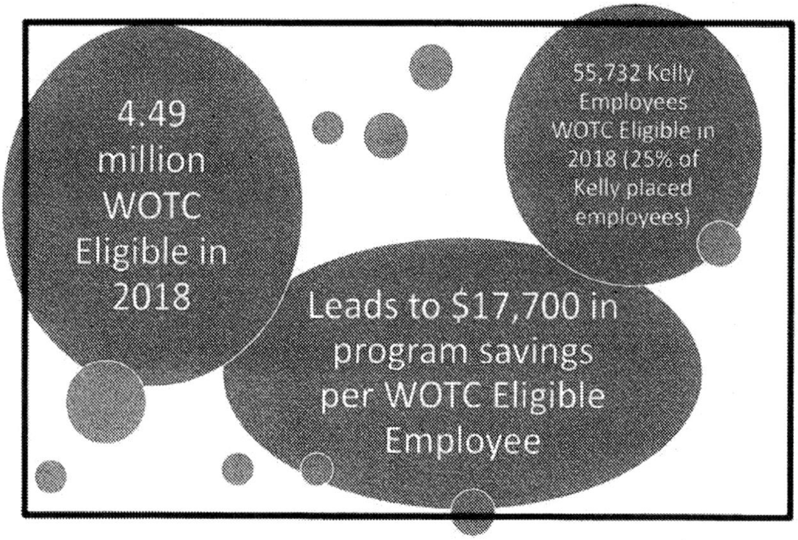

Sources: US DoL WOTC Certifications, Kelly Services data, and Cappelli study at www.wotcmeansjobs.org

Matt Harvill | Vice President, Operations Shared Services Center | Kelly Services
999 West Big Beaver Road| Troy, MI | direct: (248) 273-2615 | email: Matt.Harvill@kellyservices.com

EXECUTIVE SUMMARY SUBMITTED BY REPRESENTATIVE HALEY STEVENS: AUTOMATION AND ARTIFICIAL INTELLIGENCE HOW MACHINES ARE AFFECTING PEOPLE AND PLACES

Mark Muro, Robert Maxim and Jacob Whiton
With contributions from Ian Hathaway
January 2019

Executive Summary

The power and prospect of automation and artificial intelligence (AI) initially alarmed technology experts for fear that machine advancements would destroy jobs. Then came a correction, with a wave of reassurances.

Now, the discourse appears to be arriving at a more complicated, mixed understanding that suggests that automation will bring neither apocalypse nor utopia, but instead both benefits and stresses alike. Such is the ambiguous and sometimes-disembodied nature of the "future of work" discussion.

Which is where the present analysis aims to help. Intended to clear up misconceptions on the subject of automation, the following report employs government and private data, including from the McKinsey Global Institute, to develop both backward- and forward-looking analyses of the impacts of automation over the years 1980 to 2016 and 2016 to 2030 across some 800 occupations. In doing so, the report assesses past and coming trends as they affect both people and communities and suggests a comprehensive response framework for national and state-local policymakers.

In terms of current trends, the report finds that:

1) Automation and AI will affect tasks in virtually all occupational groups in the future but the effects will be of varied intensity—and

drastic for only some. The effects in this sense will be broad but variable:

- Almost no occupation will be unaffected by the adoption of currently available technologies.
- Approximately 25 percent of U.S. employment (36 million jobs in 2016) will face high exposure to automation in the coming decades (with greater than 70 percent of current task content at risk of substitution).
- At the same time, some 36 percent of U.S. employment (52 million jobs in 2016) will experience medium exposure to automation by 2030, while another 39 percent (57 million jobs) will experience low exposure.

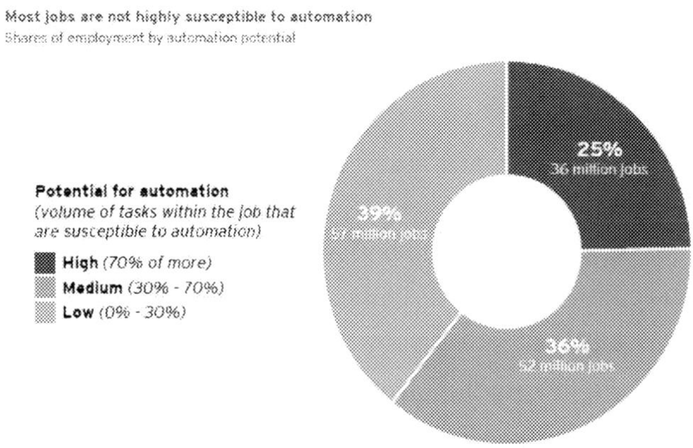

Source: Brookings analysis of BLS, Census, EMSI, and McKinsey data.

Figure 13.

2) The impacts of automation and AI in the coming decades will vary especially across occupations, places, and demographic groups. Several patterns are discernable:
   - "Routine," predictable physical and cognitive tasks will be the most vulnerable to automation in the coming years.

     Among the most vulnerable jobs are those in office administration, production, transportation, and food preparation.

Such jobs are deemed "high risk," with over 70 percent of their tasks potentially automatable, even though they represent only one-quarter of all jobs. The remaining, more secure jobs include a broader array of occupations ranging from complex, "creative" professional and technical roles with high educational requirements, to low-paying personal care and domestic service work characterized by non-routine activities or the need for interpersonal social and emotional intelligence. Near-future automation potential will be highest for roles that now pay the lowest wages. Likewise, the average automation potential of occupations requiring a bachelor's degree runs to just 24 percent, less than half the 55 percent task exposure faced by roles requiring less than a bachelor's degree. Given this, better-educated, higher- paid earners for the most part will continue to face lower automation threats based on current task content—though that could change as AI begins to put pressure on some higher-wage "non-routine" jobs.

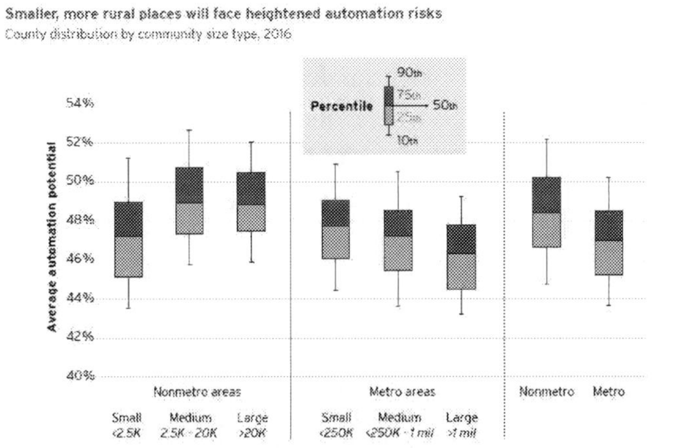

Source: Brookings analysis of BLS, Census, EMSI, Moody's, and McKinsey data.

Figure 14.

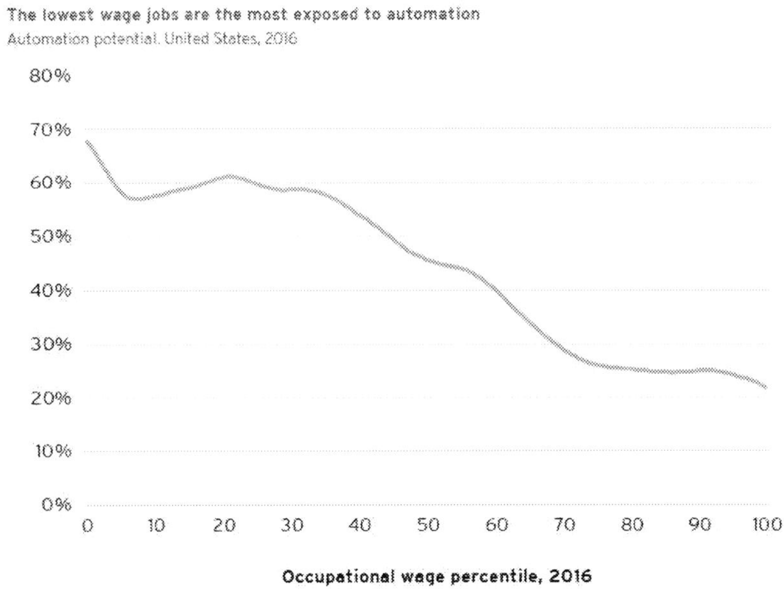

Note: Figures have been smoothed using a LOWESS regression Source: Brookings analysis of BLS, Census, EMSI, and McKinsey data.

Figure 15.

- Automation risk varies across U.S. regions, states, and cities, but it will be most disruptive in Heartland states. While automation will take place everywhere, its inroads will be felt differently across the country. Local risks vary with the local industry, task, and skill mix, which in turn determines local susceptibility to task automation.

  Large regions and whole states—which differ less from one another in their overall industrial compositions than do smaller locales like metropolitan areas or cities—will see noticeable but not, in most cases, radical variations in task exposure to automation. Along these lines, the state-by-state variation of automation potential is relatively narrow, ranging from 48.7 and 48.4 percent of the employment-weighted task load in Indiana and Kentucky to 42.9 and 42.4 percent in Massachusetts and New York, as depicted in Map 1.

Yet, the map of state automation exposure is distinctive. Overall, the 19 states that the Walton Family Foundation labels as the American Heartland have an average employment-weighted automation potential of 47 percent of current tasks, compared with 45 percent in the rest of the country. Much of this exposure reflects Heartland states' longstanding and continued specialization in manufacturing and agricultural industries.

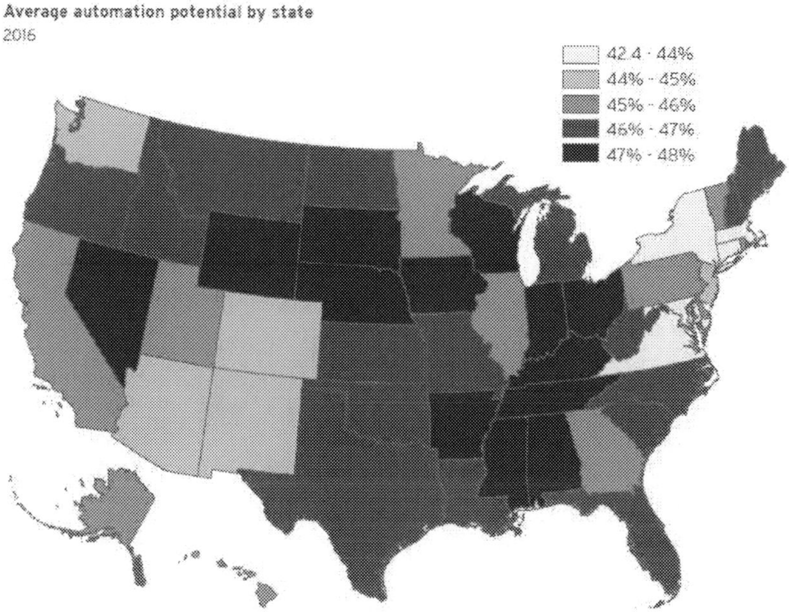

Source: Brookings analysis of BLS, Census, EMSI, Moody's, and McKinsey data.

Map 1.

- At the community level, the data reveal sharper variation, with smaller, more rural communities significantly more exposed to automation-driven task replacement— and smaller metros more vulnerable than larger ones. The average worker in a small metro area with a population of less than 250,000, for example, works in a job where 48 percent of current tasks are potentially automatable. But that can rise or decline. In small, industrial metros like Kokomo, Ind. and Hickory, N.C. the automatable share of work reaches as high as 55 percent on average. By contrast, small university towns like Charlottesville, Va. and Ithaca, N.Y., or state capitals like Bismarck, N.D. and Santa Fe, N.M., appear relatively well-insulated.

As to the 100 largest metropolitan areas, it is also clear that while the risk of current- task automation will be widely distributed, it won't be evenly spread. Among this subset of key metro areas, educational attainment will prove decisive in shaping how local labor markets may be affected by AI-age technological developments.

Among the large metro areas, employment- weighted task risk in 2030 ranges from 50 percent and 49 percent in less well-educated locations like Toledo, Ohio and Greensboro- High Point, N.C., to just 40 percent and 39 percent in high education attainment metros like San Jose, Calif. and Washington, D.C.

Following Washington, D.C. and San Jose among the larger metros with the lowest current-task automation risk comes a "who's who" of well-educated and technology- oriented centers including New York; Durham-Chapel Hill, N.C.; and Boston—all with average current-task risks below 43 percent. These metro areas relatively protected by their specializations in durable professional, business, and financial services occupations, combined with relatively large education and health enterprises.

- Men, young workers, and underrepresented communities work in more automatable occupations. In this respect, the sharp segmentation of the labor market by gender, age, and racial-ethnic identity ensures that AI-era automation is going to affect demographic groups unevenly.

  Male workers appear noticeably more vulnerable to potential future automation than women do, given their overrepresentation in production, transportation, and construction-installation occupations—job areas that have above- average projected automation exposure.

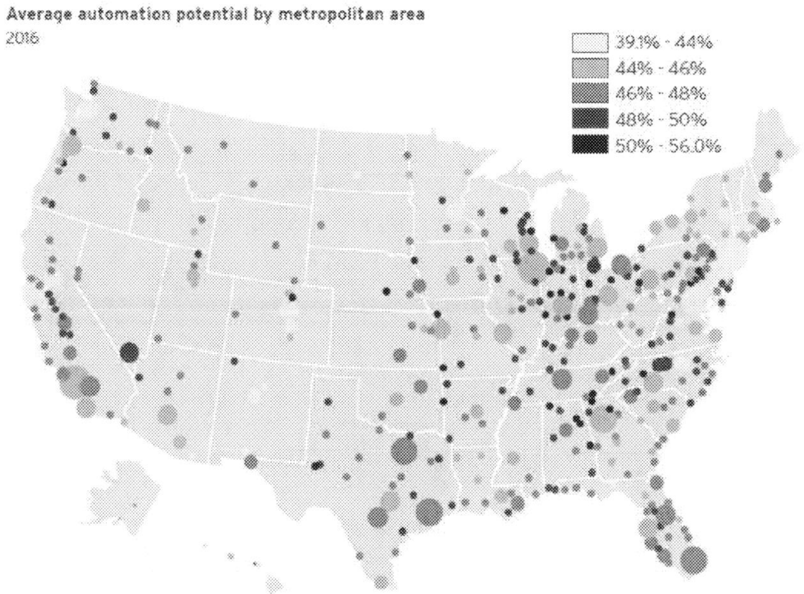

Source: Brookings analysis of BLS, Census, EMSI, Moody's, and McKinsey data.

Map 2.

By contrast, women comprise upward of 70 percent of the labor force in relatively safe occupations, such as health care, personal services, and education occupations.

Automation exposure will vary even more sharply across age groups, meanwhile, with the young facing the most disruption. Young workers between the ages of 16 and 24 face a high average automation exposure of 49 percent, which reflects their dramatic overrepresentation in automatable jobs associated with food preparation and serving.

Equally sharp variation can be forecasted in the automation inroads that various racial and ethnic groups will face. Hispanic, American Indian, and black workers, for example, face average current-task automation potentials of 47 percent, 45 percent, and 44 percent for their jobs, respectively, figures well above those likely for their white (40 percent) and Asian (39 percent) counterparts.

Underlying these differences is the stark over- and underrepresentation of racial and ethnic groups in high-exposure occupations like construction and agriculture (Hispanic workers) and transportation (black workers). Black workers have a slightly lower average automation potential based on their overrepresentation in health care support and protective and personal care services, jobs which on average have lower automation susceptibility.

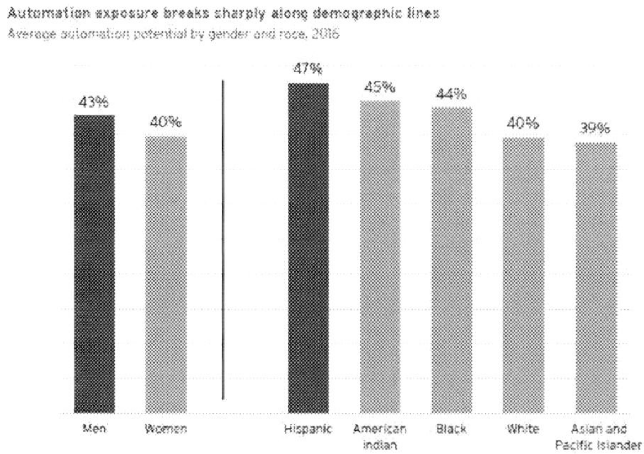

Source: Brookings analysis of 2016 American Community Survey 1-Year microdata.

Figure 16.

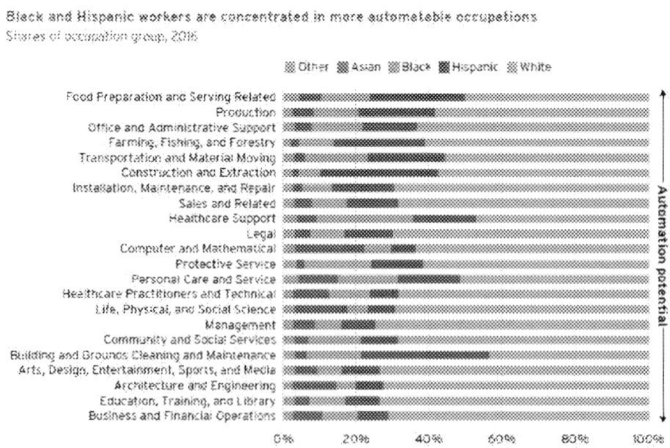

Source: Brookings analysis of American Community Survey 1-year microdata.

Figure 17.

3) To manage and make the best of these changes five major agendas require attention on the part of federal, state, local, business, and civic leaders.

To start with, government must work with the private sector to embrace growth and technology to keep productivity and living standards high and maintain or increase hiring.

Beyond that, all parties must invest more thought and effort into ensuring that the labor market works better for people. To that end, the appropriate actors need to:

- Promote a constant learning mindset
  - Invest in reskilling incumbent workers
  - Expand accelerated learning and
  - certifications
  - Make skill development more financially
  - accessible
  - Align and expand traditional education
  - Foster uniquely human qualities
- Facilitate smoother adjustment
  - Create a Universal Adjustment Benefit to support all displaced workers
  - Maximize hiring through a subsidized employment program
- Reduce hardships for workers who are struggling
  - Reform and expand income supports for workers in low-paying jobs
  - Reduce financial volatility for workers in
  - low-wage jobs
- Mitigate harsh local impacts
  - Future-proof vulnerable regional economies
  - Expand support for community adjustment

If the nation can commit to its people in these ways, an uncertain future full of machines will seem much more tolerable.

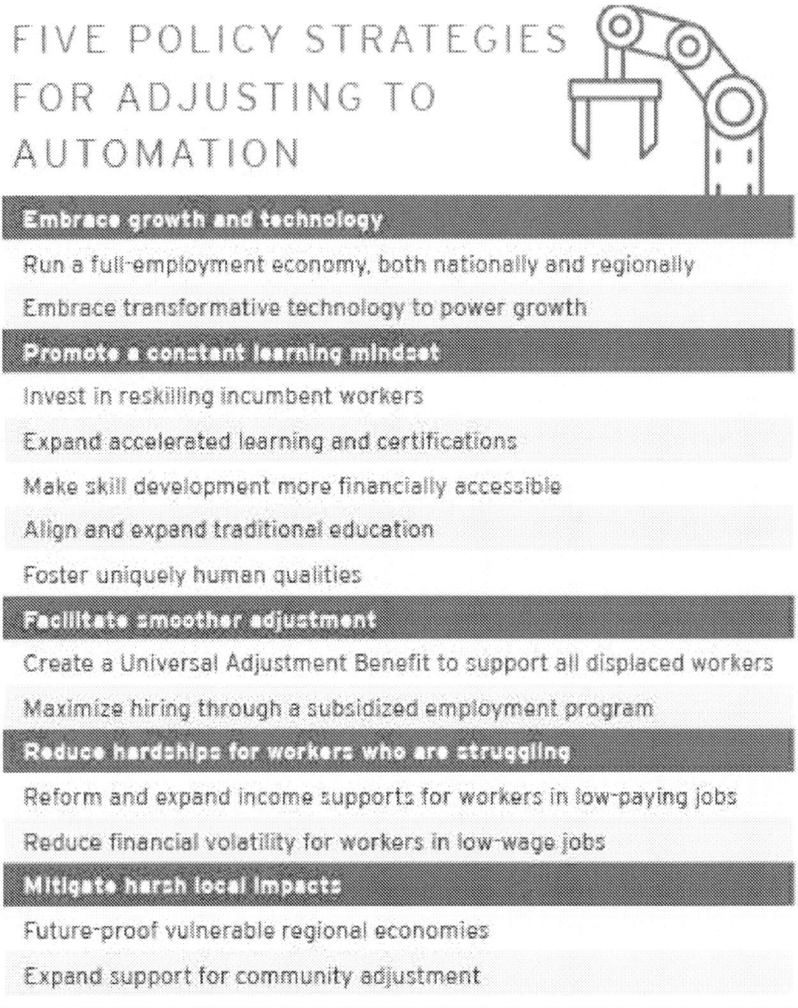

Source: Metropolitan Policy Program at Brookings.

Figure 18.

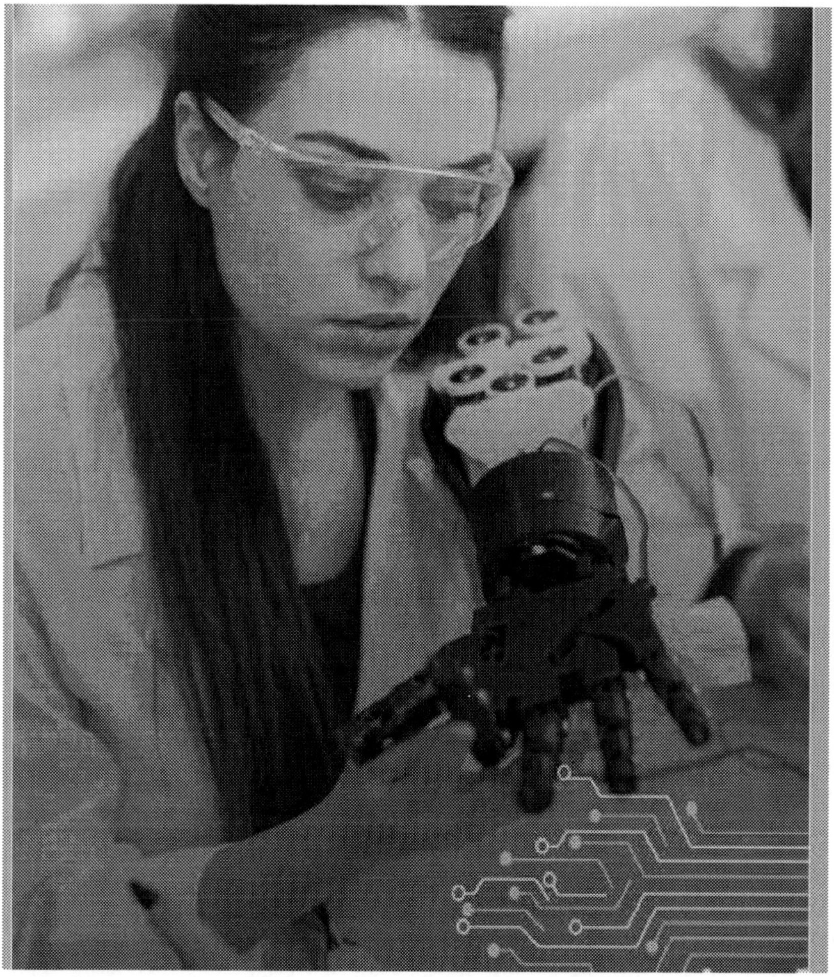

Figure 19.

Ramayya Krishnan

President, Institute for Operations Research and Management Sciences (INFORMS)

Statement Submitted to the Subcommittee on Research and Technology

Hearing on "AI and the Future of Work"

September 24, 2019

Chairwoman Stevens and Ranking Member Baird:

I appreciate the opportunity to submit this statement on behalf of the Institute for Operations Research and the Management Sciences (INFORMS) where I currently serve as President. As you may know, INFORMS is the professional society for operations research and analytics. Our 12,000 members are leveraging complex mathematical modeling to save lives, save money, and solve problems throughout academia, industry, and the federal government.

A significant amount of work within the operations research and analytics fields has been focused on the two issues this committee is reviewing today – artificial intelligence and the future of work.

In addition to my role at INFORMS, I am also the Dean of the Heinz College of Information Systems and Public Policy at Carnegie Melon University. I also serve as Director of a Carnegie Mellon Center – The Block Center for Technology and Society -- , which is focused on the study of the future of work, trust and transparency in the deployment of AI, and the solution of challenging societal problems (e.g., hunger, reskilling at scale) through technology and analytics. The center's mission is "addressing technological disruption from the perspective of economics, organizations, and public policy, the Block Center's projects will seek to ensure that the benefits of technological change are widely shared, opening new paths to prosperity for all."

There are many predictions around the impact artificial intelligence will have on the American economy and the workforce. At this point, while forecasting and speculation is fueling the discussion around AI, there is no science to show exactly what will happen in the years ahead as technologies emerge.

We do know that AI brings great opportunities in a range of sectors, from healthcare to transportation safety (and many in between). We know that these technologies will help the United States remain globally competitive and will bring advances that were unimaginable a decade ago. We shouldn't work to stall these innovations, but we should be willing to plan aggressively for them.

It is my belief that AI will certainly bring change to the workforce, but not in a manner that will result in job losses, but rather tactical changes in job responsibilities. AI, in some categories, will bring new opportunities as well. If we plan and respond appropriately, the workforce will witness AI as an addition to the workforce, not a replacement to the workforce. Much of that, however, depends on the systems we have in place to adjust for this technological reality.

I would suggest all stakeholders – government, academia, and industry – focus on three important strategies as we, together, approach the broad adoption of AI technologies: (1) evaluating the impact of AI on the future of work, (2) developing comprehensive re-skilling and re-training opportunities for workers at scale, and (3) designing teaming arrangements to ensure AI can effectively work with humans. I outline these three strategies below in some additional detail.

Evaluating the Impact of AI on the Future of Work

The first and most important step in evaluating the impacts of AI on jobs should be to map out how technology is going to affect the future of work. This comprehensive analysis will help to better understand where AI will impact the workforce and in what ways those impacts will affect employees.

There is already a significant amount of focus around the potential for job losses and I believe that is not the appropriate way to view the impact AI will have. We must focus on tasks, not jobs. Some tasks will be automated, while others will be augmented. It is important that we understand where the technological change is likely to happen – at the task level vs. at the job level. This distinction is important as we plan around these emerging technologies since jobs are a bundle of tasks. When tasks get automated or augmented, the nature of skills required to do the job changes.

Developing Comprehensive Re-Skilling and Re-Training Opportunities

Once we fully understand the sectors and tasks within them that will be augmented or automated by AI, we will need to prioritize re-skilling. This could be retraining or reskilling provided by the employer to employees or offered at societal scale to citizens seeking to acquire the skills required to find jobs. This is a fundamental change from where we are today. We don't have effective reskilling programs that can train large numbers of people (i.e., at scale) in the United States and where they exist they often do not deliver learning outcomes and skills required to acquire the jobs being produced in the economy.

Operations research can be an effective tool in determining how to deploy training and who should receive it. While AI-based educational technologies can be harnessed to deliver the training, targeting what training would deliver the most value to an individual is the province of Operations Research. This requires complex modeling to ensure that re-skilling and re-training at scale is effective for both employees/citizens and responsive to emerging job trends.

Designing Teaming Arrangements with AI

Since most jobs will not be fully replaced by AI, it is critical that AI is designed in a way to work effectively with humans. In doing so, we must develop teaming arrangements, which requires a firm understanding of and coordination with both the priorities I mentioned previously – identifying tasks within jobs that are impacted by AI and developing re-skilling and re-training opportunities.

In closing, I would like to thank the committee for the work you are doing to approach AI with a focus on the workforce. I hope you will work with academia, especially those within the operations research and analytics fields, who are aggressively leading the way on modeling the future of work as it relates to AI.

I look forward to working with the members of this committee and your staff as you think through policy decisions that relate to both AI and the future of work.

Thank you.

In: Artificial Intelligence
Editor: Tonya Randolph
ISBN: 978-1-68507-313-8

Chapter 2

MACHINES, ARTIFICIAL INTELLIGENCE, AND THE WORKFORCE: RECOVERING AND READYING OUR ECONOMY FOR THE FUTURE*

Committee on the Budget

Thursday, September 10, 2020
House of Representatives, Committee on the Budget,
Washington, D.C.

The Committee met, pursuant to notice, at 1:04 p.m., via Webex, Hon. John A. Yarmuth [Chairman of the Committee] presiding.

Present: Representatives Yarmuth, Boyle, Schakowsky, Kildee, Panetta, Morelle, Scott, Jackson Lee, Sires, Khanna; Womack, Woodall, Johnson, Flores, Hern, Burchett, and Jacobs.

Chairman YARMUTH. This hearing will come to order. Good afternoon and welcome to the Budget Committee's hearing on Machines,

---

* This is an edited, reformatted and augmented version of The Hearing Before the Committee on the Budget House of Representatives, Publication No. 116–30, dated September 10, 2020.

Artificial Intelligence, and the Workforce: Recovering and Readying Our Economy for the Future.

Before we begin, I want to welcome the newest Member of the Budget Committee, Chris Jacobs. Welcome, Chris. Before coming to Congress, Chris was a New York State Senator, and the Committee is happy to have you here.

Mr. JACOBS. Thank you.

Chairman YARMUTH. Now before I welcome our witnesses, I will go over a few housekeeping matters.

At the outset, I ask unanimous consent that the Chair be authorized to declare a recess at any time to address technical difficulties that may arise with such remote proceedings.

Without objection, so ordered.

As a reminder, we are holding this hearing virtually in compliance with the regulations for committee proceedings pursuant to House Resolution 965. First consistent with regulations, the Chair, or staff designated by the Chair, may mute participants' microphones when they are not under recognition for the purpose of eliminating inadvertent background noise.

Members are responsible for unmuting themselves when they seek recognition or when they are recognized for their five minutes. We are not permitted to unmute Members unless they explicitly request assistance. If I notice that you have not unmuted yourself, I will ask you if you would like the staff to unmute you. If you indicate approval by nodding, staff will unmute your microphone. They will not unmute you under any other circumstances.

Second, Members must have their cameras on throughout this proceeding and must be visible on screen in order to be recognized.

As a reminder, Members may not participate in more than one committee proceeding simultaneously. For those Members not wanting to wear a mask, the House rules provide a way to participate remotely from your office without being physically present in the hearing room.

Now, I will introduce our witnesses.

This afternoon we will be hearing from Dr. Susan Athey, Economics of Technology Professor at Stanford Graduate School of Business, and

Associate Director at the Stanford Institute for Human Centered Artificial Intelligence.

Dr. Daron Acemoglu, Institute Professor of Economics at the Massachusetts Institute of Technology.

Dr. Darrell West, Vice President and Director of Governance Studies at the Brookings Institution.

And Dr. Jason Matheny, Director for the Center For Security and Emerging Technology at Georgetown University and Commissioner for the National Security Commission on Artificial Intelligence, who I might add has just informed me he is from Louisville, Kentucky, so we are especially glad to have him here with us.

Thank you all for being with us today.

I will now yield myself five minutes for an opening statement.

This year Labor Day felt different than previous years. While most of us still honored our workers and celebrated their vital contributions to our nation, especially our frontline workers, we also recognize the hardships faced by millions of laid off Americans and their families struggling to get by amid global pandemic and the worst economic downturn since the Great Depression.

Yet these twin crises have amplified problems that existed long before the coronavirus: devastating healthcare inequities, the loss of stable well-paying jobs, and stagnating wages. While our economy has slowed, exacerbating these underlying issues, technological change has marched on creating even more challenges.

As we look to the future artificial intelligence, or AI, has significant potential to disrupt the world. It presents opportunities to improve lives, livelihoods, productivity, and equality. However, it also poses serious risks of large scale economic changes.

Today's hearing will help us ground our thinking in facts and better prepare for this impending economic transition.

Like the arrival of the steam engine, electricity, and computers, AI will reshape a broad swath of industries and jobs. However, history shows us that while technological advancements can create new jobs that increase productivity and growth, these benefits have been paired with the elimination of old jobs and increased inequality as some workers are left behind.

Today we are losing jobs because the administration's failed response to the pandemic and economic crisis, but as the economy eventually recovers, workers may find it difficult to get their job back as companies replace jobs with new AI enabled automation. So while advancements in AI technologies could create more opportunities for workers with advanced education or specialized skills, workers without these skills could see fewer opportunities in the near future, and it is low and middle waged jobs that are most at risk.

Since the mid–1980's, but prior to the pandemic, 88 percent of middle skilled job losses associated with the automation of routine tasks took place within 12 months of a recession. Absent concerted efforts to foster inclusive recovery, AI and automation could exacerbate income inequality, widen racial and gender income gaps, and push more people into poverty when we eventually emerge from this recession.

There is already a large and persistent racial wealth gap in America. And since Black and Latino Americans are over represented in occupations at high risk for automation, they are disproportionately at risk of job and wage losses. Additionally, there are 40 percent more women than men who work in occupations at high risk for automation.

The Organization for Economic Cooperation and Development estimates that AI and automation could eliminate upwards of 14 percent of today's jobs and disrupt an additional 32 percent.

Current AI technologies have also raised concerns around replicating human biases and discrimination in algorithms. Given the range of AI applications emerging in employment, housing, healthcare, financial services, and criminal justice, improved transparency and oversight are needed to ensure AI tools do not replicate or expand discriminatory practices.

Just like previous technological breakthroughs, AI will broadly impact the federal budget. Along with IT modernization, AI can directly improve the efficiency and effectiveness of government operations leading to savings.

With the industry set to generate additional economic activity of up to $13 trillion worldwide by 2030, Federal R&D investments will remain essential to U.S. leadership and competitiveness in AI technology. However, the benefits will only be available to all Americans if paired with strategic investments to support our workforce through this impending evolution.

The pandemic and economic crisis have already shown that income security and related programs are crucial for supporting Americans during challenging times. The shifting job landscape expected with widespread AI implementation could further demonstrate this need. This will require strong federal investments and social programs and affordable healthcare, childcare, and housing, as well as new approaches for retraining and upskilling our workforce.

IBM estimates that between 2019 and 2022, more than 120 million workers in the world's 12 largest economies may need to be retrained and reskilled as a result of AI-enabled automation. If we fail to plan ahead, the underlying problems illuminated by the pandemic and recession will continue to create barriers to success for American workers.

We have a responsibility to get Americans through the COVID crisis, but we also must address the long-term economic challenges we know are coming. These issues are complicated and nuanced, but that is why we are here today. With the help of our expert witnesses, we can begin to chart a path forward that leads to inclusive economic growth, broad social benefits, and a better prepared workforce.

I look forward to learning more about the magnitude of the potential changes to our economy and job market and the federal policies that will be needed in response.

I now yield five minutes to the Ranking Member, Mr. Womack, of Arkansas.

[The prepared statement of Chairman Yarmuth follows:]

Chairman John A. Yarmuth
Hearing on Machines, Artificial Intelligence, and the Workforce: Recovering and Readying, Our Economy for the Future
Opening Statement, September 10, 2020

This year, Labor Day felt very different than previous years. While most of us still honored our workers and celebrated their vital contributions to our nation – especially our frontline workers – we also recognized the hardships faced by millions of laid-off Americans and their families, struggling to get by amid a global pandemic and the worst economic downturn since the Great Depression.

Yet these twin crises have amplified problems that existed long before the coronavirus: devastating health care inequities, the loss of stable, well-paying jobs, and stagnating wages. While our economy has slowed – exacerbating these underlying issues – technological change has marched on, creating even more challenges.

As we look to the future, artificial intelligence (or AI) has significant potential to disrupt the world. It presents opportunities to improve lives, livelihoods, productivity, and equality. However, it also poses serious risks of large-scale economic changes. Today's hearing will help us ground our thinking in facts and better prepare for this impending economic transition.

Like the arrival of the steam engine, electricity, and computers, AI will reshape a broad swath of industries and jobs. However, history shows us that while technological advancements can create new jobs and increase productivity and growth, these benefits have been paired with the elimination of old jobs and increased inequality as some workers are left behind.

Today we are losing jobs because of the Administration's failed response to the pandemic and economic crisis. But as the economy eventually recovers, workers may find it difficult to get their job back as companies replace jobs with new AI-enabled automation. So, while advancements in AI technologies could create more opportunities for workers with advanced education or specialized skills, workers without these skills could see fewer opportunities in the near future. And it's low- and middle-wage jobs that are most at risk.

Since the mid-1980s, but prior to the pandemic, 88 percent of middle-skill job losses – associated with the automation of routine tasks – took place within 12 months of a recession. Absent concerted efforts to foster an inclusive recovery, AI and automation could exacerbate income inequality, widen racial and gender income gaps, and push more people into poverty when we eventually emerge from this recession. There is already a large and persistent racial wealth gap in America, and, since Black and Latino Americans are overrepresented in occupations at high risk for automation, they are disproportionately at risk of job and wage losses. Additionally, there are 40 percent more women than men who work in occupations at high risk for automation. The Organisation for Economic Co-operation and Development (OECD) estimates that AI and automation could eliminate upwards of 14 percent of today's jobs and disrupt an additional 32 percent.

Current AI technologies have also raised concerns around replicating human biases and discrimination in algorithms. Given the range of AI applications emerging in employment, housing, health care, financial services, and criminal justice, improved transparency and oversight are needed to ensure AI tools do not replicate or expand discriminatory practices.

Just like previous technological breakthroughs, AI will broadly impact the federal budget. Along with IT modernization, AI can directly improve the efficiency and effectiveness of government operations, leading to savings. With the industry set to generate additional economic activity of up to $13 trillion worldwide by 2030, federal R&D investments will remain essential to U.S. leadership and competitiveness in AI technology. However, the benefits will only be available to all Americans if paired with strategic investments to support our workforce through this impending evolution.

The pandemic and economic crisis have already shown that income security and related programs are crucial for supporting Americans during challenging times. The shifting job landscape expected with widespread AI implementation further demonstrates this need. This will require strong federal investments in social programs, in affordable health care, child care, and housing, as well as new approaches for retraining and upskilling our workforce. IBM estimates that between 2019 and 2022, more than 120 million workers in the world's 12 largest economies may need to be retrained and reskilled as a result of AI-enabled automation.

If we fail to plan ahead, the underlying problems illuminated by the pandemic and recession will continue to create barriers to success for American workers. We have a responsibility to get Americans through the COVID crises, but we also must address the long-term economic challenges we know are coming.

These issues are complicated and nuanced, but that's why we are here today. With the help of our expert witnesses, we can begin to chart a path forward that leads to inclusive economic growth, broad societal benefits, and a better-prepared workforce. I look forward to learning more about the magnitude of the potential changes to our economy and job market, and the federal policies that will be needed in response.

Mr. WOMACK. And I thank the Chairman for holding this hearing and my thanks to the witnesses who will be with us today.

I would like to also add my bit of welcome to Chris Jacobs, the newest Member of the Committee, native of Buffalo, New York. Long history of public service, Erie County clerk, state Senator now joining us as a Member of Congress. This isn't his first tour of duty at the Capitol. He began his career working for former Congressman and Buffalo Bill quarterback Jack Kemp.

Chris, welcome to the Budget Committee. To your wife and daughter, Martina and Anna, thank you for allowing your husband and father to continue his public service career by spending time in Washington with all of us. Chris, we welcome you to the Committee.

We are here to talk about AI capabilities, both current and future, and the impacts on the economy and the federal budget. It is a critical technology to be sure that will benefit the lives of many Americans and touch nearly every sector of the U.S. economy. While it will likely change the way many jobs are performed as technological advances have for many decades, we must harness the capabilities of AI to help drive our economy and society forward.

Congress has to ensure that its actions do not stifle innovation, rather government should work in partnership with the private sector to move our country forward in AI research and development.

By making strategic federal investments in AI R&D, Washington can help unleash America's pioneering and entrepreneurial spirit. It also means creating a regulatory environment that supports, not hinders, private industry by allowing technological advancements to flourish in a safe, trustworthy, and effective way. Congress should also move to encourage more American high-tech manufacturing in general.

The U.S. currently relies on countries located in geopolitical hot spots for many critical components and as the coronavirus pandemic has shown with medical supplies, we need to ensure we have reliable, secure, and diverse supply chains for vital materials.

Now while this is an interesting, important topic, it should not be the reason why the Budget Committee is convening this afternoon, in my strong opinion.

The dire fiscal outlook—notably the recent deficit and debt projections—and the discussion on how to tackle these challenges should be the focus of today's Committee meeting. Last week the Congressional Budget Office released its budget outlook update, and let me tell you the findings are incredibly sobering, but not surprising.

We did not do our job when this pandemic—before the pandemic hit. This Committee is charged with writing a budget to put our country on a responsible fiscal path, but we failed in that duty. Once COVID hit, we were obligated to respond to the crisis. For those of you who don't know, let me summarize where our nation stands fiscally. And let me just warn you, it isn't good.

The deficit for fiscal 2020 is protected to be $3.3 trillion, more than triple the previous year's deficit and by far the highest in American history. Every single year for the next 10 years, CBO is projecting that annual deficits will exceed a trillion dollars and total $13 trillion over this period.

The public debt is projected to be larger than the size of the entire economy by next year, that is 104 percent of GDP, and will continue to increase to more than $33 trillion by fiscal 2030. That is 109 percent of projected GDP. Once again, CBO confirmed the driver of the fiscal problem, federal spending, particularly mandatory spending.

Mandatory spending, including interest payments on the debt is expected to account for 75 percent of total federal spending by 2030. And I don't need to be the guy to tell you, you already know. That is squeezing resources for many discretionary priorities. The job of this Committee is to write a budget resolution that sets a fiscal path for the government to follow. We didn't write one. We don't have one. Instead of considering a budget resolution, we are talking about artificial intelligence, which is, as I mentioned before, while an interesting topic and an important topic, it is not the mandate of this Committee.

The Democrat majority has neglected to do a budget resolution for the past two years. CBO's projections illustrate the necessity for the Democrat majority to do its job—write and pass a budget resolution that provides a responsible, fiscal framework to correct this current, fiscal trajectory.

With that, I look forward to hearing from our witnesses, and always look forward to the discussion. Thank you, Mr. Chairman.

I will yield back the balance of my time.

[The prepared statement of Steve Womack follows:]

OPENING STATEMENT OF RANKING MEMBER STEVE WOMACK (R-AR)

As Prepared for Delivery

Thank you, Chairman Yarmuth, for holding this hearing, and thank you to our witnesses for joining us today.

I would like to welcome one more person – Representative Chris Jacobs, the newest member of the Committee. A native of Buffalo, New York, Chris has a long history of public service – as Erie County Clerk, a state senator, and now joining us as a Member of Congress. This isn't his first tour of duty in the Capitol. He began his career working for former Congressman – and Buffalo Bills quarterback – Jack Kemp. Chris – welcome to the Budget Committee.

And to your wife and daughter, Martina and Anna, thank you for allowing your husband and father to continue his public service career by spending time in Washington. Chris, welcome.

We are here today to talk about artificial intelligence (AI) capabilities – both current and future – and the impacts on the economy and federal budget.

AI is a critical technology that will benefit the lives of many Americans, and touch nearly every sector of the U.S. economy. While it will likely change the way many jobs are performed, as technological advances have for many decades, we must harness the capabilities of AI to help drive our economy and society forward. Congress must ensure that its actions do not stifle innovation. Rather, government should work in partnership with the private sector to move our country forward in AI research and development (R&D).

By making strategic federal investments in AI R&D, Washington can help unleash America's pioneering and entrepreneurial spirit. This also means creating a regulatory environment that supports – not hinders – private industry by allowing technological advancements to flourish in a safe, trustworthy, and effective way.

Congress should also move to encourage more American high-tech manufacturing in general. The U.S. currently relies on countries located in geopolitical hotspots for many critical components, and as the coronavirus pandemic has shown with medical supplies, we need to ensure we have reliable, secure, and diverse supply chains for vital materials.

While this is an interesting and important topic, it should not be the reason why the Budget Committee is convening this afternoon.

The dire fiscal outlook – notably the recent deficit and debt projections – and a discussion on how to tackle these challenges should be the focus of today's Budget Committee meeting. Last week, the Congressional Budget Office (CBO) released its budget outlook update, and, let me tell you, the findings are incredibly sobering but not surprising. We did not do our job before the pandemic hit. This Committee is charged with writing a budget to put our country on a responsible fiscal path. We failed that duty. Once COVID-19 hit, we were obligated to respond to the crisis. For those of you who don't know, let me summarize where our nation stands fiscally. It isn't good.

The deficit for fiscal year 2020 is projected to be $3.3 trillion, more than triple the previous year's deficit and by far the highest in American history. Every single year, for the next 10 years, CBO is projecting that annual deficits will exceed one trillion dollars and total $13 trillion over the period. The public debt is projected to be larger than the size of the entire economy by next year (104 percent of GDP) and will continue to increase to more than $33 trillion by fiscal year 2030 (109 percent of GDP). Once again, CBO confirmed the driver of the fiscal problem: federal spending, particularly mandatory spending.

Mandatory spending, including interest payments on the federal debt, is expected to account for 75 percent of total federal spending by 2030, squeezing out resources for important discretionary priorities, including investments in AI.

The job of this Committee is to write a budget resolution that sets a fiscal path for the government to follow. We didn't write one; we don't have one. Instead of considering a budget resolution, we are talking about artificial intelligence, which, as I mentioned before, while an interesting topic, is not the mandate for this Committee. The Democrat Majority has neglected to do a budget resolution for the past two years. CBO's projections illustrate the necessity for the Democrat Majority to do its job: write and pass a budget resolution that provides a responsible fiscal framework to correct the current trajectory.

With that, I look forward to hearing from our witnesses, and I look forward to today's discussion. Thank you, Mr. Chairman. I yield back.

Mr. WOMACK. Chairman, you'll need to unmute, I think. Chairman YARMUTH. Thank you. Should be up to that by now.

In the interest of time, once again, if any additional Member has an opening statement, you may submit those statements electronically to the Clerk for the record.

Once again, I want to thank our witnesses for being here this afternoon. The Committee has received your written statements and they will be made a part of the formal hearing record. Each of you will have five minutes to give your oral remarks. As a reminder, please unmute your microphone before speaking.

I now introduce and yield five minutes to Dr. Susan Athey. Please unmute your mike and begin when you are ready.

STATEMENTS

Susan Athey, PhD, Economics of Technology Professor, Stanford Graduate School of Business, and Associate Director, Stanford Institute for Human-Centered Artificial Intelligence (HAI);

Daron Acemoglu, PhD, Institute Professor of Economics, Massachusetts Institute of Technology;

Darrell West, PhD, Vice President and Director of Governance Studies, Brookings Institution;

Jason Matheny, PhD, Founding Director, Center for Security And Emerging Technology at Georgetown University, and Commissioner, National Security Commission on Artificial Intelligence.

Statement of Susan Athey, PhD

Dr. ATHEY. Hello, Chairman Yarmuth, Ranking Member Womack, and Members of the Committee. Thank you so much for inviting me to speak today.

Artificial intelligence seems to inspire extreme views. Some focus on a future where robots take all the jobs, while others point out that so far its effects on the economy are barely detectable. My own view is that AI has enormous positive potential for society and for the efficiency and finances of government, and that governments and universities have a crucial role to play in ensuring that the potential is realized.

AI, of course, also creates challenges, contributing to an era where workers transition more frequently and require more reskilling throughout their careers. So we need to ensure that our institutions are prepared to meet this reality, especially in light of the many fiscal and labor market challenges created by an aging population and workforce. But when R&D is directed at technology that augments human workers and support citizens in their lives and health, we may be able to expand the circumstances in which people engage in rewarding work while experiencing a high-quality of life in areas with a more moderate cost of living.

Some of the most promising areas where technology can be part of the solution include education, training, remote work, medicine, and government services. In each case, digital technology powered by AI can be used to make services cheaper to provide, higher quality, more tailored to the individual need, and substantially more accessible and convenient.

The accessibility matters particularly to people with limited time, like working people with caregiving responsibilities and especially rural residents who face a dual burden of high transportation costs and insufficient density to support specialized services and job opportunities in their local communities.

One reason the potential is so great for these problems is that digitization and the adoption of AI can lead to low marginal cost scalable and thus more efficient services.

Digitization and AI are inextricably linked to measurement and optimization, which naturally improves the accountability and effectiveness of the organizations who adopt them, including the government. In addition, general trends that have led to the rapid diffusion of AI relate to the lowered fixed cost in time required to adopt it.

One trend is just a digitization of everything from consumer interactions to supply chains. That creation of data is what powers and makes possible AI to be an optimization. The way IT is implemented has also changed. Cloud computing allows companies to rent computing as they need it rather than buy allowing infrastructure to be shared across firms and that reduces cost.

Software as a service lets companies subscribe to services and purchase the best products use case by use case and that software as a service then can also make available AI and machine learning innovation without firms having to do that R&D themselves.

Finally, we have seen a big expansion of open source software and, in general, data management analytics tools are widely available. They are shared across firms and across academia, and thus diffuse very quickly. The latest machine learning algorithms are typically free. For example, for my class we used algorithms that we downloaded that were trained using Facebook's image data setting computing infrastructure allowing the students to move on to the analytics on top of the image recognition.

The reason that firms are willing to share those types of algorithms is that it is customer relationships and data, as well as know-how to optimize the algorithms at large scale that give companies their competitive advantage.

And the general purpose technologies in algorithms have actually been fairly widely available. That means the cost of developing services is reduced as these general purpose innovation from academia and for-profit organizations can be repurposed by entrepreneurs, governments, and social impact organizations.

Now an important precursor to a policy discussion is demystifying the technology. In practice, rather than sort of general intelligence, most of what we have seen in the past 15 years can be thought of as more automation on steroids. For software, automation is like following prespecified rules without real-time human direction, but the latest innovations have concerned implementing automation using decision rules that are learned from past data using machine learning.

And a common example of machine learning and algorithm might take as input a digital photo and output a guess of what animal is in the photo.

Traditionally, analysts had to do a lot of manual work to customize the statistical models so the models were simplified, but modern machine learning allows the analyst to just feed in raw data and the algorithm does a lot of work to determine what is important for the task. This makes things general purpose, but the fact that they are general purpose also means they are black boxed and sometimes even the engineers building them don't understand them. Thus we need a lot more research and best practices to make sure that this technology is implemented safely and without unintended consequences.

Just to close, machine learning is diffusing across the economy use case by use case, but in most cases, this has led to an incremental innovation and incremental changes over time rather than sudden shifts.

So I look forward to continuing the discussion in the question and answer. Thank you.

[The prepared statement of Susan Athey follows:]

Susan Athey, the Economics of Technology Professor, Stanford Graduate School of Business: Written Testimony House Committee on the Budget

Chairman Yarmuth, Ranking Member Womack and Members of the Committee,

Thank you for inviting me to speak today. Artificial intelligence (AI) seems to inspire extreme views among policy analysts: some focus on a future where robots take all the jobs, while others argue that its effect will be no different than previous rounds of technological innovation. My own view is that AI has enormous positive potential that should not be ignored, and that governments and universities have a crucial role to play in ensuring that the potential is realized. At the same time, it will create some challenges, contributing to an era where workers transition more frequently and require more ongoing training and reskilling throughout their careers. If we invest carefully in making technology and innovation part of the solution, AI can achieve its potential and even contribute to addressing a variety of societal and fiscal challenges that loom before us.

An important precursor to a policy discussion about AI is a grounding in the technology, including a clear framework for understanding what it can and cannot do. Once AI is demystified, it is easier to assess its potential for impact, both positive and negative, as well as to interpret the data we have so far about how it affects the economy.

Artificial Intelligence, Automation and Software

Ideally, artificial intelligence refers to intelligent machines, where by "intelligent" we mean truly smart, for example capable of reasoning. In practice, most of what we've seen in the past fifteen years, and what I believe we will continue to see in the near future, can be better thought of as "automation on steroids." Thinking in terms of automation can guide the discussion in a more realistic direction, and also helps remind us of the limitations of AI.

Traditional automation in turn refers to physical machines or software that follow pre-specified rules or routines for interacting with its environment without real-time human direction.

One kind of automation that has expanded dramatically over the last few decades consists of a set of rules conceived of and written by humans, and executed by software. An automated telephone system that requires you to choose from a series of menus is a simple example of this; these systems evolved from phones, to websites, and more recently to chatbots. However, more complex systems have also been programmed using human-specified rules; some of the earliest self-driving cars encoded in software a set of scenarios and correct responses. Many educational technology applications that advertise their ability adapt to the level of the student simply specify what the next learning exercise should be as a function ofthe student's answers to previous questions using a large decision tree created manually by human experts (Golub Capital Social Impact Lab, 2020).

Although most people wouldn't consider a phone menu either inspiring or enjoyable, over time, automation through websites and apps have created substantial customer value and saved consumers large amounts of time and money. Being able to check a bank balance quickly on the go can prevent an overdraft fee; and when airlines finally adopted technology to pull up your flight information based on your mobile phone number, it made it much faster to make last-minute changes to a travel itinerary. Although it can be frustrating to deal with pre-specified menus when you have a non-standard request, a well-designed automated system can allow consumers to get their needs met quickly, and on their own time, which may be especially important for people working long hours or for working parents. As more and more services digitize, we expect that a larger share of services directly provided by government or indirectly funded by government will be accessed through automated systems.

This automation, while not sexy, can have an impact on employment. As more people have mobile phones and learn to use bank mobile apps for more and more functions, there is less need for a bank branch or call center with human beings available to answer questions. Indeed, Totty (2020) documented that bank teller employment declined by 26% in the last decade, from 600,000 jobs in 2010 to about 442,000 in 2019, while the Bureau of Labor Statistics projects a further decline of 15 percent between 2019 and 2029 (BLS, 2019). Numerous analysts have predicted large declines in financial services employment in the near future, including not just front-line workers but also back-office workers whose jobs involve relatively routine information processing (Kelly, 2019).

This type of automation has increased substantially over the last decade, but much of the change is not directly due to advances in artificial intelligence. Instead, in my view the most impactful changes have resulted from an expansion of digitization of interactions and recording of digital data.

As firms interact with customers digitally, use software to manage supply chains, GPS to track locations, and have digital recordings of many processes, it becomes natural for them to use software to manage the data. There is an evolution through the steps of digitization, using software to automate and process data, to more sophisticated optimization of digital processes and machine learning from data. Although sometimes firms take several steps simultaneously, it is more common to evolve slowly through these steps.

Alongside digitization, some other important trends include the rise of cloud-based services (where according to analysts the global cloud computing market increased from under $1 billion to several hundred billion dollars annually over a single decade, and today provides services to the vast majority of businesses.) The U.S. leads the world in both supply of cloud computing services and in adoption (IDC, 2019). Software as a service replaced the need for company-owned computers and specialized software to do things like manage email, customer databases, and call centers.

Even technology firms often adopt "software as a service" solutions for many purposes rather than building their own applications. This can be efficient, as software development is done once by a specialized team of developers and then used across many organizations. It is also increasingly common for different software products to interact and share data through application programming interfaces (APIs), allowing for more of a "plug and play" environment and enabling firms to take advantage of the best software for each need. This in turn makes it easier for firms to enter in both the technology and non-technology sectors, as they can purchase the products they need off-the-shelf and scale their usage as they grow. This can reduce costs associated with functions ranging from email to human resources to accounting to marketing and sales; it can also position governments and firms to more easily take advantage of innovations in AI.

Artificial Intelligence and Machine Learning

The largest innovations in AI in the past decade have concerned automation using decision rules learned from data, rather than human-specified rules. This is called machine learning. For an educational application, machine learning might be used to learn what types of reading material to recommend to a student based on past reading. With machine learning, an algorithm takes data as input and performs tasks such as prediction and classification.

For example, an analyst building a machine learning algorithm might feed in "training data" consisting of digital files that represent photos together with the corresponding labels for the photos such as "cat" and "dog." Once trained, the algorithm will take as input an unlabelled photo and output its best guess of the label (that is, its guess of whether the photo is a cat or a dog). Or, an algorithm might take in data about patients in a hospital from their electronic medical records, and output a predicted probability of death for each patient or the predicted number of days each patient will stay, predictions that can be important in a time of scarce hospital capacity, as in the COVID-19 pandemic.

Scientists and industry practitioners have built models like this for many decades, for applications like predicting the probability that a consumer will repay a loan. However, traditionally, the analyst had to do a lot of work to determine which variables were most important, and models were often overly simplified. Recent advances in machine learning allow the analyst to just feed in raw data, and the algorithm does a lot of the work to make sense of the data. In other words, the newer tools figure out what is important from the data, and then use the important factors to make predictions. This allows the same general purpose tools to be used across a wide range of applications. These tools work best when there is plenty of data, as well as a stable environment, so that the model's performance in the future is well approximated by how well it performs on a set of held out "test data" that is hidden from the analyst when building the model.

The fact that the algorithms take over a lot of the work of refining statistical models implies that algorithms can be very "general purpose," meaning that the same general approaches can be applied to a wide range of settings (see, e.g., Agarwal, Gans, and Goldfarb (2018) or Brynjolfsson, Rock, and Syverson (2020) for further discussion of this). For this reason, we have seen a rapid diffusion of machine learning across industries and applications.

At the same time, the fact that the algorithms are general purpose and emerge from data also create weaknesses. For example, the models can be difficult to interpret and understand without substantial additional effort and analysis; they are "black boxes" that translate input into output, making it challenging for even the engineers who build them to identify potential weaknesses. The goal of training is for the algorithms to perform well on average, but predictions may be poor for some realizations of input data, which can be a problem for individual decisions with certain characteristics, but further can create more widespread difficulties if the world changes in a way that makes the realizations of certain characteristics more likely. For example, unemployment or business failure may become more likely in sectors that previously did not experience it. In general, machine learning might make predictions based on relationships that are not stable in the long run. For example, factors that predict loan default may be different during the COVID-19 pandemic than at other times. In an image classification application, cats may be associated with indoor photographs, so that an algorithm bases its classification of a photo as showing a cat versus a dog using the background of the photo rather than characteristics of the animals, where characteristics of the animals themselves are more likely to remain constant across different countries, cultures, and environments for photo sharing.

It may be difficult for the engineers that build machine learning models to even understand the extent to which their models are fragile or unstable, let alone address the problems or prevent them. Well-documented examples where image classification failed for humans with darker skin highlight the pitfalls; once identified, many technology firms addressed the particular problems that had been pointed out, but other problems likely remain to be identified and fixed. This remains an active and important area of research in both academia and industry.

For related reasons, off-the-shelf machine learning models are often not suitable for learning about cause and effect. A small research community focuses on addressing such challenges, and indeed much of my own research focuses on how to adapt machine learning to make it more useful for scientific discovery (Athey, 2017), disentangling cause and effect (Athey, 2018; Athey and Imbens, 2019), and to make prediction more stable and reliable (Chipman, 2018; Kuang et al, 2018; Kuang et al, 2020); but the most commonly applied algorithms in practice suffer from challenges that come with the territory of black-box, general purpose machine learning.

In spite of their limitations, there are many advantages of general purpose algorithms, and the general purpose nature of machine learning is complementary with the trends of digitization, cloud computing, and open source software. There has been a dramatic increase in the availability of open source software that provides tools to manage and analyze large datasets, as well as software to implement machine learning algorithms. Although it might at first seem surprising, large technology firms have put a large number of software packages and algorithms into the public domain, including algorithms that have been trained on their own large datasets.

Even a few years ago, an engineer might need to spend a lot of time to train an algorithm that classifies images, but now it is possible to use off the shelf algorithms that companies like Facebook have trained on their large datasets of pictures. That frees engineers to focus on other parts of the problem, and can make it easier for academics to do research as well as for other AI firms to enter.

For example, as a university researcher I can store terabytes of data in public cloud infrastructure for research projects, and for just hundreds or thousands of dollars, I can analyze it in ways that would have only been possible inside large corporations a decade ago. Tools exist now that manage a lot of the work for distributing workloads and optimizing performance for statistical algorithms, and I can just focus on the analytic questions without worrying so much about the computational issues. My students can use publicly available image classifiers developed by Facebook to detect objects in images. Anyone from a student to a startup to a large company can use the technology. It is easy to experiment or prototype new models. What is often scarce is not the know-how or the infrastructure, but the data or the user base.

On the other hand, some of the most computationally intensive and cutting-edge applications of AI can be too expensive for startups or university researchers to carry out due to large computing needs, or they may require the types of data only available within large technology firms. For that reason, certain types of AI research have been challenging to carry out in academia, reducing the pace of publicly available innovation in those areas (see Lazer et al, 2020 for further discussion of policy issues around access to data and infrastructure for social science research). Some have called for a greater investment in public infrastructure for AI to support research and innovation (Etchemendy and Li, 2020).

Overall, digitization has decreased the costs of implementing AI, which reinforces the advancement of practical applications of AI and facilitates the diffusion of AI across industries and applications. Cloud infrastructure has made it easier for companies to enter and compete providing software as a service. In turn, companies providing software as a service invest in research and development, over time adding features including those powered by machine learning, thus making the benefits of machine learning available more broadly. As long as markets are competitive, a lot of those benefits accrue to the businesses and consumers who use the products. Of course, and this is a topic for another day, market power can sometimes be a concern, particularly in situations where a single firm controls access to a large group of consumers and/or their data. However, in many cases, consumers have seen the quality and convenience of digitally-delivered services rise or the costs fall as a result of all of this innovation, as digital services often have low marginal cost of delivery. This potential is what captures the imagination of AI optimists. However, there are also many unintended consequences of all of this innovation that require careful attention, as I will discuss further below.

Artificial Intelligence and the Generation of Novel Creations

An even more recent set of advances in artificial intelligence concerns algorithms that are used to create original digital objects, such as stories, art, photographs or music. It is easy to see why an observer might get the impression that AI is truly intelligent when we see a computer create an original digital image that looks like a photograph of real human. Some of the photo filters my children enjoy on their smartphones are another example of this technology, where the apps produce an image of a person that is altered to look younger or older. This type of creation is often the result of what is known as a "generative adversarial network" or GAN (Goodfellow et al, 2014). This type of AI solves a very challenging problem; it is much easier for an algorithm to distinguish between images of cats and dogs than to create an original image of a cat. Telling images of cats and dogs apart might boil down to understanding the shape of cat ears, nose, and eyes separately, without needing to specify how they relate to one another within an image; but creating a believable photograph of a cat requires generating ears, nose and eyes that make sense together in terms of proportions, locations relative to one another in the image, colors, and shadows.

GANs work by combining two distinct, dueling algorithms, the generator and the discriminator, where the discriminator has access to a dataset of objects that are labelled as real. The generator algorithm creates fake objects, and while the discriminator builds a model that classifies objects as real and fake based on a dataset of including the generator's fake objects and those that it knows are real. The algorithms battle amongst themselves. The one that creates fake objects keeps trying to make objects that trick the latest model built by the discriminator, and the discriminator keeps trying to find different ways to distinguish real from fake. The fact that the discriminator is automated (rather than a human judge) means that the generator can try a very large number of different options, and eventually it can find something that looks good in the sense that the discriminator can't distinguish it from something fake. But much like the example you've heard that a monkey would eventually write a classic novel if it typed long enough, the algorithm creating fake stuff is not smart, it just did a lot of trial and error against a computerized judge.

GANs already have a wide array of applications (Alqahtani et al, 2019; Brownlee, 2019), and we may expect more to be introduced, as they have only gained widespread use in the last few years. GANs can be useful when it is helpful to have lots of options to select from, but it is important that the objects are original or distinct. They can generate designs for images, fabrics, music, cartoons, email subject lines, etc. that are likely to be pleasing, but typically when applied, humans screen the generated options in a second step. GANs can also can make variants of existing objects with desired characteristics, e.g., a handbag with a specified shape decorated in a certain color or style, and GANs can also convert text to an image.

In scientific applications, GANs can be used to generate fake datasets for replication of studies, to test algorithms, or to protect privacy of, e.g., health data. Constraints can be added to the GAN, so that a GAN can be trained to generate objects that have desired scientific properties. They have been used for generating potential chemical or biological compounds with useful properties, for example candidate drug compounds that might deserve further research (Schmelzer, 2019).

GANs can be problematic as well. They can be used for "deep fakes," where convincing videos or images appear to show politicians or celebrities in a negative light, as well as to generate fake comments or social media posts, creating discord and anger among citizens. They can create fake identities that can be used for financial crimes or fraud as well. The fact that GANs can produce a large number of unique fakes make them particularly useful for applications where an actor repeatedly attempts to get past anti-fraud systems or algorithms designed to screen out robots from review systems and social media.

As impressive as GANs may be, there is a big gap between being able to, say, help a customer with a non-standard request and being able to spit out sentences that mimic human sentences. The technology doesn't think or reason, it just mimics patterns.

Artificial Intelligence and Autonomy

Autonomy, whereby an algorithm governs behavior of software or hardware in reaction to a changing environment, is another key concept in artificial intelligence. A robot that navigates obstacles to deliver an object is called autonomous; and recent advances have improved the ability of autonomous agents to learn decision rules. A type of algorithm known as reinforcement learning is designed to solve a problem like winning a board game or climbing over a wall. The algorithms actively experiment, and learn by trial and error. They break a problem down into a set of "states of the world," e.g., the location of chess pieces on a game board, or what objects are perceived by a robot in a hallway. The algorithm then considers what states it can move to from the current state, and either moves to the best option, or experiments among alternatives to learn more about what the value is of being in different states.

Reinforcement learning generally requires a lot of training in a setting where mistakes are not too dangerous, for example when a computer can play billions of games of chess against other computers in order to learn what works. As impressive as it sounds, reinforcement learning still relies heavily on pattern recognition; it isn't developing theories of the world. The core ideas behind reinforcement learning have been around a long time, but its performance has advanced dramatically in large part because of improvements in machine learning that help the algorithm automatically learn ways to effectively simplify the state space. The algorithms learn simpler representations of the possible positions of chess pieces; just as chess students learn a point system to determine how good their position is in a game, the algorithms assign scores to different positions and suggest game moves that optimize the scores. The AI accomplishments are especially impressive when there are billions of billions of possible configurations of a game board, since human brains can't remember that much information, but fundamentally the algorithms are still just adding up wins and losses using a scoring system learned from many replications of the game. Algorithms created in this way might perform arbitrarily badly if something small changes about the environment, and they are only as good as the data they have seen in the past, whether through simulated game play, their own experiments in previous games, or data from past games played by humans. Thus, they still may not do well in never-experienced environments.

Artificial Intelligence Applications and Impact

We have seen that the most commonly used categories of AI either implement human-created decision rules, or make use of pattern recognition to derive predictions or decision rules. Despite the inherent limitations of these categories of AI, some awe-inspiring accomplishments have emerged; yet, it is important not to conclude from the accomplishments to date that some sort of general intelligence will follow quickly. As discussed above, pattern recognition has limitations, particularly performance in changing circumstances.

Machine learning and AI have had especially widespread adoption for applications when it is possible to update the model more quickly than the environment changes, and when prediction and classification tasks play an important role (Agrawal, Gans, and Goldfarb, 2018). Examples of applications include digitizing input from people, including handwritten forms and voice recognition. Image classification has many applications across industries ranging from finance (e.g., images for insurance claims) to medicine (diagnosis). For example, AI has been used in medical imaging, detecting diseases or anomalies with specialist-level accuracy in some cases (Ruamviboonsuk et al., 2019). It is also used to predict the likelihood of a chemical reaction (Hao, 2020).

Machine learning and AI can be particularly useful in a setting where, in the absence of AI, human workers would need to make decisions in limited time. Although in principle, a human worker could make a better decision than an algorithm with sufficient investment of time, they might not have enough time to gather and absorb all of the relevant data in practice. An example is resume screening, where often a human screener might only briefly scan a resume before deciding if it should be prioritized for further consideration. The screener might not know all relevant information about the quality of the secondary or university school attended by the applicant, and they might not be familiar with the skills required for work at a particular firm in the worker's employment history. In contrast, an algorithm might be trained on thousands of resumes, and can quickly process a large set of characteristics of the individual. Of course, it is important to consider issues of bias that can arise when using algorithms in this way; careful attention to training data and active investment in expanding the pool of workers who advance to higher levels of the interview process are examples of approaches that may mitigate these issues.

A related application is in automation of worker screening for qualifications and availability. Alain Dehaze, CEO of Adecco, recently reported that his firm quickly recruited 16,000 workers in Europe using a purely digital process during the COVID-19 pandemic (Michaels, 2020).

AI is also used to prioritize resource allocation according to the risk posed by an individual or entity. It has been used in a variety of government applications, including the allocation of health inspectors to restaurants or home visits by child protective services workers (Schwartz et al, 2017). AI has also been used to help judges make bail decisions (Kleinberg et al, 2018). In principle, they can improve decision quality, accountability, and equity, as they replace rapid decisions by humans who may not have the time to consider all relevant information.

However, it should also be obvious that these types of applications require great care to implement fairly and effectively (Glaberson, 2019), and more work is needed both by academics and regulators to ensure that implementations of these algorithms follow best practices and are evaluated for unintended consequences.

Applications of reinforcement learning include digital marketing, where reinforcement learning is commonly used to figure out which of many email subject lines or headlines work best to attract consumer clicks; and autonomous drones, robots, and delivery vehicles.

More broadly, according to McKinsey's 2019 AI impact survey across hundreds of firms, AI had been adopted in nearly every industry by 2018. Retail is growing most quickly, with 60 percent of respondents from retail reported that their companies have embedded at least one AI capability in one or more functions or business units, a 35-percentage-point increase from the 2018 survey (Cam et al., 2019). Funding of AI startups in the U.S. spans a wide range of industries. AI startups received $19.8B of investment in 2019, with top focus areas including Data Tools (8.1% of all startups); Medical Technology (5.3%); Fashion and Retail Technology (4.7%); Text Analytics (4.7%), and Chatbots (3.9%) (Perrault et. al 2019, p. 92).

Impact on the Efficiency and Accessibility of Service Delivery

The impacts of automation and AI arise not just in terms of the cost of providing services, but also in the costs of receiving services. In particular, individuals seeking services like health and education often bear substantial costs in terms of transportation and time, which translate into lost income, outlays for child care, or lost sleep. For those with full-time jobs or caregiving responsibilities, it can be extremely frustrating and create economic hardship to waste time in waiting rooms, lines, or traveling in order to access services.

Providing services digitally allows people to access services when it is convenient, avoiding the need to take time off of work or obtain child care. Otherwise unused blocks of time can be used to accomplish tasks such as filling out forms or acquiring job-relevant skills, and a parent might engage in these activities while children are sleeping to avoid the need for child care. Citizens may be more satisfied with digital services in many cases, and lower income consumers in particular can benefit from improved access (Kuziemski, M., & Misuraca, G., 2020). For example, Medicaid patients may experience long travel times or waits to access health care, while providing access to telehealth has shown promising results in pilot studies (Koehn, 2016), and the widespread adoption of telehealth during COVID has opened up new possibilities to expand this access while simultaneously reducing costs. Access to high-quality medical care in rural areas is another important application.

In contrast, the lack of ability to reach consumers digitally can interfere with efficient provision of services. For example, poor IT infrastructure hampered state governments in their efforts to provide COVID relief to individuals quickly, and it limited the scope of early programs to deal with the pandemic (Bollag and Wilner, 2020). Even where digital provision was enabled, as in telemedicine, concerns remain about inequality of access (Weigel et al, 2020; Anderson and Kumar, 2017). This type of infrastructure and access must be addressed for governments to be able to take the next step and optimize service provision using artificial intelligence.

It is perhaps more straightforward to assess the potential for efficiency benefits in terms of reducing the cost of providing services through digitization and automation, which (after technology is developed) reduces the number of government workers needed to provide a service. This reduction in employment is obviously a challenge for the affected workers, but it increases the efficiency of government. In some cases, government funds can be reallocated to provide additional services in areas where it is harder for automation to substitute for human workers, as in the area of education or child care.

A number of studies have attempted to assess the state of digitization as well as the efficiency gains that are possible for governments (see, e.g., analyses of the degree of digitization of government services in the US (OECD, 2019); the extent of potential efficiency and cost savings (Eggers et al, 2017); citizen preferences and satisfaction with government services (BCG, 2018); the use of AI in government services in developing countries (Lauron and Stamboel, 2018)). Deloitte estimates that automation of federal government employee tasks could save between 96.7 million and 1.2 billion hours annually, with potential savings between $3.3 billion and $41.1 billion (Eggers et al, 2017). Categories of potential benefits include reducing the labor cost of providing government services and avoiding corruption.

There are some challenges to undertaking large-scale digitization programs. First, the infrastructure underlying digitization has the feature of requiring up front investments that pay off over years, which can be difficult for companies, let alone governments, to manage well, especially in an environment of changing technology. There are large risks for governments undertaking large IT projects, although there are also substantial risks of retaining antiquated systems, as described in testimony before this committee in July (Gerton, 2019). It is also important to remain attentive to inequality in IT skills, access and adoption that make for an uneven playing field when it comes to accessing digital services (Anderson and Kumar, 2017).

Impact on Productivity and Measurement Challenges

Like many previous technologies, it is hard to isolate the impact of AI in productivity numbers. Despite impressive improvements in AI, not to mention many other technologies, productivity growth has actually slowed down in the last fifteen years, from an average of over 2.4% per year between 1995-2005 to less than 1.3% per year since then (Brynjolfsson,

Rock and Syverson, 2019). That is to say, the data appears to rule out very large productivity gains from AI or digitization in general. One explanation is that realizing the potential of new technologies "requires large intangible investments and a fundamental rethinking of the organization of production itself. Firms must create new business processes, develop managerial experience, train workers, patch software, and build other intangibles. This raises productivity measurement issues because intangible investments are not readily tallied on a balance sheet or in the national accounts." (Brynjolfsson, Rock and Syverson, 2020, p.2) In addition, all of the investments required to achieve the full potential of AI may be characterized by up front investments whose benefits take many years to realize, making it more difficult to isolate the impact.

Opportunities

Several types of opportunities stand out where AI can be an important part of the solution to societal challenges. A first area is finance. The financial services sector is on the front line of employment impacts from AI, but there are also a wide range of opportunities for technology to improve access to services and to reduce costs to the point that more low-income consumers can be served. However, challenges remain, in part because the regulatory framework for our financial system is designed around regulating processes followed by human workers, not regulating algorithms and automated systems. Many financial regulators lack experience and expertise in AI, and the existing regulatory structure is not designed to handle situations where algorithms have a small but positive chance of making mistakes. Cost-benefit analysis is not the primary framework used by regulators to evaluate AI projects, and firms slow their investment in the face of regulatory uncertainty. Financial technology has the potential to be very progressive, reducing costs of serving low-income consumers and small businesses, providing opportunities for new startups, and introducing competition. Automation can ensure compliance and avoid a role for human biases, while well-designed algorithms can avoid introducing new forms of bias. A regulatory framework needs to address the benefits as well as the risks of new technology and innovation. Of course, risks are real, as AI can be used to automate the creation of exploitive or manipulative marketing as well as financial crimes (FINRA, 2020).

A second area where AI can be quite impactful is in the area of education and training.

The COVID-19 pandemic dramatically accelerated adoption of a wide range of educational technology applications (Gilchrist, 2020), ranging from preschool applications like Khan Kids or IntellectoKids (Kotlov, 2020) to upskilling programs. Companies like Coursera expanded their free offerings and partnered with governments to allow unemployed workers to acquire new skills, such as basic technical skills identified by employers (Training Industry, 2020). The United States could do more to study the impact of such programs, and if effective, scale up access to a larger group of unemployed Americans.

Many educational technology companies are in a relatively early stage of growth.

However, with the new, larger user bases they have attracted during the pandemic, companies have the opportunity to introduce more automation and artificial intelligence into the learning process, personalizing educational experiences, adapting to the student, and also potentially innovating in certification and interview practice (as artificial intelligence can be used evaluate students or create interactive scenarios for students to practice their skills). Given its outsized impact on society, it will be important to continue to nurture the industry providing education and training digitally, and to consider complementary investments that reduce frictions for workers in job transitions.

More generally, the changes brought by AI will contribute to increasing rates of worker transitions between jobs. As automation changes the organization of work, some jobs are likely to be eliminated, and newly created jobs may require different skills. If, as in the case of call centers, a large number of jobs in a single category is eliminated in a short period of time, workers may need to transition to a different type of work. The use of cloud computing and software as a service may lead to a variety of employers in the same industry automating processes at the same time, making the transitions more challenging for affected workers. A variety of frictions might interfere with their ability to transition.

Simon (2020) reviews research on labor market frictions, and finds that many causes of frictions are related to individuals needing to adapt by (1) learning new skills or (2) moving to new geographies with better opportunities. There is potential for AI and digitization more generally to provide solutions to both of these frictions, (1) by providing convenient, accessible, enticing and personalized education and training solutions, (2) reducing the importance of geography by providing remote work opportunities, and (3) improving worker access to information and support in order to guide workers to better decisions and reduce the risk associated with transitions.

A variety of evidence (Chen et al, 2019) also points to the importance of flexibility of schedules for many workers, particularly workers who need to balance school or caregiving responsibilities with work. Remote work and technology-related work may lend themselves to flexibility, and the new approaches to work developed during the COVID-19 pandemic may enable more such flexibility. Other policies that complement worker flexibility may also become important, for example policies that facilitate continuous access to health care while workers combine retraining and part time work.

Artificial Intelligence for Worker Safety and Monitoring

Another category of application of AI concerns monitoring the activities and experiences of workers. Although the primary motivation for the introduction of AI might be worker safety or regulatory compliance, there are a number of potential unintended consequences.

First, consider some of the ways in which AI can be used to monitor workers. Worker communication is increasingly digital, as it takes place through email, company-sponsored chat platforms, or over digital conferencing systems. A variety of companies provide services designed to translate conference calls into written notes, and it is straightforward to use machine learning to learn to create risk scores for written communication. The relevant type of risk to be predicted may vary by industry, but, for example, AI is already being productively deployed to monitor communication within financial services companies to ensure compliance with regulations, such as prohibitions on insider trading or other illegal activities (IBM and Chartis Research, 2018; FINRA, 2020). Indeed, the term "regtech" has been coined for technology that helps firms comply with regulations, something that ultimately will be important to consider when thinking about cost-benefit analysis from regulations. Some regulations may become easier and cheaper to comply with and enforce in the digital era, especially when compliance processes can be automated and included in software as a service provided to firms in a given industry. On the other hand, compliance failures may occur at a larger scale when many firms use the same software.

It is also relatively straightforward for an employer to create a training dataset for a machine learning algorithm based on video or audio recordings of employee interactions with customers. A sample of video or audio can be watched and manually scored by human judges to create a labelled training dataset. After training, an algorithm can be applied to all video, creating a "predicted customer satisfaction score" for every minute of every recorded interaction. This allows large-scale, low-cost scoring of workers. Another application would be safety violations. Video can be labelled, or assembly line accidents or errors can be used as "labels" in training datasets for algorithms designed to identify undesirable actions by workers. Once trained, the algorithms can be applied to all recorded video, and those video segments that received poor scores could be manually reviewed to assess whether the incident was, in fact, an example of undesirable employee behavior. This dramatically increases the efficiency of worker monitoring by focusing human time on the portions of video most likely to be associated with problems.

A related example concerns safety for fleets of drivers. A variety of companies sell software that is installed on the mobile phones of drivers, where drivers are required to use the software during working hours. The software uses the telemetry from the phone to identify whether the driver was speeding, or whether the other safety violations took place. Drivers with poor safety can be assigned to safety courses, or if necessary, terminated.

Similar algorithms could in principle be used in governments to ensure that government workers provide proper service, follow rules, and don't take bribes, similar to the use of body cameras for police. This type of application is in an earlier stage, but there have been some promising case studies in recent years (Aarvik, 2019).

However, as a society we will need to consider the broader implications and substantial risks that arise alongside the large scale monitoring of workers. A variety of problems might emerge, ranging from bias, as might occur if algorithms perform poorly on women, shorter people, or people with darker skin; to the potential that the existence of all of this tracking can create fodder for blackmail or extortion. It is hard to imagine that nothing embarrassing ever happens if you are constantly monitored as a worker or as a citizen. Privacy and security of data is already important to individuals in their leisure time, but it takes on different considerations in the workplace.

A final issue worth considering when AI is used to augment humans in the workforce is the extent to which reliance on AI reduces human attentiveness. Just as humans might "fall asleep at the wheel" when using an autopilot feature in a car, workers may fail to gain experience in certain types of tasks when the tasks are automated, or they may be insufficiently incentivized to pay attention and gather information when AI is introduced to assist them with tasks. Thus, it is important for firms and governments to consider the way in which AI changes both the information and incentives for workers when it is introduced into organizations and decision processes (Athey, Bryan, and Gans, 2020).

Additional Policy Considerations

A common mistake in thinking about AI is to focus on the harm to a small group of people, without considering the benefits that accrue to many. Many AI applications can be progressive, because automation and digital provision of services reduce marginal cost. On the other hand, technical change is taking place in a context where the costs of essentials such as housing and health care are rising faster than wages, and some of the consumer products and services made available through technology are consumed by wealthier individuals. It is thus important to consider overall effects as well as the context in which the innovation occurs.

AI raises a variety of additional opportunities and challenges for our economy. One is a misalignment of incentives by firms in the type of research and development that is prioritized. Firms have incentives to invest in cost reduction, but don't consider broader societal consequences; thus, they may be more likely to invest in labor-replacing technology. Research that helps explore labor augmenting technology may receive insufficient investment by the private sector. The Stanford Institute for Human-Centered Artificial Intelligence, where I am associate director, is attempting to prioritize research on labor-augmenting technology, but much more investment in this type of research and development would be beneficial and more aligned with societal objectives.

Another set of considerations concerns the geographic distribution of research, entrepreneurship, and investment. Historically, the United States has been a leader in AI innovation, but there is no guarantee that will continue without support for universities as well as high-skilled immigration. Given that some parts of the AI industry are prone to concentration due to scale economies, it can be important that the U.S. retains its leadership position in innovation if the U.S. hopes to be the home of the world's leading companies in the future.

Furthermore, there is no guarantee that jobs created by AI will have broad geographic distribution within the U.S. For example, Bloom et al. (2019) suggests that between 1990 and 2007, large multinational firms offshored their production while creating new service-sector jobs. However, the lost jobs were in the U.S. heartland, while the new service jobs were created in high-education areas along the coasts, and were therefore taken up by very different people.

Despite this shift in the location of jobs, geographic mobility has not been a widespread way of adjusting to the shock (Autor, Dorn, and Hanson, 2013; Autor et al., 2014).

Gruber and Johnson (2019) argue that universities, especially those with large medical centers, can anchor cities that are large enough to grow and create jobs, and that research and development investment (including investment funded by the government) can be effective at spurring the innovation that drives this growth. With high cost of living and congestion in the existing tech centers, together with tech firms embracing remote work, there may be opportunities for timely investments in these locations that contribute to their success, expanding the set of geographies where firms open offices with AI jobs. Technology companies consider the size of the engineering workforce as well as the opportunities to hire from universities when locating new satellite offices, and it has been common for veterans of larger technology companies to start new ventures after gaining experience, which can seed new communities of entrepreneurs outside the traditional technology hubs.

A further set of challenges facing the U.S. is related to demographics. Overall, our working population is aging. Several countries, including the United States, may face fiscal challenges due to demographics unless they increase either the birth rate or immigration. Varian (2018) did analysis to suggest that using the most aggressive estimates for the impact of automation, we are still more likely to face a worker shortage than surplus in the coming decades. He points out that it may be hard to predict the future impact of AI, but we have a lot of certainty about how many 40 year olds there will be in 20 years, and our population is very likely to be much older. According to the Congressional Budget Office, the federal government spent about one-third of its budget on seniors in 2005 (Congressional Budget Office, 2019, pp. 12-14). By last year, the share grew to 40 percent, or $1.5 trillion. The share is forecast to rise to half of all non-interest spending, or $3 trillion, by 2029. This amounts to spending 10 percent of the nation's Gross Domestic Product on older adults.

Countries with aging workforces tend to invest more in automation. To mitigate demographic challenges, we may want to consider investments in research and development that supports the efficient provision of services to older populations, perhaps assisted by technology to make services safer and more affordable. In addition, AI can be used to augment older workers, making it possible for older workers to have second careers without compromising their health. For example, robots can help workers with challenging physical tasks, while AI can assist with tasks that traditionally required memory or attention to detail, as it can warn of anomalies and monitor performance in real time. This removes some of the more challenging components of work, allowing older workers to focus on activities that emphasize human interaction and provide fulfillment and stimulation.

Conclusion

As AI is adopted through government and the economy, it will be important for governments to keep a close eye on the myriad challenges raised by AI. Some of them have been raised in my testimony today, including bias, privacy, security, investment risk, reliability and fragility of machine learning models, and the need for thoughtful regulation that includes cost-benefit analysis. Other challenges, such as concerns about market power of large firms who have unique access to data, are important, but beyond the scope of this testimony.

In the coming decades, as AI plays a larger and larger role in our economy and in the provision of government services, transitions will be the new normal for workers. It will be important for governments to address the challenges faced by workers, and also to make the necessary investments to ensure that AI fulfills its potential as part of the solution. Since digitally provided services have low marginal cost of delivery, AI is well positioned to contribute to providing scalable and effective education, training, and access to government-provided and government-funded services.

References

Agrawal, A., Gans, J. and Goldfarb, A., 2018. *Prediction machines: the simple economics of artificial intelligence*. Harvard Business Press.

Alqahtani, H., Kavakli-Thorne, M. and Kumar, G., 2019. Applications of generative adversarial networks (gans): An updated review. *Archives of Computational Methods in Engineering*, pp.1-28.

Anderson, M. and Kumar, M., 2017. Digital divide persists even as lower-income Americans make gains in tech adoption. *Pew research center, 22.*

Aarvik, P., 2019. Artificial Intelligence a promising anti-corruption tool in development settings. *U4 Report* 2019:1. https://www.u4.no/publications/artificial-intelligence-a-promising-anti-corruption-tool-in-develo pment-settings.pdf.

Athey, S., 2017. Beyond prediction: Using big data for policy problems. *Science*, *355*(6324), pp.483-485.

Athey, S., 2018. The impact of machine learning on economics. In *The economics of artificial intelligence: An agenda* (pp. 507-547). University of Chicago Press.

Athey, S. and Imbens, G.W., 2019. Machine learning methods that economists should know about. *Annual Review of Economics*, *11*, pp.685-725.

Athey, S.C., Bryan, K.A. and Gans, J.S., 2020, May. The allocation of decision authority to human and artificial intelligence. In *AEA Papers and Proceedings* (Vol. 110, pp. 80-84).

BCG, 2018. Realizing the Power of Digital Government, *Digital Government Citizen Survey* 2018. https://www.bcg.com/en-us/industries/public-sector/digital-transformation-technology.

Bloom, N., Kurmann A., Handley, K. and Luck, P., 2019. The Impact of Chinese Trade on U.S. Employment: The Good, The Bad, and The Debatable, *Stanford mimeo.*

Bureau of Labor Statistics, U.S. Department of Labor, *Occupational Outlook Handbook*, Tellers, on the Internet at https://www.bls.gov/ooh/office-and-administrative-support/ tellers.htm.

Brownlee, J., 2019. 18 Impressive Applications of Generative Adversarial Networks (GANs) *Machine Learning Mastery*, June 14, 2019. https://machinelearningmastery.com/impressive-applications-of-generative-adversarial-networks/.

Brynjolfsson, E., Rock, D., & Syverson, C. (2019). Artificial intelligence and the modern productivity paradox: A clash of expectations and statistics. In A. Agrawal, J. Gans, & A. Goldfarb (Eds.) *The economics of artificial intelligence: An agenda* (pp.23– 57). National Bureau of Economic Research Conference Report. University of Chicago Press.

Brynjolfsson, E., Rock, D. and Syverson, C., 2020. The productivity J-curve: How intangibles complement general purpose technologies, *AEJ: Macroeconomics* (forthcoming).

Cam, A., Chui, M. and Hall, B., 2019. Global AI Survey: AI proves its worth, but few scale impact. *McKinsey Analytics.*

Chen, M.K., Rossi, P.E., Chevalier, J.A. and Oehlsen, E., 2019. The value of flexible work: Evidence from uber drivers. *Journal of Political Economy*, *127*(6), pp.2735-2794.

Chipman, Ian, 2018. Susan Athey: Why Business Leaders Shouldn't Have Blind Faith in AI. *Insights by Stanford Business*. https://www.gsb.stanford.edu/insights/susan-athey-why-business-leaders-shouldnt-have-blind-fai th-ai.

Congressional Budget Office. 2019. *The budget and economic outlook: 2019 to 2029.* Washington, DC: Congress of the United States, Congressional Budget Office.

Eggers, W.D., Schatsky, D. and Viechnicki, P., 2017. AI-augmented government. Using cognitive technologies to redesign public sector work. *Deloitte Center for Government Insights.* https://www2.deloitte.com/us/en/insights/focus/cognitive-technologies/artificial-intelligence-gov ernment.html.

Etchemendy, J. and Li, F., 2020. *National Research Cloud: Ensuring the Continuation of American Innovation.* https://hai.stanford.edu/blog/national-research-cloud-ensuring-continuation-american-innovation

FINRA, 2020. Artificial Intelligence (AI) in the Securities Industry, *FINRA RegTech White Paper.* https://www.finra.org/rules-guidance/key-topics/fintech/report/artificial-intelligence-in-the-securi ties-industry.

Gerton, T.W., 2019. Testimony of Teresa W. *Gerton President and Chief Executive Officer National Academy of Public Administration Before the Budget Committee U. S. House of Representatives July 15, 2020.* https://budget.house.gov/sites/democrats.budget.house.gov/files/documents/Gerton_Testimony.pdf.

Gilchrist, K. 2020. These millennials are reinventing the multibillion-dollar education industry during coronavirus, *CNBC*, June 8, 2020. https://www.cnbc.com/2020/06/08/edtech-how-schools-education-industry-is-changing-under-co ronavirus.html.

Golub Capital Social Impact Lab, 2020. What really is 'adaptive learning'? *Medium*, January 22, 2020. https://medium.com/@gsb_silab/what-really-is-adaptive-learning-68e64c1f78c3.

Glaberson, S.K., 2019. Coding over the cracks: predictive analytics and child protection. *Fordham Urban Law Journal*, *46*, p.307.

Goodfellow, Ian, Jean Pouget-Abadie, Mehdi Mirza, Bing Xu, David Warde-Farley, Sherjil Ozair, Aaron Courville, and Yoshua Bengio. "Generative adversarial nets." *In Advances in neural information processing systems*, pp. 2672-2680. 2014.

Gruber, J. and S. Johnson, 2019. *Jump Starting America. How Breakthrough Science Can Revive Economic Growth and the American Dream,* Public Affairs.

Hao, K., 2020. IBM has built a new drug-making lab entirely in the cloud. *MIT Technology Review*, August 28, 2020. https://www.technologyreview.com/2020/08/28/1007737/ibm-ai-robot-drug-making-lab-in-the-cl oud/.

Kelly, J. 2019. From Layoffs To Declining Revenues, Banks Are In Trouble: Here Are Some Hiring Bright Spots, *Forbes*, September 12, 2019. https://www.forbes.com/sites/jackkelly/2019/09/12/wall-street-banks-are-in-trouble-employees-a xed-and-revenues-down-heres-some-hiring-bright-spots/#6f7b5de6dd44.

Kleinberg, J., Lakkaraju, H., Leskovec, J., Ludwig, J. and Mullainathan, S., 2018. Human decisions and machine predictions. *The Quarterly Journal of Economics, 133*(1), pp.237-293.

Kuziemski, M., & Misuraca, G., 2020 . AI governance in the public sector: Three tales from the frontiers of automated decision-making in democratic settings. *Telecommunications Policy,* 44(6), 101976. https://doi.org/10.1016/j.telpol.2020.101976.

Koehn, A. 2016. Apps and Technology Help Low-Income People Access Healthcare. *Medill Report Chicago*, March 1, 2016. https://news.medill.northwestern.edu/chicago/apps-and-technology-help-low-income-people-acc ess-healthcare/.

Kotlov, M., 2020. Is the Rise of Preschoolers' App Usage a Pandemic Boom or a Paradigm Shift?, *Hackernoon*, July 31, 2020. https://hackernoon.com/is-the-rise-of-preschoolers-app-usage-a-pandemic-boom-or-a-paradigm-s hift-lh8l3eqx.

Kuang, K., Cui, P., Athey, S., Xiong, R. and Li, B., 2018, July. Stable prediction across unknown environments. In *Proceedings of the 24th ACM SIGKDD International Conference on Knowledge Discovery & Data Mining* (pp. 1617-1626).

Kuang, K., Xiong, R., Cui, P., Athey, S. and Li, B., 2020, January. Stable Prediction with Model Misspecification and Agnostic Distribution Shift. In *AAAI* (pp. 4485-4492).

Lauron, C. and Stamboel, I. 2018. Digitalization of government - Suits The *C*-Suite, *Business World*, February 18, 2018. https://www.bworldonline.com/digitalization-of-government/.

Lazer, D.M., Pentland, A., Watts, D.J., Aral, S., Athey, S., Contractor, N., Freelon, D., Gonzalez-Bailon, S., King, G., Margetts, H. and Nelson, A., 2020. Computational social science: Obstacles and opportunities. *Science*, *369*(6507), pp.1060-1062.

Michaels, D., 2020. Remote Work Forever? Not So Fast, Jobs Guru Says, *The Wall Street Journal*, June 10, 2020. https://www.wsj.com/articles/remote-work-forever-not-so-fast-jobs-guru-says-115917 90405.

IBM and Chartis Research, 2018. *AI in RegTech: A Quiet Upheaval.* https://www.ibm.com/downloads/cas/NAJXEKE6.

IDC 2019, *Worldwide Public Cloud Services Spending Forecast to Reach $210 Billion This Year, According to IDC*, https://www.idc.com/getdoc.jsp?containerId=prUS44891519.

Totty, M., 2020. Rapid Change Is Coming to the Service Sector, *UCLA Anderson Review*, July 08, 2020. https://www.anderson.ucla.edu/faculty-and-research/anderson-review/service-industrialization.

Training Industry, 2020. *CINDE Announces: Coursera And Costa Rica Launch A Joint Program To Strengthen Industry 4.0 Skills And Train – Free Of Charge – 50,000 People To Confront The COVID-19 Crisis. June 16, 2020.* https://trainingindustry.com/press-release/it-and-technical-training/cinde-announces-coursera-an d-costa-rica-launch-a-joint-program-to-strengthen-industry-4-0-skills-and-train-free-of-charge-5 0000-people-to-confront-the-covid-19-crisis/

OECD, 2019. Going Digital: Shaping Policies, Improving Lives, *OECD Publishing,* Paris, https://doi.org/10.1787/9789264312012-en.

Schmelzer, R. 2019. 3 GAN use cases that showcase their positive potential. *E-Handbook: Neural network applications in business run wide, fast and deep*, August, 20, 2019. https://searchenterpriseai.techtarget.com/feature/3-GAN-use-cases-that-showcase-their-positive- potentia.

Schwartz, I.M., York, P., Nowakowski-Sims, E. and Ramos-Hernandez, A., 2017. Predictive and prescriptive analytics, machine learning and child welfare risk assessment: The Broward County experience. *Children and Youth Services Review*, *81*, pp.309-320.

Simon, L. 2020. Sources of Labor Market Upheaval - and How the Workforce Can Adapt to Constant Change. *Medium*, August 17, 2010. https://medium.com/@gsb_silab/sources-of-labor-market-upheaval-and-how-the-workforce-can-adapt-to-constant-change-b1d4366a9eba.

Perrault, R., Shoham, Y., Brynjolfsson, E., Clark, J., Etchemendy, J., Grosz, B., Lyons, T., Manyika, J., Mishra, S. and Niebles, J.C., 2019.

The AI Index 2019 Annual Report. AI Index Steering Committee, Human-Centered AI Institute, Stanford University, Stanford, CA.

Raghu, M., Blumer, K., Corrado, G., Kleinberg, J., Obermeyer, Z. and Mullainathan, S., 2019. The algorithmic automation problem: Prediction, triage, and human effort. *arXiv preprint arXiv: 1903.12220*.

Ruamviboonsuk, P., Krause, J., Chotcomwongse, P., Sayres, R., Raman, R., Widner, K., Campana, B.J., Phene, S., Hemarat, K., Tadarati, M. and Silpa-Archa, S., 2019. Deep learning versus human graders for classifying diabetic retinopathy severity in a nationwide screening program. *NPJ digital medicine*, 2(1), pp.1-9.

Varian, H., 2018. *Automation vs. Procreation*. http://conference.nber.org/conferences/2018/AIf18/f114523.slides.pdf.

Webb, M., 2019. *The Impact of Artificial Intelligence on the Labor Market.* Available at SSRN 3482150.

Weigel, G., Ramaswamy, A., Sobel, L., Salganicoff, A., Cubanski, J. and Freed, M., 2020. *Opportunities and barriers for telemedicine in the US during the COVID-19 emergency and beyond*. Washington, DC: Kaiser Family Foundation, May, 11, 2020. https://www.kff.org/womens-health-policy/issue-brief/opportunities-and-barriers-for-telemedicine-in-the-u-s-during-the-covid-19-emergency-and-beyond/.

Chairman YARMUTH. Thank you for your testimony.

I now recognize Dr. Acemoglu for five minutes. Please unmute and the floor is yours.

Statement of Daron Acemoglu, PhD

Dr. ACEMOGLU. Chairman Yarmuth, Ranking Member Womack, and Members of the Committee, thank you for inviting me to testify on this important subject.

The U.S. economy today and U.S. workers are suffering from what I view as excessive automation. The extent of automation is excessive in that it is not leading to sufficient productivity growth, creating new tasks for humans or increasing wages.

Automation, the substitution of machines and algorithms for tasks previously performed by labor, is nothing new. It has often been an engine of economic growth, but in the past, for example, during the year of the mechanization of agriculture, it was part of a broad technology portfolio and its potentially negative effects on labor were counterbalanced by other technologies. Not today.

Recent advances in AI and machine learning are not responsible for these trends. In fact, AI, a broad technological platform with great promise, can be used for helping human productivity in creating new human tasks. But it could exacerbate the same trends if we use it just for automation.

The COVID–19 pandemic will also contribute to this predicament as there are now more reasons for employers to look for ways of substituting machines for workers and recent evidence suggests that they are already doing so.

Excessive automation has already been a major drag for the U.S. economy. Private sector spending on workers, which increased steadily and rapidly almost every year in the four decades following World War II, has been essentially stagnant over the last 20 years. The decline in the share of labor in national income, the stagnation of middle class wages, and a huge increase in inequality are all connected to our recent unbalanced technology portfolio prioritizing automation and not much else.

Excessive automation is not an inexorable development. It is a result of choices and we can make different choices. While there is no consensus on exactly what brought us to this state, we know of a number of factors that have encouraged greater automation. Chief among these has been the transformation in the technology strategies of leading companies.

American and world technology is shaped by the decisions of a handful of very large and very successful tech companies with tiny workforces and business models centered on the substitution of algorithms for humans.

There is, of course, nothing wrong with successful companies pushing their vision, but when this becomes the only game in town, we have to watch out. Past technological successes have often been fueled by a diversity of perspectives and approaches. The dominance of the paradigm of a handful of companies has been exacerbated by the dwindling support of the U.S. Government for fundamental research. The transformative technologies over the 20th century, such as antibiotics, sensors, modern engines, and the internet have the fingerprints of the government all over them. The government funded and purchased these technologies and often set the agenda, but no longer.

Last but not least, government policies encouraging automation excessively through its tax code. The U.S. tax system has always treated capital more favorably than labor. My own research estimates that over the last 40 years, via payroll and federal income taxes, labor has paid an effective tax rate of over 25 percent.

Even 20 years ago, capital was taxed more lightly, with equipment and software facing tax rates around 15 percent. This differential has significantly widened with tax cuts on high incomes, the shifts of many businesses to S-Corporation status that are exempt from corporate income taxes, and very generous depreciation allowances.

Software and equipment are now taxed at about 5 percent, and in some cases corporations can get a net subsidy when they invest in capital. This generates a powerful motive for excessive automation. One result of this has been the disappearance of good jobs, especially for workers without postgraduate degrees or very specialized skills.

The only way to alter this technology is to redirect technological change. That will require changes in federal policy. A first step would be to correct the asymmetric taxation of capital and labor. This would go a long way, but is not sufficient by itself.

A second step is to re-evaluate the role of big tech companies in our lives, including in the direction of technology. This, of course, goes beyond debates about automation and AI as it relates to the issue of limiting the size and dominance of big tech.

These measures can be strengthened with government R&D policies specifically targeting technologies that help human productivity and increase labor demand. Research policies that target specific classes of technologies are rightly controversial. They may be particularly challenging in the context of choosing between automation and human-friendly technologies since identifying these is nontrivial.

Nevertheless, I would like to end my comments by emphasizing that such policies have been adopted and have had successes in the past. Four decades ago, renewable energy was prohibitively expensive and the basic know-how for green technology was lacking. Today, renewables already make up 19 percent of energy consumption in Europe and 11 percent in the United States, and have costs in the ballpark of fossil fuel based energy. This has been achieved thanks to a redirection of technological change away from a singular focus on fossil fuels toward greater efforts for advances in renewables.

In the U.S., the primary driver of this redirection has been the government subsidies to green technologies, as well as the changing norms of consumers in society. The same can be done for the balance between automation and human-friendly technologies.

Thank you.

[The prepared statement of Daron Acemoglu follows:]

Daron Acemoglu Institute Professor, MIT Written Testimony House Committee on the Budget Hearing on Machines, Artificial Intelligence, and the Workforce: Recovering & Readying Our Economy for the Future September 10, 2020

Chairman Yarmuth, Ranking Member Womack and Members of the Committee,

Thank you for inviting me to testify today on this important subject. Today, the U.S. economy— and U.S. workers — are suffering from what I view as excessive automation. The extent of automation is excessive in that it is not leading to increased productivity, creating new tasks for humans or increasing wages.

Automation — the substitution of machines and algorithms for tasks previously performed by labor — is nothing new. Ever since the weaving and spinning machines that fueled British Industrial Revolution, automation has often been an engine of economic growth. However, in the past it was part of a broad technology portfolio, and its potentially negative effects on labor were counterbalanced by other technologies boosting human productivity and employment opportunities. Not today.

Recent advances in AI and machine learning are not responsible for these trends. In fact, AI, a broad technological platform with diverse applications and great promise, can be used for helping human productivity and creating new human tasks and competencies in education, health care, engineering, manufacturing and elsewhere. But it could exacerbate the same trends if we use it exclusively for automation.

The COVID-19 pandemic will also contribute to this predicament as there are now more reasons for employers to look for ways of substituting machines for workers, and recent evidence suggests that they are already doing so.[1]

Excessive automation has had major costs for the U.S. economy. One aspect of this can be seen in Figure 1, which plots private sector spending on workers (the private sector wage bill) normalized by population. The left panel shows that private sector wage bill increased, on average, about 2.5% faster than population in the four decades following World War II. This meant over 2% real wage growth for the majority of the U.S. workforce during these years. This growth (and resulting wealth) was very broadly shared. The real wages of all demographic groups (by education, gender and race) grew more or less in tandem, and if anything, overall inequality contracted.

---

[1] See https://assets.ey.com/content/dam/ey-sites/ey-com/en_gl/topics/ey-capital-confidence-barometer/pdfs/22/ey-22nd-global-capital-confidence-barometer-march-2020.pdf, https://www.nytimes.com/2020/04/10/business/coronavirus-workplace-automation.html and Alex Chernoff and Casey Warman (2020) "COVID-19 and Implications for Automation" NBER working paper.

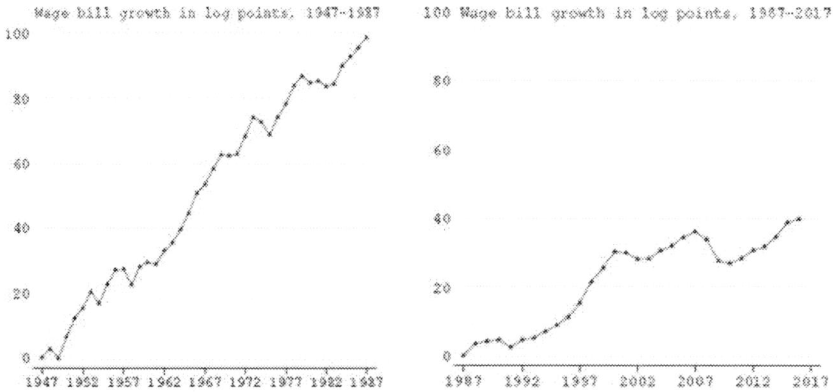

Figure 1. Evolution of US Labor Demand. From Acemoglu, Daron and Pascual Restrepo (2019) "Automation and New Tasks: How Technology Changes Labor Demand." Journal of Economic Perspectives, 33(2): 3--30.

The right panel of the figure shows a very different picture after the mid-1980s: slower growth of private sector spending on labor, and subsequently, almost no growth from the late 1990s onwards. This drying up of labor demand in the U.S. economy has many causes, but it is fundamentally related to the changing nature of technology. From the mid-1980s onwards, there is faster automation and automation-related displacement of workers from U.S. industry, and much less rapid introduction of other technologies that would increase human productivity and opportunities.[2]

The adoption of industrial robots, a typical example of automation technologies, illustrates these implications. Robots have raised productivity in many parts of modern manufacturing. But their impact on labor has been more mixed. Local communities where businesses have adopted more robots have experienced employment and wage declines (relative to the rest of the U.S.)[3]

---

[2] Acemoglu, Daron and Pascual Restrepo (2019) "Automation and New Tasks: How Technology Changes Labor Demand." *Journal of Economic Perspectives*, 33(2): 3--30.

[3] Acemoglu, Daron, and Pascual Restrepo (2020) "Robots and jobs: Evidence from US labor markets." *Journal of Political Economy* 128(6): 2188-2244.

While robots impacted a relatively narrow segment of the US workforce (manufacturing workers specialized in production tasks), the substitution of algorithms and software for white-collar tasks probably had even more sweeping consequences.

The next phase of automation, relying on AI and AI-powered machines, such as self-driving cars, can be even more disruptive, especially if it is not accompanied with other types of more human-friendly technologies.

The imbalance of technology may also be partly responsible for the disappointing productivity performance of the American economy. Despite the bewildering array of new machines and algorithms all around us, productivity growth in the U.S. economy has much lower rates of productivity growth over the last 20 years than during the decades that followed World War II.[4] Even though information and communication technology (ICT) has advanced rapidly and is used in every sector of the economy, industries that use ICT more intensively have not performed better in terms of productivity, output or employment growth.[5] The reasons for slow productivity growth over the last two decades are not well understood. But one contributing factor appears to be that many automation technologies, such as self-checkout kiosks or automated customer service, are not generating much productivity growth.

The implications of our recent unbalanced technological portfolio and the resulting slowdown in private sector labor demand are widespread and include: the sizable decline in the share of labor in national income (driven partly by the reduced role of labor in the production process); the stagnation of middle-class wages and the huge increase in inequality, which has also meant large declines in the real wages of low-education men.[6]

---

[4] Gordon, Robert J. The Rise and Fall of American Growth: The US Standard of Living Since the Civil War. Princeton University Press, Princeton, NJ, 2017.

[5] Acemoglu, Daron, David Autor, David Dorn, Gordon H. Hanson and Brendan Price (2014) "Return of the Solow Paradox? IT, Productivity, and Employment in US Manufacturing" American Economic Review, 104(5), 394-99.

[6] Acemoglu, Daron and David Autor (2011) "Skills, Tasks and Technologies: Implications for Employment and Earnings." *Handbook of Labor Economics*, 4: 1043--1171, and

Excessive automation is not an inexorable development. It is a result of choices of researchers who have focused on automation applications at the expense of other uses of technologies and companies that have built their business models on automation and reducing labor costs rather than broad-based productivity increases. We can make different choices.

While there is no consensus on exactly what brought us to this perilous state, we know of a number of factors that have pushed the economy towards greater automation.

Chief among these has been the transformation in the corporate strategies of leading companies in the U.S. American and world technology is shaped by the decisions of a handful of very large and very successful tech companies, with tiny workforces and a business model built on automation.[7] Big tech companies are responsible for more than two out of every three dollars spent globally on AI and their vision, centered on the substitution of algorithms for humans, influences not only their own spending but also what other companies prioritize and the aspirations and focus of hundreds of thousands of young students and researchers specializing in computer and data sciences.[8] There is of course nothing wrong with successful companies pushing their vision, but when this becomes the only game in town, we must be on guard. Past technological successes have more often than not been fueled by a diversity of perspectives and approaches, and if we lose this diversity, we will also risk losing our technological edge.

The dominance of the paradigm of a handful of companies has been exacerbated by the dwindling support the US government is providing for fundamental research.

The transformative technologies of the 20th century, such as antibiotics, sensors, modern engines, and the Internet, have the fingerprints

---

Acemoglu, Daron and Pascual Restrepo (2019) "Automation and New Tasks: How Technology Changes Labor Demand." *Journal of Economic Perspectives*, 33(2): 3--30.

[7] Acemoglu, Daron, and Pascual Restrepo (2020) "The Wrong Kind of AI? Artificial Intelligence and The Future of Labour Demand." Cambridge Journal of Regions, Economy and Society 13.1: 25-35.

[8] Artificial Intelligence: The Next Digital Frontier? McKinsey & Company.

of the government all over them.[9] The government funded and purchased these technologies and often set the research agenda. This is no longer the case.[10]

Last but not least, government policy is encouraging automation excessively, especially through its tax code. The U.S. tax system has always treated capital more favorably than labor, encouraging firms to substitute machines for workers, even when workers may be more productive. As Figure 2 shows, over the last 40 years, via payroll and federal income taxes, labor pays an effective tax rate of over 25%. Even twenty years ago, capital was taxed more lightly, with equipment and software facing tax rates around 15%. This differential has widened even more with tax cuts on high incomes, the shift of many businesses to S-Corporation status making them exempt from corporate income taxes, and very generous depreciation allowances. As a result of these changes, software and equipment are taxed close to zero now and in some cases, corporations can get a net subsidy when they invest in capital. This generates a powerful motive for excessive automation.

A critical consequence of these trends has been the disappearance of good jobs, the lifeblood of the American workforce.[11] Today it has become exceedingly difficult for workers without post-graduate degrees or very specialized skills to obtain jobs with decent wages, prospects for promotions and wage growth, and a reasonable amount of job security. The only way to change this trajectory is to redirect technological change. That will require changes in federal policy.

---

[9] Lerner, Josh. Boulevard of Broken Dreams: Why Public Efforts to Boost Entrepreneurship and Venture Capital Have Failed and What to Do about It. Princeton University Press, New York, 2009, and Mazzucato, Mariana. The Entrepreneurial State: Debunking Public Versus Private Sector Myths. Public Affairs, New York, 2015.

[10] Gruber, Johnson, and Simon Johnson. Jump-Starting America: How Breakthrough Science Can Revive Economic Growth and the American Dream. Public Affairs, New York, NY, 2019.

[11] Acemoglu, Daron (2001) "Good Jobs Versus Bad Jobs" Journal of Labor Economics, 19(1): 1-21.

Figure 2. Evolution of effective taxes in the U.S. From Acemoglu, Daron, Andrea Manera and Pascual Restrepo (2020) "Does the US Tax Code Favor Automation" *Brookings Papers on Economic Activity*.

A first step would be to correct the differential taxation of capital and labor. This would go a long way but is not sufficient by itself. A second step is to reevaluate the role of big tech companies in our lives, including in the direction of technology. This of course goes beyond debates about automation and AI, as it relates to the issue of limiting the size and the dominance of big tech companies.

These measures can be strengthened with government R&D policies specifically targeting technologies that help human productivity and increase labor demand. Research policies that target specific classes of technologies are controversial and difficult. They may be particularly challenging in the context of choosing between automation and human-friendly technologies, since identifying these may be nontrivial. Nevertheless, I would like to end my comments by emphasizing that such policies have been adopted and have had successes in the past.

Four decades ago renewable energy was prohibitively expensive and the basic know-how for green technologies was lacking. Today renewables already make up 19% of energy consumption in Europe and 11% in the U.S., and have costs in the same ballpark as fossil-fuel based energy.[12] This has been achieved thanks to a redirection of technological change away from a singular focus on fossil fuels towards greater efforts for advances in renewables. In the U.S. the primary driver of this redirection has been government subsidies to green technologies, as well as the changing norms of consumers in society.

The same can be done for the balance between automation and human-friendly technologies, but as in the case of climate change, change must start with a broader societal recognition that our technology choices have become highly unbalanced, with myriad adverse social consequences, and with a clear commitment by the federal government to redress some of these imbalances.

Chairman YARMUTH. Thank you very much for your testimony. I now recognize Dr. West for five minutes.

Statement of Darrell West, PhD

Dr. WEST. Chairman Yarmuth, Ranking Member Womack, and Members of the Committee, thanks for the opportunity to testify. I am coauthor with Brookings' president, John Allen, of a new AI book entitled, "Turning Point: Policymaking in the Era of Artificial Intelligence." And I also am the co-editor of the Brookings technology policy blog Tech Tank and coproducer of the Tech Tank Podcast.

In my testimony, I am going to argue that artificial intelligence is one of the transformative technologies of our time and likely to have major ramifications for the workforce. AI is being deployed in a number of different sectors, and its usage will accelerate in coming years. Its development is going to necessitate rethinking our policies in the areas of

---

[12] Renewable Power Generation Costs in 2018, International Renewable Energy Agency; Global renewable energy consumption, Our World in Data. See also https://www.lazard.com/perspective/lcoe2019/; https://irena.org/publications/2020/Jun/ Renewable-Power-Costs-in-2019; https://www.sciencedirect.com/science/article/abs/pii/S1364032111003492?via%3Dihub.

budgeting, infrastructure, healthcare, education, workforce development, and economic development.

As AI and other emerging technologies become widely deployed, there are several possible ramifications for the workforce—job loss, job dislocation, job redefinition, job mismatch, and job churn.

For example, there could be job losses in entry level positions as firms automate routine tasks. There can be geographical dislocations as positions migrate to urban population centers and there can be job churn as people move from company to company.

In an economy where benefits are tied to full-time employment, any increase in job churn will create instability in people's ability to maintain income and benefits.

Most of the issues noted above have grown worse with the advent of COVID–19. The pandemic has revealed stark inequities in access to online education, telemedicine, and opportunities for remote work. As an illustration, African Americans are far less likely than Whites to access online educational resources, but far more likely to suffer from the coronavirus.

It is hard to estimate the precise impact of technology innovation on the federal budget because there is so many ramifications for government revenues and expenses. But one thing that appears clear is we are going to need greater investment by both the private and the public sectors.

One area is digital infrastructure. Right now there are around 18 million Americans who lack sufficient access to the internet. You need an online connection to apply for many jobs. A number of people do not have the connectivity required for online education, telemedicine, and remote work. So it is vital that we close that gap so that all can benefit from the digital economy.

The emerging economy presents challenges with respect to ensuring health and retirement benefits. Any increases in unemployment or people having part-time jobs will create some hardships. In today's digital world, workers need benefit portability to survive a turbulent working environment.

Organizations need to shorten their vesting periods for people to become eligible for company retirement contributions. Right now many organizations do not vest employees until they have worked at the firm for one or two years, and if there is increased joblessness, lengthy vesting periods will lead to shortfalls in retirement income.

In the world of rapid change, it is imperative that people engage in lifelong learning. The traditional model in which people focused their learning on the years before age 25 and then get a job and devote little attention to education thereafter is becoming obsolete. In the contemporary world, people can expect to see whole sectors disrupted and they will need to develop additional skills. The type of work that people do at age 30 is going to be very different from what they will be doing at ages 40, 50, and 60.

One possibility to encourage continuing education is through the establishment of lifelong learning accounts. They would be analogous to individual retirement accounts or state government-run 529 college savings plans, but the owners of the account could draw on that account to finance online learning, certificate programs, or job retraining expenses.

As America deploys AI and moves to a digital economy, its two coasts have fared much better economically than the heartland. According to research by my Brookings colleague, senior fellow Mark Moro, only about 15 percent of American counties generate 64 percent of GDP. Far too many parts of the United States are being left behind. One way to address this is through regional innovation districts. These are public-private partnerships that boost innovation in heartland cities. And the districts include regulatory relief, tax benefits, workforce development, and infrastructure.

To summarize, it is crucial to think proactively as tech changes unfold. The longer we wait, the more painful the transition will be. Now is the time to start having the discussions required to make meaningful changes. And I applaud the Committee for providing a platform for this important conversation.

[The prepared statement of Darrell West follows:]

The Prepared Statement of Darrell M. West, PhD, Vice President of Governance Studies Brookings Institution Washington, D.C.

Chairman Yarmuth, Ranking Member Womack, and members of the Committee. Thank you for the opportunity to testify at this hearing. I am Vice President of Governance Studies at the Brookings Institution and co-author with John R. Allen of Turning Point: Policymaking in the Era of Artificial Intelligence (Brookings Institution Press, 2020) and the author of The Future of Work: Robots, AI, and Automation (Brookings Institution Press, 2018). I am the co-editor with Nicol Turner-Lee of the Brookings technology policy blog TechTank and co-producer with her of the TechTank Podcast.

In my testimony, I argue that artificial intelligence is one of the transformative technologies of our time and likely to have major ramifications for the workforce and the economy. AI is being deployed in a number of different sectors and its usage will accelerate in coming years with advances in computer storage and processing capabilities. It will necessitate rethinking our policies in the areas of budgeting, taxes, infrastructure, agency modernization, health, education, workforce development, economic development, and market competition. The remainder of this memo outlines a series of suggestions for moving forward.[13]

What is Artificial Intelligence?

Artificial intelligence is automated software that analyzes data, text, and/or images and makes decisions based on those insights. It is characterized by several qualities that separate AI from traditional computer software: intentionality, intelligence, autonomy, and adaptability. It is these features that enable AI algorithms to find patterns

[13] For more details on the analysis and recommendations, see Darrell M. West and John R. Allen, *Turning Point: Policymaking in the Era of Artificial Intelligence*, Brookings Institution Press, 2020 and Darrell M. West, *The Future of Work: Robots, AI, and Automation,* Brookings Institution Press, 2018.

or associations through "neural networks" that group data based on common similarities and act on them. In addition, AI-based systems learn from insights gathered via "deep learning" techniques that use statistics to spot underlying trends or patterns in data and apply that knowledge to changing circumstances. And it is not just numbers that can be mined as AI can employ "natural language processing" (NLP) that has the capacity to ingest massive amounts of text or video to find patterns and meanings. NLP may be one of the most powerful derivative capabilities to emerge from the AI constellation.[14]

AI Impact on the Workforce

As AI and other emerging technologies become widely deployed, there are several possible ramifications for the workforce: job loss, job dislocation, job redefinition, job mismatch, and/or job churn. For example, there can be job losses in entry-level and mid-level positions as firms automate routine tasks and apply computational processes to augment or replace human activities. There also can be geographic dislocations as positions migrate to urban population centers clustered on the coasts and in a few metropolitan areas scattered around the heartland.

Some positions will get redefined as AI performs tasks that currently are conducted by humans. There certainly will be new jobs created by technology, such as in data analytics and machine learning, but most people do not have the skills necessary to fill those positions so there will be job mismatches. And there could be job churn as people move from company to company. In an economy where benefits are tied to fulltime employment, any increase in job churn would create instabilities and insecurities in people's ability to maintain their income and their health and retirement benefits.

---

[14] John R. Allen and Darrell M. West, "The Brookings Glossary of AI and Emerging Technologies," Brookings TechTank, July 13, 2020. https://www.brookings. edu/blog/techtank/2020/07/13/the-brookings- glossary-of-ai-and-emerging-technologies/.

COVID-19, the Workforce, and the Economy

Most of the issues noted above have grown more worrisome with the advent of the COVID-19 pandemic and the resulting recession. Unemployment has grown and millions are suffering economically. Huge segments of the population are "financially unanchored" without sufficient monetary protection. The health and economic devastation coupled with tech disruption creates considerable urgency in making future policy changes that address the workforce in general but the negative consequences for individual workers in particular.

The pandemic has revealed stark inequities in access to online education, telemedicine, and opportunities for remote work. As an illustration, African-Americans are far less likely than Caucasians to access online educational resources and are far more likely to suffer from the coronavirus.[15] They also are more likely to have jobs in sectors where the work cannot be performed from home and a number are not able to afford the technologies required to work from their personal residence.

Tech Ramifications for the Federal Budget

It is hard to estimate the precise impact of technology innovation on the federal budget because there are so many direct and indirect ramifications for government revenues and expenses. Shifts in one area undoubtedly will affect expenditures and revenues in other parts of the budget. A detailed answer to that question would require sophisticated budget modeling.

But one thing that appears clear is we are going to need greater investment by the private and public sectors in several key areas. As I outline below, these areas will include infrastructure, agency modernization, healthcare, education, economic development, and market competition. With the increased importance of lifelong learning in a rapidly changing digital economy, for example, we will need to figure out

---

[15] Rashawn Ray, "How to Reduce the Racial Gap in COVID-19 Deaths," Brookings FixGov, April 10, 2020. https://www.brookings.edu/blog/fixgov/2020/04/10/how-to-reduce-the-racial-gap-in-covid-19- deaths/.

ways to invest in and deliver effective workforce training, job upskilling, and continuing education.

At the same time, there are likely to be revenue ramifications as the economy shifts toward digital sectors. Many large technology platforms pay a relatively small percentage of their overall revenues in taxes and if that sector grows as a part of the overall economy while firms paying a larger tax share shrink, that could negatively impact government revenues. To deal with that possibility, it may be necessary to close business tax loopholes and/or reenact an alternative minimum tax for large companies.

As an illustration of misaligned tax incentives, research by economists Daron Acemoglu, Andrea Manera, and Pascual Restrepo finds "the U.S. tax code systematically favors investment in robots and software over investments in people." The reason, according to them, is capital investment in equipment is taxed at 5 percent, while the effective labor tax is around 28.5 percent. The result is a tax code that encourages automation far beyond any efficiency gains represented by the software.[16]

There also could be ramifications for the Social Security Trust Fund if there are job losses that reduce the inflow of payroll taxes. The Congressional Budget Office estimates the program could run out of funds in 2031 due to COVID-related job reductions. Any AI-related job disruption could harm the 40 percent of retired Americans for whom Social Security is their only income source.[17]

Improving Infrastructure

Right now, there are around 18 million Americans who lack sufficient access to the internet.[18] This creates problems in terms of economic development, education, healthcare, and employment. You need an online connection to apply for many jobs and a number of people do not have the

---

[16] Daron Acemoglu, Andrea Manera, and Pascual Restrepo, "Does the US Tax Code Favor Automation?", Brookings Institution, March 18, 2020. https://www.brookings.edu/bpea-articles/does-the-u-s-tax-code- favor-automation/.

[17] Megan Henney, "Social Security Benefit Cuts Could Be Coming," *Fox Business*, September 4, 2020, https://www.foxbusiness.com/economy/social-security-benefit-cuts-could-be-coming-heres-who-it-will- affect-first?ocid=uxbndlbing.

[18] Federal Communications Commission, 2020 Broadband Deployment Report, April 20, 2020, https://assets.documentcloud.org/documents/6878120/FCC-20-50A1.pdf.

connectivity required for online education, telemedicine, and remote work. The Federal Communications Commission has estimated that it would take $40 billion to close the bulk of that connectivity gap.[19]

In addition, many people lack laptops, notebooks, smart phones, or electronic devices that allow them to stream videos and take advantage of online service delivery. They are not able to utilize new opportunities in virtual education, telemedicine, and remote work and are stuck in low-paying jobs with little opportunity for advancement.

It is vital to close gaps based on race, income, and geography so that all can benefit from the digital economy. As noted by Nicol Turner Lee, those who lack online access fall behind, are not able to utilize digital resources, and suffer greatly during pandemics and economic downturns.[20] For individuals falling on the "wrong side" of the digital divide based either on income or race, it is very difficult to advance economically.

Agency Modernization

Government agencies need to modernize their operations and infrastructure in order to become more efficient and effective. Many state and federal organizations have antiquated information technology that is not user-friendly and does not deliver a high quality of service. Tools that have enabled innovation in the private sector, such as cloud computing, artificial intelligence, machine learning, and data analytics, are not widely deployed in most agencies, which harms agency performance and weakens public confidence in government.

This year, there were vivid examples of these problems in the COVID response. Many states had unemployment systems that were not up to the task of delivering assistance to those who filed jobless claims. Across the country, people reported long wait times, IT systems that crashed, and processes that were hard to understand. We need to modernize government

---

[19] Federal Communications Commission, "Improving the Nation's Digital Infrastructure," January 19, 2017. https://www.fcc.gov/document/improving-nations-digital-infrastructure.

[20] Nicol Turner Lee, "What the Coronavirus Reveals about the Digital Divide Between Schools and Communities," Brookings TechTank, March 17, 2020. https://www.brookings.edu/blog/techtank/2020/03/17/what-the-coronavirus-reveals-about-the-digital- divide-between-schools-and-communities/.

agencies so systems can handle citizen needs, are easy to use, and process information efficiently.

Portable Health Benefits and Faster Vesting
of Retirement Benefits

The emerging economy presents challenges with respect to ensuring health and retirement benefits. With a number of employers moving toward greater use of temporary staffing with limited benefits, it is vital that we figure out ways to provide essential benefits. Since most benefits are tied to fulltime employment, any increases in temporary jobs or long-term unemployment will necessitate attention to benefit delivery models.

A key to any reform is the idea of benefit portability. In the digital economy, people are moving across employers, and these movements could accelerate in the future. As noted by analysts Daniel Araya and Sunil Johal, "Introducing portable benefits for independent workers so that pension and health care benefits can be taken from gig to gig while requiring contributions from technology platforms that employ these workers" is an important feature of the emerging landscape.[21] In today's world, workers need benefit flexibility to survive in a working environment that can be turbulent and chaotic.

In addition, organizations need to shorten their vesting periods for people to become eligible for company retirement contributions. Right now, many organizations do not vest employees until they have worked at the firm for one or two years. If there is increased joblessness or job churn resulting from tech disruption, lengthy vesting periods will short-change workers, rob them of the benefits of compound interest, and lead to shortfalls in retirement income.

Lifelong Learning and Continuing Education

In a world of rapid technological, organizational, and economic transition, it is imperative that people engage in lifelong learning. The

---

[21] Daniel Araya and Sunil Johal, "Work and Social Policy in the Age of Artificial Intelligence," Brookings TechTank, February 28, 2017. https://www.brookings.edu/blog/techtank/2017/02/28/work-and-social- policy-in-the-age-of-artificial-intelligence/.

traditional model, in which people focus their learning on the years before age twenty-five, then get a job and devote little attention to education thereafter, is obsolete and dangerously out of tune with the emerging digital era. In the contemporary world, people can expect to switch jobs, see whole sectors disrupted, and need to develop additional skills as a result of major economic shifts. The type of work they do at age thirty likely will be different from what they do at ages forty, fifty, or sixty.

For this reason, it is important that people develop new capabilities throughout their lives. People need to stay abreast of the latest developments and understand that employers will look for different skills as the economy changes. Skills that might be perfectly suited for a certain time may become obsolete due to AI or machine learning and thereby force individuals to update their abilities.

Community colleges are vital in the contemporary situation because they train many adults who need additional coursework. With their lower cost and practical orientation, they are a venue of choice for people of limited financial means and working-class adults wanting to develop new skills. Since they are important in a workforce undergoing transition, it is crucial they be adequately funded so that they can fulfill their mission.

Vocational education and apprenticeship programs also help provide valuable skills and smooth people's transition into the workforce. Students in these programs can join the workforce with the particular skills that are needed and so can contribute to the economy right away.

One possibility to encourage continuing education is the establishment of a lifelong learning account. In an era of fast technological innovation and rapid job displacement, there needs to be a way for people to gain new skills throughout their working lifetime. When people are employed, their companies could contribute a set amount to an individual's fund. This account could be augmented by contributions from the person him or herself. The funds would be analogous to individual retirement accounts or state government-run 529 college savings plans, but the owner of the account could draw on the account to finance online learning, certificate programs, or job retraining expenses. The account would be portable, so that if the person moved across state lines or switched jobs, the account would migrate with that individual.

Closing Geographic Disparities

As America deploys AI and moves to a digital economy, its two coasts have fared much better economically than the heartland. Much of the technology innovation and resulting economic activity is focused on the East and West coasts and a few metropolitan areas in between.

According to research by Brookings senior fellow Mark Moro and analyst Sifan Liu, about 15 percent of American counties generate about 64 percent of GDP economic activity.[22]

That leaves little activity in large parts of the country. Having major geographic inequities is not healthy from an economic or political standpoint. The limited economic activity in rural areas, for example, spawns public discontent and a sense that the system is rigged against those places.

Several communities have sparked economic growth through regional innovation districts. As noted in a 2019 Brookings paper by Robert Atkinson, Mark Muro, and Jacob Whiton, just five cities "Boston, San Francisco, San Jose, Seattle, and San Diego - accounted for more than 90% of the nation's innovation-sector growth during the years 2005 to 2017."[23]

To improve economic opportunity, these researchers propose public-private partnerships that boost innovation centers in heartland cities. The districts would include regulatory relief, tax benefits, workforce development funding, and infrastructure support designed to spur growth. Some places already have launched innovation districts and been successful at creating new jobs. This approach represents a way to use

[22] Mark Muro and Sifan Liu, "Another Clinton-Trump Divide: High-Output America vs. Low-Output America," Brookings The Avenue, November 29, 2016. https://www.brookings.edu/blog/the-avenue/2016/11/29/another-clinton-trump-divide-high-output-america-vs-low-output-america/.

[23] Robert Atkinson, Mark Muro, and Jacob Whiton, "The Case for Growth Centers: How to Spread Tech Innovation Across America," Brookings Institution, December 9, 2019. https://www.brookings.edu/research/growth-centers-how-to-spread-tech-innovation-across-america/

technology and other sectors to boost growth and better prepare young people for the emerging economy.

Boosting Market Competition

The dominance of large internet platforms complicates the economic situation for small and medium-sized businesses. In a 2020 House Judiciary Antitrust Subcommittee hearing, there were allegations of unfair competition and predatory business practices that hurt these firms. Several legislators suggested greater attention to the "consumer welfare" standard that has guided antitrust enforcement and clarification of the rules regarding possible harms to individuals and businesses.

During a recent Brookings TechTank podcast, Subcommittee Chair David Cicilline called for a Glass-Steagall Act for the internet that would separate the functions of selling goods and services from setting the overall rules of the marketplace. He suggests it is time to have clearer, fairer, and more transparent rules of the digital marketplace and that we need more inclusive policies to rebuild the overall economy.[24]

The Need for Action

To summarize, America is headed for significant economic disruption due to AI and machine learning, and shifts in business models. It is crucial to think proactively as these changes unfold. The longer we wait, the more stressful and painful the transition will be. Now is the time to start having the national discussions required to make meaningful changes. I applaud this committee for providing a platform for this important conversation. Thank you for your time.

Chairman YARMUTH. Thank you, Dr. West, for your testimony. I now recognize Dr. Matheny from Louisville, Kentucky.

---

[24] Brookings TechTank Podcast, "Why Rep. David Cicilline Thinks We Need a Glass-Steagall Act for the Internet," September 2, 2020. https://www.brookings.edu/blog/techtank/2020/09/02/techtank-podcast-episode-3-why-rep-david-cicilline-thinks-we-need-a-glass-steagall-act-for-the-internet/.

Statement of Jason Matheny, PhD

Dr. MATHENY. Thank you, Chairman Yarmuth, thank you Ranking Member Womack, and Members of the Committee. And thanks also to my colleagues at the Center for Security and Emerging Technology at Georgetown whose research I will be drawing from today.

AI is a general purpose technology with a broad range of applications in healthcare, agriculture, energy, transportation, national security, and scientific discovery. Advances in AI are likely to be applied across many sectors of the economy spurring growth and enabling new technologies. Policies to strengthen U.S. leadership in AI have enjoyed bipartisan support, at least during the decade that I have worked on the topic.

I worked on AI strategies for both the current administration and the last administration, and there are more similarities than there are differences. Both administrations emphasize the points that I will make here today and each had a positive outlook on the potential for AI to improve American health and prosperity.

As Michael Kratsios, the U.S. chief technology officer recently said, our future rests on getting AI right. AI will support the jobs of the future. Jason Furman, the previous chair of the Council of Economic Advisers in the last administration said that his biggest worry about AI is that we do not have enough of AI.

So while AI will cause changes to the labor market, this has been true of every technology since the industrial revolution and this country has adapted. I believe we will adapt to AI and will be helped by more economic research on the likely effects of AI and automation on the labor force. And by benchmarking to assess progress in various applications of AI.

The United States is in a strong position globally. By most measures, we lead the world in AI and our lead is key—is due to key structural advantages. We have an open society that attracts the world's top scientists and engineers. The National Science Foundation shows that over the half of the master's and Ph.D.-level computer scientists who are employed in the United States were born abroad. We have a competitive private sector that spurs innovation, and we maintain strong international partnerships.

While the U.S. alone funds only 28 percent of global R&D, with our allies we fund more than half. We should double down on these strengths. We should ensure that we remain an attractive destination for global talent by broadening and accelerating the pathways to permanent residency for scientists and engineers. Most research suggests that increases in high skilled immigration yield increases in jobs and wages for Americans due to immigrants' contributions to economic growth and the creation of new companies.

We should also ensure that small and mid-sized businesses have access to the computing power needed for AI applications. We can leverage the purchasing power of the federal government to buy commercial cloud computing credits in the private market and award them through federal grants and contracts competitively as the National Science Foundation has done through its cloud bank program. We should also strengthen our alliances and foster the responsible use of AI through organizations, such as the Global Partnership on AI, of which the United States is a founding member. China has made extraordinary technological progress in recent decades and its future prospects should not be underestimated, but U.S. policy should be based on an appreciation of the strengths that have driven our leadership in AI thus far and how they can be leveraged in the future.

While our private sector leads in AI, the federal government plays a key supporting role. Federal research funding laid the foundation for the current wave of AI progress. Federal funding should continue to focus on areas where the private sector is likely to underinvest. That includes basic research, safety and security, testing and evaluation, and verification and validation.

The National Institute of Standards and Technology should be given the resources needed to lead interagency and public-private collaborations on AI testing and evaluation, including establishment of a national AI test bed: A digital platform containing public and nonpublic data sets, code, and testing environments on which AI systems from industry, academia, and the government can be developed, stored, and tested.

Fourth and last, the United States should ensure that it has access to leading edge microelectronics. This country is the birthplace of microelectronics and we continue to design most of the world's leading edge systems, but most devices are now manufactured elsewhere.

Offshoring most of our semiconductor industry has increased the risk of supply chain disruptions during crises. The United States should strengthen U.S. based semiconductor manufacturing to reduce supply chain risks and to increase the number of high-quality jobs at home.

At the same time, we should work with our allies to ensure that democracies remain at the leading edge of microelectronics by investing in joint research programs and by enforcing multilateral export controls on the manufacturing equipment needed to produce advanced chips.

The United States and our allies produce more than 90 percent of this equipment, so we are in a particularly strong position. Legislation, such as the bipartisan proposals for the CHIPS for America Act and the American Foundries Act can help maintain that position.

With these four points on the benefits of AI as a general purpose technology, the sources of U.S. leadership in AI, the federal government's role in supporting the private sector, and the importance of microelectronics, I thank the Committee for the opportunity to speak with you today, and I look forward to your questions.

[The prepared statement of Jason Matheny follows:]

Prepared Statement of Jason Matheny Founding Director, Center for Security and Emerging Technology (CSET) Walsh School of Foreign Service, Georgetown University September 10, 2020

Chairman Yarmuth, Ranking Member Womack, members of the committee: Good afternoon, and thank you for the opportunity to talk with you today. I'm the founder and director of the Center for Security and Emerging Technology (CSET), a think tank at Georgetown University, that studies the security implications of new technologies, with a focus on artificial intelligence. I also serve as a Commissioner on the National Security Commission on Artificial Intelligence, to which I was appointed by the Senate Select Committee on Intelligence in 2018. I previously worked on similar topics in the federal government as Assistant Director of National Intelligence, and Director of the Intelligence Advanced Research Projects Activity.

In the next few minutes, I'll make four points that I hope we'll return to during the Q&A. They concern the benefits of AI as a general purpose technology, the sources of U.S. leadership in AI, the federal government's role in supporting the private sector, and the importance of microelectronics.

First, AI is a general purpose technology with a broad range of potential applications in healthcare, agriculture, energy, transportation, national security, and scientific discovery. Advances in AI are likely to be applied across many sectors of the economy, spurring growth and enabling new technologies. Policies to strengthen U.S. leadership in AI have enjoyed bipartisan support during the decade that I've worked on the topic. I worked on AI strategies for both the current administration and the last administration, and there are more similarities than there are differences. Both administrations emphasized the points I'll make here today, and each had a positive outlook on the potential for AI to improve American health and prosperity. As Michael Kratsios, the Chief Technology Officer of the United States, has said, "Our future rests on getting AI right. AI will support the jobs of the future."[25] Jason Furman, previous Chair of the Council of Economic Advisors, has said, "the biggest worry I have about it [AI]: that we do not have enough of AI."[26] While AI will cause changes to the labor market, this has been true of every technology since the Industrial Revolution, and this country has adapted. I believe we will adapt to AI. We'll be helped by more economic research on the likely effects of

[25] Michael Kratsios, Remarks at the Center for Data Innovation Forum on AI, September 18, 2019, Washington, DC, https://www.datainnovation.org/2019/09/remarks-by-michael-kratsios-u-s-cto-at-center-for-data-innovation-forum-o n-ai/.

[26] Jason Furman, "Is This Time Different? The Opportunities and Challenges of Artificial Intelligence," Remarks at *AI Now: The Social and Economic Implications of Artificial Intelligence Technologies in the Near Term*, July 7, 2016, New York, NY, https://obamawhitehouse.archives.gov/sites/default/files/page/files/20160707_cea_ai_furman.pdf.

AI and automation, and by benchmarking to assess progress in various applications of AI.

Second, the United States is in a strong position—by most measures, we lead the world in AI.[27] Our lead is due to key structural advantages:

- We have an open society that attracts the world's top scientists and engineers. National Science Foundation data show that over half of the master's- and PhD-level computer scientists employed in the United States were born abroad.[28]
- We have a competitive private sector that spurs innovation.
- We maintain strong international partnerships—while the US, alone, funds only 28% of global R&D, with our allies we fund more than half.[29]

We should double down on these strengths:

- We should ensure that we remain an attractive destination for global talent by broadening and accelerating the pathways to permanent residency for scientists and engineers.[30] Most research suggests that increases in high-skilled immigration yield increases

[27] See, for example, Saurabh Mishra, et al., "The AI Index: Global AI Vibrancy Tool" (Stanford University, 2019), http://vibrancy.aiindex.org/; Daniel Castro, Michael McLaughlin, and Eline Chivot, "Who Is Winning the AI Race: China, the EU or the United States?" (Center for Data Innovation, August 2019), https://www.datainnovation.org/2019/08/who-is-winning-the-ai-race-china-the-eu-or-the-united-states/; Andrew Haynes and Luke Gbedemah, "The Global AI Index" (Tortoise, December 2019), https://www.tortoisemedia.com/intelligence/ai/; Jeff Ding, "Deciphering China's AI Dream" (Centre for the Governance of AI, Future of Humanity Institute, University of Oxford, March 2018), https://www.fhi.ox.ac.uk/wp-content/uploads/Deciphering_Chinas_AI-Dream.pdf.

[28] Remco Zwetsloot, Roxanne Heston, and Zachary Arnold, "Strengthening the U.S. AI Workforce" (Center for Security and Emerging Technology, September 2019), https://cset.georgetown.edu/research/strengthening-the-u-s-ai-workforce/.

[29] Melissa Flagg, "Global R&D and a New Era of Alliances" (Center for Security and Emerging Technology, June 2020), https://cset.georgetown.edu/research/global-rd-and-a-new-era-of-alliances/.

[30] Zachary Arnold, Roxanne Heston, Remco Zwetsloot and Tina Huang, *Immigration Policy and the U.S. AI Sector* (Center for Security and Emerging Technology, September 2019), https://cset.georgetown.edu/research/immigration-policy-and-the-u-s-ai-sector/

in jobs and wages for Americans, due to immigrants' contributions to economic growth and the creation of new companies.[31]

- We should ensure that small- and mid-sized businesses have access to the computing power needed for AI applications. We can leverage the purchasing power of the federal government to buy commercial cloud computing credits in the private market and award them through federal grants and contracts, as the National Science Foundation has done through its CloudBank program.
- We should strengthen our alliances[32] and foster the responsible use of AI through organizations such as the Global Partnership on AI, of which the United States was a founding member.

China has made extraordinary technological progress in recent decades, and its future prospects should not be underestimated. But U.S. policy should be based on an appreciation of the strengths that have driven our leadership in AI thus far, and how they can be leveraged in the future. Imitating China is not a winning strategy. Instead, as writer and scholar James Fallows recommended, "We should be more like us."

Third, while our private sector leads in AI, the federal government plays a key supporting role. Federal research funding laid the foundation for the current wave of AI progress. Federal funding should continue to focus on areas where the private sector is likely to underinvest, including basic research, safety and security, testing and evaluation, and verification and validation. The National Institute for Standards and Technology (NIST) should be given the resources needed to lead interagency and public-private collaborations on AI testing and evaluation, including establishment of a national AI test bed—a digital platform containing public and non-public datasets, code, and testing environments on which AI systems can be developed, stored, and tested.

---

[31] William Kerr, The Gift of Global Talent: How Migration Shapes Business, Economy & Society (Stanford Business Books, 2018).

[32] Andrew Imbrie, Ryan Fedasiuk, Catherine Aiken, Tarun Chhabra and Husanjot Chahal, *Agile Alliances: How the United States and Its Allies Can Deliver a Democratic Way of AI* (Center for Security and Emerging Technology, February 2020), https://cset.georgetown.edu/research/agile-alliances/.

Fourth and last, the United States should ensure that it has access to leading-edge microelectronics. This country is the birthplace of microelectronics, and we continue to design most of the world's leading-edge systems, but most devices are now manufactured elsewhere. Offshoring most of our semiconductor industry has increased the risk of supply chain disruptions during crises. The United States should strengthen U.S.-based semiconductor manufacturing to reduce supply chain risks and create high-quality jobs at home. At the same time, we should work with our allies to ensure that democracies remain at the leading edge of microelectronics by investing in joint research programs and by enforcing multilateral export controls on the semiconductor manufacturing equipment needed to produce advanced chips.[33] The United States and our allies produce more than 90% of this equipment, so we are in a strong position.

Legislation, including bipartisan proposals such as the CHIPS for America Act and American Foundries Act, can help maintain our position.

With these four points on the benefits of AI as a general purpose technology, the sources of U.S. leadership in AI, the federal government's role in supporting the private sector, and the importance of microelectronics, I thank the Committee for the opportunity to speak with you today. I look forward to your questions.

Chairman YARMUTH. Thank you for your testimony.

Once again, I thank all the witnesses for those statements. We will now begin our Q&A session.

As a reminder, Members can submit questions to be answered later in writing. Those questions and their responses will be made part of the formal hearing record. Any Members who wish to submit questions for the record may do so by sending them to the Clerk electronically within seven days.

---

[33] Saif Khan and Carrick Flynn, "Maintaining China's Dependence on Democracies for Advanced Computer Chip" (Brookings Institution and Center for Security and Emerging Technology, April 2020), https://cset.georgetown.edu/research/maintaining-chinas-dependence-on-democracies-for-advanced-computer-chips/.

As we usually do, the Ranking Member and I will hold our question periods till the end.

So I now yield five minutes to the gentleman from Pennsylvania, Mr. Boyle.

Mr. BOYLE. Thank you. I hope you can hear me OK, Mr. Chairman.

All right.

Chairman YARMUTH. Yes.

Mr. BOYLE. Thank you.

So whoever said this in the very beginning was right, that no topic, perhaps more—while exciting some people, I would say, inspires more fear, consternation/paranoia than AI. So all of the presentations were very interesting. I want to go back, though, to a point that was made very early on by one of the witnesses because something that I learned, certainly today if you look at our tax code, we treat capital and labor very differently and certainly make it much more attractive for capital versus labor.

I didn't realize that that is not just been a recent tendency, which was always my impression, but one of the witnesses stated that that goes back a ways.

So I was wondering what any of the witnesses would think about constructive ways that we could bring equality to our tax code, ideas like treating capital gains as ordinary income. There is a discussion right now obviously, perhaps started unintentionally by the President in terms of the use of the payroll tax for funding Social Security and Medicare.

I am curious about these ideas because as my line of questioning probably suggests, I am certainly one who thinks that, at the very least, labor and capital should be treated equally in our tax code and we shouldn't have our thumb on the scale, which in my view we heavily do in treating capital more favorably and thus making it actually more attractive for companies to replace the McDonald's worker with the touch screen that I now use—I am advertising my bad eating habits, but—that now we have at so many of our fast food restaurants.

So I will open that up to any of the witnesses and certainly any ideas or proposals you would have, and if you agree with my view that capital and labor should be treated more equally in our tax code.

Chairman YARMUTH. Who wants to take that?

Dr. Acemoglu. Unmute, please.

Dr. ACEMOGLU. OK. Yes. Somehow I was muting and unmuting and muting myself at the same time. Thanks for that question.

Yes, I was the one who talked about the taxation of capital and labor and it is a complex topic. Economists actually differ, in allfull disclosure. There are some economists who passionately think that capital should be taxed at the very low rate or not at all, but I think in the age of automation, the asymmetric treatment of capital and labor in the tax code has a lot of costs.

If you live in a world where every piece of capital needs to be combined with some human operators, there are still problems with asymmetric treatment of capital and labor, certainly distributional consequences, but there is a better case that increased demand for capital equipment is going to trickle down to workers.

But during our current era where automation is so prevalent from the McDonald's checkout kiosks, to customer service, to machinery, numerically controlled machinery, robots and algorithms everywhere, I think the asymmetric treatment of capital and labor does create more severe problems.

Now if that wanted to be reversed, for example, going back to the 1980's or the 1990's when capital and labor were still treated asymmetrically, but the gap was smaller, you know, a couple of items would help a lot. For example, reversing the very generous depreciation allowances which were often introduced during recessionary times as temporary measures and then weren't completely reversed later. That would be a very major step.

Then there is also the issue of, you know, why we have corporations that choose their own tax status, S-corporations versus C-Corporations, and that has changed a lot over recent decades.

And often that is a way of reducing the tax base for capital through some sort of tax arbitrage and I think that is something that needs to be followed through especially since Ranking Member Womack said this Committee is going to look for ways of increasing tax revenues.

And exactly like you have expressed, Representative Boyle, one has to also consider the taxation of capital gains and other items. If you wanted to go on the other side, there has been a long line of argument in economics going back several decades that payroll taxes are particularly problematic. And in the United States that is actually a very important part of the taxes that labor faces, but, of course, I recognize that right now, with the budget deficit, makes more sense to think of, you know, creating that symmetry by increasing the taxation of capital especially broadening the tax base for capital rather than eliminating taxes, but certainly payroll taxes are something to think about in the future as well. Thank you.

Chairman YARMUTH. All right. The gentleman's time is expired. I now recognize the gentleman from Georgia, Mr. Woodall, for five minutes. Is Mr. Woodall on? Unmute if you are on. Not answering. Well, then, I will recognize the gentleman from Ohio, Mr. Johnson for five minutes.

Mr. JOHNSON. Well, thank you, Mr. Chairman. And I appreciate you holding this hearing today and many thanks to our witnesses too.

I am in my car, so I apologize if things are jumping around, but I am an IT guy. I was in undergraduate and graduate school in the late 1970's, early 1980's when AI first came on the horizon. And today there is no doubt, we all know it, technology spans every sector of our economy.

Investments and emerging technologies, such as AI, blockchain, and the internet of things have the exciting potential to drastically improve our economy, national security, and our very way of life through greater efficiency, increased global competitiveness, and creating countless other applications.

In addition to domestic uses for AI, the Department of Defense has been developing and utilizing AI applications for a range of military capabilities, including intelligence collection and analysis, cyber and information operations, logistics, command and control and also for semi or fully autonomous vehicles, but we all know, the United States is not the only country developing AI capabilities.

China, in particular, is investing billions in AI. It is imperative to our national security that the United States continues to be the leader in developing AI and other emerging technologies. However, China resorts to stealing innovation or subsidizing state-owned enterprises. This is not the role of America's federal government, nor should it be given the innovative spirit of the American people and the exciting advances in technology already occurring right here at home.

Rather it is imperative that our federal government enable the private sector to flourish by removing barriers to innovation, something that President Trump and his Administration has taken important steps to do so.

And supporting private sector research and development collaboratively through strategic federal investments in agencies such as the National Institute of Standards and Technology.

So I am very pleased to have introduced H.R. 6940, the Advancing Tech Startups Act, which is part of a larger public energy and tech agenda to create policies that foster American innovation, secure our supply chains, and protect American consumers.

Specifically, my legislation promotes a national strategy for encouraging more tech focused startups and small businesses in all parts of the United States. It is vital to our national security to reduce our reliance on other countries, such as China. And as I have stated, we don't need to rely on any other country. We should, once again, tap into American ingenuity and unleash the American innovation and entrepreneurship that we are famous for.

So Dr. Matheny, some suggest that the United States may be at risk of falling behind in AI development. For example, some experts predict China could in the near future surpass the U.S. and take the lead in AI development. In your opinion, where does the U.S. currently stand globally on AI? Are we leading the way or falling behind?

Dr. MATHENY. Thank you, Congressman Johnson. I think that the U.S. has a strong lead, but that we can maintain it by drawing on our structural advantages compared to China.

First, most scientists and engineers in the world weren't born in either the U.S. or China, and many more of those scientists and engineers would prefer to work and live in the United States than they would like to live or work in China. That is a great advantage to the United States.

High-skilled immigration was key to our victory during World War II and during the cold war. We were simply able to get more scientists and engineers on our side to win.

Second, as we do have a more competitive private sector and, sir, I think your efforts to empower small businesses where there is so much innovation is really key to our success.

Thank you.

Mr. JOHNSON. OK. Are there some actions that we, in Congress, can take or do we need to do more to maintain our global competitive edge in AI, especially given where China's going and the major investments that are in place?

Dr. MATHENY. I think there are two things that I would emphasize. The first is just how important our immigration policy is to allowing us to lead globally given that this is one of the asymmetric strengths that the United States has compares to China.

And the second is our lead in microelectronics. It would be very difficult for China to match us if we play our cards right. We shouldn't rest on our laurels, but if we pursue policies that strengthen our semiconductor industry while also placing the appropriate controls on the manufacturing equipment that China doesn't have and that China currently doesn't have the ability to produce itself and is probably a decade away from being able to produce itself, we will be in a very strong position.

Thank you.

Mr. JOHNSON. OK, well, thanks. Mr. Chairman, I yield back.

Chairman YARMUTH. The gentleman's time is expired.

And I now recognize the gentlewoman from Illinois, Ms. Schakowsky, for five minutes.

Ms. SCHAKOWSKY. Thank you, Mr. Chairman, and thanks to our witnesses.

So technology has certainly addressed some of the isolation problems that people have felt during the pandemic, and look how we are communicating today, so there has been a lot of important changes that technology and opportunities that technology has provided for us, but even before the pandemic, I think there were many, many consumers that reported feelings of helplessness when it comes to with respect to the digital economy.

You know, on my subcommittee in Energy and Commerce, which is the Consumer Protection Subcommittee, we have talked a lot about technology and its ups and downs, and we know that big tech has actually allowed fraud and fake news and fake reviews and counterfeit and stolen products that are thriving on their platforms.

And we have talked about—they come in and talk about self-regulation, and I think it is pretty clear that we need—that that isn't working very well.

But here is the other question. They ask about consumers are concerned about privacy.

So Dr. West, I want to ask you. A functioning AI needs data, but we also need to protect consumer privacy.

So in your view, what are the main issues related to consumer privacy and control and ownership of data that we need to consider through as we think through the use of AI technology?

Dr. WEST. Thank you, Congresswoman, for that question. It is a great question. Privacy is very important to consumers. You can look at any set of public opinion surveys and that often ranks very high on the list next to security.

The problem with our current approach to policy at the national level is it is mainly based on what is called notice and consent. Like when you download software or even install an ad, you get this 20-page document that nobody reads and at the bottom, if you want to use the app, you basically have to agree to it.

Nobody reads these. We did a national public opinion survey and basically found that that to be the case. So my Brookings colleague Cam Kerry has been doing a lot of work on thinking about new privacy legislation and what he proposes is basically get rid of the notice and consent because it is not effective in protecting peoples' privacy and basically holding companies responsible for their data sharing practices.

Improving transparency so consumers know more about what is going on, improve everybody's sense of how—what kind of data practices are being deployed.

I mean, there are all sorts of geolocation features that are now built-in to apps. Like if you check the weather, basically the weather app is localized to you so there is a geolocation feature there, there is all sorts of privacy problems that get developed there. So basically we suggest a greater accountability for companies.

California, of course, at the state level has adopted a much tougher law than what we have had nationally. We really encourage Congress to embrace the issue of privacy at the national level. We don't want to end up in a situation where there are 50 different privacy laws. I mean, that creates havoc for the tech companies, makes it difficult for them to innovate. We need a national privacy law that can really address the concerns that consumers have.

Ms. SCHAKOWSKY. Thank you.

In the remaining time that I have, I wanted to really ask any of you who wanted to comment on this. You know that AI is used in policing, in social work, in banking, in healthcare, and we also know that this is a time of racial reckoning in this country, disparities that we see, and we had a hearing in my subcommittee on the issue of discrimination built into algorithms, built into our technology, built into AI.

And I wanted to just ask whoever to talk about how we can ensure that there is accountability to make sure that there is not the kind of built-in bias that discriminates against many in our population?

Someone grab this.

Chairman YARMUTH. Anyone want to handle that real quickly?

Dr. ATHEY. I can speak quickly. I think that we have to consider what the algorithms are replacing, and in some cases they are replacing human decisions, which have perhaps a different set of biases sometimes driven by the fact that the humans are using less information or don't have a full view of someone's circumstance like in resume screening being too superficial.

So in principal, when well-designed, when training data is carefully selected and when best practices are used, actually digitization can improve the situation and reduce bias, but it has to be done well and it has to be done carefully.

So I believe that we need more research, we need more best practices, and whenever they are used in government situations or regulated situations, we do need to include accountability and ongoing monitoring in order to make sure there are no unintended consequences.

Often engineers themselves don't understand the source of the problem and they won't look for it unless they are asked to, but they also like to use best practices if those are delineated and available. And so this is partly just a maturation of the industry and a maturation of the best practices.

So I am long-term optimistic, but we have to do the hard work to make it improve things rather than make them worse.

Ms. SCHAKOWSKY. Thank you so much. I yield back.

Chairman YARMUTH. The gentlewoman's time is expired.

And I yield five minutes to the gentleman from Georgia, Mr. Woodall.

Mr. WOODALL. Thank you, Mr. Chairman, for giving me a second chance. You have always been gracious in that way.

Chairman YARMUTH. Of course.

Mr. WOODALL. Mr. Matheny, I wanted to thank you for mentioning the stability in national AI policy between the two administrations that you have had an opportunity to serve. We tend to focus on the chaos, which I think leads to less confidence as opposed to the leaders in the room who are working hand-in-hand administration to administration.

Could you talk a little bit about that? We are about to come up on another major election. Do you anticipate that stability in policy continuing whether it is into a second term of the Trump Administration or the first term of a Biden Administration?

Dr. MATHENY. Thank you, Congressman Woodall. I would expect there to be continuity in the U.S. strategy on AI. I think there really has been a bipartisan consensus that I have seen and a lot of continuity at the Office of Science and Technology policy, in particular, which I think has done a great job both in the last administration and in this administration continuing much of the strategic work that was laid out.

Michael Kratsios and Lynn Parker, in particular, at the office had been outstanding in coordinating the interagency. They led a smart and ambitious AI strategy, which I hope to see continued. It is, I think, one of the best cases of bipartisan coordination around a key technology topic.

Thank you.

Mr. WOODALL. I very much appreciate that.

Dr. Athey, you mentioned not just in your response to Ms. Schakowsky, but also in your opening statement a need to be aware of unintended consequences.

Are there particular unintended consequences that weigh on you in your work or is that just a general admonition as we plow new ground?

Dr. ATHEY. Well, I think maybe one—one answer relates back also to the question about labor versus capital and excessive auto mation. In general, firms are going to be thinking primarily about their bottom line and they are often short-term.

So it is going to be—you know, a firm might be indifferent between a worker and a machine from a cost perspective and if they are indifferent they will go with the machine. But, of course, from society's perspective, we care about the jobs and we care about the people and we care about their transitions.

So we do want to think about how are we investing in this R&D generally. We can't always count on companies to take the longer term perspective and our national innovation strategy and R&D strategy can, in principal, develop this general purpose technology in a way that focuses more on augmentation of humans.

So one thing about this general purpose technology is that somebody makes better AI and then lots of people adopt it. And so if somebody makes AI that helps replace humans, lots of other people can copy it. But if universities or a particular company or government invests in AI that augments humans, it is also the case that that can diffuse.

So I think that we can—we need to be intentional about our strategies and recognize the places where we as a society care about the direction of technological innovation so that it pushes more and makes it cheaper and easier for the private sector to then pick up augmenting technologies.

A second thing that I worry a lot about is just that the most recent innovation has been in black box technology. It is powerful in general purpose because it does the work for you.

An engineer who doesn't know anything about a domain can plop down modern machine learning and the machine learning will spit something out, but if it is just applied without a context, without domain experts, without ethical experts or legal experts or people who are thinking about your national security consequences, we might end up in dangerous situations.

And so actually like the privacy and security issues, I think, are especially concerning when we realize that all of us are being observed and monitored sort of 24/7 by our phones and by everything that we do as it all gets digitized. That can create national security issues in that somebody always does something wrong, so we are available for blackmail.

And we are also going to see in the future, because it is so easy and cheap, a lot more worker monitoring, which can be good for safety. We can make sure people are driving safely. We can make sure truck drivers aren't asleep. We can make sure that workers aren't going to be injured on an assembly line if we use video to monitor them.

But, again, we are creating this massive corpus of information about people. And we also need to make sure that that information is applied in a fair way and for benefit rather than being exploiting in various ways.

Mr. WOODALL. Mr. Chairman, I know Dr. Acemoglu referenced companies that were doing it wrong. I hope as this hearing continues we will have an opportunity to talk about some of those companies that are doing it right so that we can benefit from that experience.

I yield back, Mr. Chairman.

Chairman YARMUTH. Absolutely. I will make sure we do that. Thank you, Mr. Woodall.

I now recognize the gentleman from Michigan, Mr. Kildee, for five minutes.

Mr. KILDEE. Well, first of all, thank you, Mr. Chairman. I assume you can hear me OK?

Chairman YARMUTH. We can.

Mr. KILDEE. I very much appreciate you holding this hearing. It is a very interesting and, I think, obviously very important topic. I represent an area that has seen a pretty drastic drop in manufacturing jobs over the last 30 or so years. Often, and almost exclusively, attributed to trade policy. And while trade has clearly contributed to the loss of manufacturing jobs in my region of East Central Michigan, Flint, Saginaw, Bay City area, clearly technology has played a pretty significant role in that job loss. We have gone from, in my hometown, of about 80,000 direct manufacturing employees in the auto sector to something around 10,000 right now; but we still produce about half the cars that we used to produce. So that technology disruption obviously has had a pretty dramatic impact on my community, and now we are trying to imagine and you are thinking and researching about how AI may have that same disruptive effect. So I am curious about any thoughts that any of you have about the pace of development of AI as it relates to manufacturing and specifically around the production of automobiles. I know this might require some speculation, but I think it is really important that we engage in that speculation.

And I am particularly interested, Dr. West, your references to the work of Mark Moro, I have a past relationship with Brookings and did a lot of work around this space, particularly around communities being left behind.

So I am curious if, maybe starting with you, Dr. West, but others might comment on those two aspects: The pace of these trends as they might relate to heavy manufacturing, particularly the auto sector, and then any thoughts you have on compensating interventions that we can deal with that might add to the way we typically deal with trade disruption through trade adjustment assistance, or something like that, how we might think about support for those communities that are being disproportionately impacted by these trends.

So maybe starting with Dr. West.

Dr. WEST. Thank you, Congressman.

I do worry about job losses, and manufacturing is one of the areas where there is already a lot of automation and AI that is being introduced, and we fully expect that to accelerate.

When you look around the world, there are countries that have almost fully automated factories right now where it is basically a bunch of robots driven by AI technology and a handful of humans just monitoring the computer control panels.

But it is not just manufacturing. Finance is going to be disrupted. The retail sector, Amazon already has opened a number of stores with basically no retail clerks. They basically use computer vision to see what you have put in your bag or, you know, what it is that you are purchasing, and they automatically charge you as you are exiting it. So there certainly is going to be, I believe, an acceleration of job losses.

And in terms of the geographic thing, the thing I would worry about here is if you look at venture capital investment, three-quarters of it now is going into New York, California, and Massachusetts. So, if anything, the geographical inequity is going to accelerate. Already, you know, much of the high tech industry is centered on the East Coast and West Coast and a few metropolitan areas in between, but much of the country is being left behind. My Brookings' colleagues in our Metro Program have done a lot of work on this. This is very worrisome. It creates political anger. People get upset. They feel the system is rigged. They feel like they are being left behind.

So we do need to think about public policies that will address the geographic aspects. Now, one positive development is the growing tendency to move toward remote work. It turns out you no longer have to live in Seattle or San Francisco or Boston or New York in order to work for these tech companies.

In fact, you know, the real estate is growing so expensive in those areas that they are kind of pricing a lot of employees out of that market. So they are starting to rely more on remote work and telework, and so I think public policy can contribute to that.

There is a rural digital divide where people living in the country have less access to broadband and less access to high-speed broadband. They are less able to take advantage of these remote work things. So Congress should definitely invest in infrastructure, development in the broadband area just to reduce that digital divide so that, as companies start to move to telework and remote work, everybody can take advantage of that, including people living in the heartland.

Mr. KILDEE. Thank you. It is a fascinating subject. I look forward to pursuing it further.

My time has expired, so I yield back. Thank you, Mr. Chairman.

Chairman YARMUTH. I thank the gentleman. The gentleman's time has expired.

I now recognize the gentleman from Texas, Mr. Flores, for five minutes.

Mr. FLORES. Thank you, Chairman Yarmuth, and I appreciate you holding this informative hearing today.

I want to note something that you said at the beginning, that the government moves at 10 miles an hour when the rest of the economy is moving at 100 miles an hour, and I will talk about that in a minute.

I personally am excited about the opportunities that AI brings moving forward. I know that several people are apprehensive about it, but I think that we as policymakers need to be excited about it. A couple of things I want to comment on before I go on to my questions. Number one is, I think that there has been a lot of discussion about R&D, and I think one of the essential roles of the federal government is robust investment in basic research and development, and I say this from the perspective that I represent two large tier 1 research and education institutions and also have a great high tech footprint in several parts of my district that rely on that, and those discoveries that come out of the search for basic knowledge from basic R&D.

The second thing is I think we as policymakers need to be very careful about trying to get into adjusting the mix of capital versus labor because, as you said early on, Chairman Yarmuth, the government moves slowly, and I think we as policymakers could wind up being well behind where the economy is if we are not careful with that.

I would like to thank all of the witnesses for participating. Dr. Matheny, I have a couple of questions for you. As we are all aware, Taiwan through its TSMC Foundry is a leading semiconductor manufacturer for many countries, and particularly we in the U.S. rely on them for AI development.

The first question is this: Does the U.S. rely too heavily on other countries for AI development, and what can the U.S. do to put less of this reliance on other countries?

Dr. MATHENY. Thank you. Thank you, Congressman Flores. And, first, thanks also for your emphasis on research. I think one of the most exciting opportunities is for AI to be applied to research itself, to accelerate science and engineering. I think some of the more exciting demonstrations that we have seen on this include DeepMind's use of AI to solve protein folding problems, which are really important for biomedical research. So I hope we will see more of that in ways that can expand the economy and produce jobs.

To your very good question about Taiwan Semiconductor Manufacturing Corporation. I think the U.S. does rely too much on imported semiconductors, which introduces at least three risks.

The first is that our dependence on manufacturing in Taiwan means that we have a supply chain that could be disrupted by a conflict with China.

The second is that Taiwan is vulnerable to having its workforce and its IP poached because of its proximity to China.

And third is we risk having our own know-how vanish in a key industry the more we import.

I think Intel's recent announcement that they were considering outsourcing their most advanced manufacturing, which would be really the only U.S. based advanced manufacturing of semiconductors, is extremely worrying. So I think it is prudent to reshore some semiconductor manufacturing to the United States, particularly the leading edge chips that are used to power many of the AI applications that will be valuable in the future.

And beyond the security benefits, this would also create new manufacturing jobs for Americans.

Thank you.

Mr. FLORES. Thank you.

You know what, you actually answered the second part of my question that talked about the economic and national security threats that exist if we rely on other regions and other countries. Let me ask a second question.

As you are aware AI development requires talented workers with particular skill sets. In order for the U.S. to continue leading the way in AI development, it is critical that we continue to develop domestic talent in addition to attracting talent from abroad.

When you answered Mr. Johnson's question a minute ago, you talked about attracting the best talent from abroad. What policy recommendations do you have to ensure that the U.S. successfully cultivates a domestic talent supply for AI?

And, for instance, talk in particular about what the education system will look like for that group of persons.

Dr. MATHENY. Thank you for asking the question.

My sister is a school teacher and a great one, so I have a deep sympathy for school teachers who are trying to teach computer science and mathematics. These are difficult topics to teach, but we need to find ways of teaching more of our students the strong math skills that they are going to need.

Mathematics is really the discipline that is most useful to succeeding in AI. And we simply need to find better ways of teaching math to our students and finding ways to teach more of it.

We also need to address the AI labor needs that aren't in research and development. I know discussions around tech talent often center around the scarcest and most educated parts of the workforce; but a critical talent gap also sits in skilled labor, and for our skilled labor to compete globally, it will need help from technology.

China enjoys a manufacturing advantage due to its vast workforce, which is about 11 times the size of the U.S. manufacturing workforce. But despite its larger size, the Chinese manufacturing sector only produces about twice the amount of value-adds. So the average U.S. manufacturing worker is about six times as productive as the average Chinese manufacturing worker.

So reshoring manufacturing will require that we both increase the parts of our labor force while also increasing the productivity per worker, which is going to have to be achieved through both training and technology. One example is cobots, robotic systems that complement human workers in order to increase their productivity per person.

Thank you.

Mr. FLORES. OK. Thank you, Dr. Matheny. And my time has expired.

Chairman YARMUTH. The gentlemen's time has expired.

I now recognize the gentleman from California, Mr. Panetta, for five minutes.

Mr. PANETTA. Great. Thank you, Mr. Chairman. I appreciate this hearing, appreciate this opportunity, Ranking Member Womack. I apologize if my connection is spotty, but I have two daughters learning remotely, sucking up a lot of the bandwidth. I guess it would be in more ways than one, not just virtually but mentally for their parents; but that is a whole other story.

Let me just say I appreciate this opportunity to have this type of hearing, especially when it comes to the risks of automation for workers, especially for those jobs where automation only provides a marginal cost in productivity benefit over the human worker.

Now, I think we all sort of agree that we need to focus on these workers and how such changes will affect them, but we need to be very careful not to discourage automation or technological progress because I think all of us agree that automation and, yes, AI hold tremendous promise when it comes to improving our lives and our economy.

Now, it can also eliminate, as we know, some very tedious tasks so that workers can focus on being more productive, and it does lower prices for consumers, improving our daily lives, and raising the standard of living for low-income families. So because automation has that ability to increase worker productivity, it is our responsibility to ensure that workers benefit from their increased value.

But taxing or otherwise disincentivizing automation I don't think saves jobs, and I do think it will make our economy less nimble and risk us falling further behind our competitors, like China.

And that is why I believe we need to continue to invest in automation and cutting edge technology like artificial intelligence. That is why we should continue to keep the U.S. competitive in these areas for the sake of our security.

And yet if the successes in these areas do lead to displacement, it is our responsibility to help those workers, and we should be prepared to support those workers, rethinking our social safety net, how we retrain those workers, bolstering their workers' rights, strengthening collective bargaining for higher wages and job security so that the productivity increases.

That also means we need to study how workers can best complement automation and artificial intelligence, but we should not, we should not shy away from these fundamental challenges by stunting progress and protections for our national, economic, and food security.

Now, here on the Central Coast, when it comes to food security, we live up to our jobs, we live up to our responsibilities. We have a lot of farms, farmers, and farm workers. And as Dan Kildee will tell you, I live in the salad bowl of the world because of it. We have a lot of specialty crops that cannot be harvested like traditional row crops in the Midwest, concerning corn, soy, and wheat. We have crops where human discernment as to what is a ripe, safe, and aesthetically pleasing product is really difficult to replace.

But our Ag workforce is very necessary right now. Unfortunately, though, it is an age thing and it is shrinking. And the pandemic is highlighting not just how valuable that workforce is but how vulnerable they are.

Now, obviously, it is a two-prong solution. Yes, one is immigration reform, looking at the Farm Workforce Modernization Act that passed out of the House this year. The other, though, is investment in specialty crop mechanization, dealing with how you can harvest those types of very difficult to harvest crops.

Now, obviously, the private industry is working more to develop these technologies and to fulfill that labor gap, but I believe the federal government has a critical role to play in helping oversee and scale up these investments, if I may say so.

Now my first question, Dr. Athey, is as we develop these types of technologies to save labor, to save our food security, what steps do you think are necessary to protect existing farm workers and for them to transition and adapt to these new types of existing circumstances?

Dr. ATHEY. Thank you for that question.

I believe that historically we have not really done the greatest job in dealing with displaced workers in general. In economics class we teach about, you know, all of the benefits from trade and, you know, more efficient production of products; but then as a society we forget about that second step where you actually get the redistribution done and deal with the consequences.

But where I am optimistic is that I think we have a lot more tools at our disposal now to reach people, to use data to figure out what is the best next step for a worker, what types of up-skilling will actually work for a person in this circumstance. And that in turn can help people feel comfortable in the investment because, of course, for a worker to take their scarce time and invest in trying to acquire a skill, they need to have confidence that if they do make that effort and take that scarce time and money, they will be able to use that to get a new job.

And so I think we have just had services in the past that haven't really responded to the individual worker, to the individual worker's circumstance, and then provided them with effective training and relocation services.

But I believe that we can do better. I am collaborating with a project in Rhode Island working with the state government to try to improve both the data to evaluate training programs and as well try to help workers to have better information for making choices. And I think that with technology and data we can do better, and we can also reduce the cost of delivery by bringing services to people remotely in their homes at a time that is convenient for them, so they don't have to get in their car, they don't have to hire a babysitter and, you know, sacrifice income in order to receive the training that they need.

So I am optimistic about the future, but we have to be intentional about it, and we actually have to execute and follow through on those types of promises.

Mr. PANETTA. Agreed. Thank you, Doctor. Thank you, Mr. Chairman. I yield back.

Chairman YARMUTH. The gentleman's time has expired.

I now recognize the gentleman from Oklahoma, Mr. Hern, for five minutes.

Unmute. Mr. Hern, unmute. Oh, you need to be helped?

Mr. HERN. I did it twice. It is good. OK. We are good again.

Chairman YARMUTH. There you go.

Mr. HERN. Thank you, Chairman, Ranking Member Womack, for holding this important hearing today, and thanks to all of our witnesses for being her today. This is a topic that I find quite fascinating, being an engineer myself.

Unfortunately, due to the unforeseen spread of a particular virus from China, economic growth has been stunted, and so this really gets to be a real exacerbated issue right now that it is up to us really to fix.

The U.S. economy has been forced—it is force built by hard working, first starting Americans, and we only move forward as a country if we continue to support innovation and encourage workers to get back into the workforce.

AI can act as a great catalyst to both needs, and the U.S. Government should create a regulatory environment which enables growth and innovation, rather than creating hurdles to both, if we want and would like to beat China and others in this space as our own available workforce declines.

My question now is—there has been many answers to the questions that I had; but one of the witnesses really is pretty fascinating as we get into it. We talked a lot about the technical aspects of this.

But, Dr. Athey, let's just talk about the workforce. There has been a lot of talk about workforce replacement, but we haven't talked at all about the lack of workforce. And for the first time in at least a generation government figures show a larger of open jobs than people out of work. Obviously, this was pre COVID, but it was only six months ago. And certainly a lot of us, probably all of us, hope we get back there very quickly.

And part of that problem is demographics, labor and market growth. The U.S. birth rate has been falling and is at a 30-year low, and simultaneously baby boomers are hitting retirement age, a big force behind the falling number of unemployed. Some would argue it is the real problem of our Medicare issues and our Social Security issues. We don't have enough people working to fund those programs, along with the aging population.

In fact, McKinsey Global Institute research on the automation potential of the global economy focuses on 46 countries representing about 80 percent of the global workforce and has examined more than 2,000 work activities and quantified the technical feasibility of automating each of them. But the proportion of occupations that can be fully automated using current technology is actually pretty small, only about 5 percent.

And if you could speak to that AI as our workforce continues and declines and our need for consumption grows, I would like to get what your thoughts are on policies—and I am being flippant in this; but, you know, if you go back to the McKinsey group, it forces higher fertility and prevent us all from getting older, which are two driving forces. And while that is ridiculous, you can't, there is at least one—and I would like to piggyback off on my colleague from California when he talks about immigration. You know, there is a big push, and the President has pushed for this, for merit-based immigration, bringing people in that can add to where we need to go from a technology standpoint to help us continue our drive for AI.

So as you are aware, AI requires talented workers from particular skill sets so that we can continue to lead the way as our witnesses have testified. And so what policy recommendations do you have to ensure the U.S. successfully cultivates a domestic talent supply in this space? Will students need a different education to pursue careers in AI versus what they are doing right now?

Dr. ATHEY. Thank you, Congressman, for the question. And you raised a number of really crucial issues.

Of course, everyone on the Budget Committee I am sure is acutely aware that the amount of our budget that we are spending on older Americans is increasing dramatically, and so we need to really think about how we are going to deliver services to our aging population more efficiently and also what can we do to keep people in the workforce, preferably in the workforce longer, which might be in a second career or a part-time job that looks very different than how work was done in the past.

So I think the first important consideration is to think about what will all of these elderly people need and how can we help them live independently, live fulfilling lives, and get of the services they need. I think AI and automation can actually help quite a bit because some of the things that make it difficult to work as you age include, you know, physical challenges, as well as memory challenges and, you know, certain cognitive aspects of the job, all of which can be alleviated through augmenting AI or physical robots, which might allow humans to work longer and focus on the aspects of the job that involve interpersonal relationships, comforting seniors, helping them get their psychological needs met.

So you might have seniors helping seniors. It is also the case that actually there is a lot of service work at that time that in the end may not be fully replaced by automation.

So I see that this aging population is a challenge, but it also points our way toward solutions for those people. And, more broadly, the demographic crisis highlights for us that immigration will be important because we see a shortage of workers on the horizon and a shortage of taxpayers in the working age when you look at the demographics.

It is much harder to predict what is exactly going to happen to automation in 10 years, but we already know how many 20-year- olds we have in the country who will be 40 in 20 years. Unless we bring in more 40-years-old, you know, we are kind of stuck with what we have got.

So we can expand immigration, but we can also think about how to most effectively use the people we have and allow our aging population to contribute in meaningful ways as they age.

Thank you.

Mr. HERN. Thank you so much. Mr. Chairman, I yield back.

Chairman YARMUTH. The gentleman's time has expired.

I now recognize the gentleman from New York, Mr. Morelle, for five minutes.

Mr. MORELLE. Thank you very much, Mr. Chairman, for holding another really, really important issue facing the country.

Before I begin, I do want to also add my welcome to Representative Jacobs, who I had the privilege of serving with in the New York State Legislature, and I am delighted that he has joined this Committee. I am looking forward to continuing to work with my neighbor to the west in upstate New York.

I just want to say a couple of things. I think some of the comments by the other members have been really, really provocative, and there are a ton of questions here. To me this isn't a question of whether or not AI, machine learning, robotics, and innovative technology will reshape the landscape economically and as it relates to the workforce. It is doing it. It will continue to do it. It is happening, in many respects, at breakneck speed. And I think then the question for us, we have always marketed ourselves as a nation of opportunity, a nation of innovation.

So the question is, as public policy challenges emerge because of it, what do we do? How do we think through this? I think that is why this hearing is so critical.

The way I see AI, I guess I think about it in a couple different buckets. One is, to the extent that it could displace human beings in some jobs and in some occupations, the more I see it as ways to create tools that will allow people to do their jobs faster, better, more efficiently. But there is no question it is going to have an impact and we need to think about it.

One of the things, as it relates to the budget—and perhaps people can talk about this—you know, the President has talked about elimination or deferral of payroll taxes. Obviously, that has an impact on Social Security.

It has an impact on Medicare. But even beyond the call for reduction of payroll taxes, to the extent that there is a displacement of workers or lessening of wages because jobs become a focus of commodity-like activities, what I am struck by is so much of what we have built on the safety net, Medicare and Social Security being two of the most obvious, built into a system where we get revenues based on payroll.

So, you know, there have been suggestions by some folks looking at this, to the extent that we look at displacement, should there be alternative ways of looking at taxation so we can continue to provide resources to Social Security, to Medicare to make sure that particularly as the baby boom generation starts to move into some of these programs, you are going to see this significant percentage of the population in Medicare, in Social Security, and given the reproduction rate in the United States is at an all-time low, and mix that in with AI and machine learning, robotics.

Could anyone—and perhaps, Dr. West, maybe you can help answer this. Is there something we should be looking at in terms of a replacement for payroll taxes that is based on—I know people have talked about the difference between capital and people when it comes to investment and tax payments.

Can you talk a little bit how we can make sure that our revenue base doesn't decline if we see jobs displaced by either AI, robotics, machines, et cetera.

Dr. WEST. That is a great question, Congressman.

I think we do need to think about the tax system both in terms of tax rates, tax credits but possibly also new types of taxes. And if you go back a hundred years to the start of the industrial revolution, you know, we found our tax system to be inadequate at that time, and so we developed new taxes, we developed new social programs. And I think now as we are moving to the digital economy, we need to be asking big questions like that.

So I am not sure exactly what the kind of new taxes could be, like people propose a financial transactions tax that would kind of help with income inequality in general. Some countries are implementing digital services taxes. So there is a lot of new ideas that are being formulated there.

And on the first part of your question, you are right about the importance of market competition, and the key in innovation has always been small and medium size enterprises. We are worried about a loss of market competition, and so I think Congress should really think about ways to promote small and medium size enter prises just so we can maintain the startup the economy that has fueled American prosperity for several decades.

Mr. MORELLE. Yes, thank you. I think that is a really important comment.

And I would just say in the few seconds that I have left, what I do worry about is we don't want to create disincentive for investment in innovative technologies. We also don't want to put ourselves in a position where, as a result of that, we have displaced workers and the payroll taxes that support much of our social infrastructure.

So I want to thank the panelists. Thank you, Mr. Chair, for a great hearing. I yield back.

Chairman YARMUTH. Thank you. The gentleman's time has expired.

And now I recognize, in his debut Budget Committee appearance, Mr. Jacobs from New York.

Mr. JACOBS. All right. Can you hear me, or no?

Chairman YARMUTH. You are live.

Mr. JACOBS. I am having some problems here. Chairman YARMUTH. You may have muted yourself. Now you are fine. You should be good.

Mr. JACOBS. Can you hear me?

Chairman YARMUTH. Yes.

Mr. JACOBS. OK. Sorry about that.

Thank you, Mr. Chairman. Thank you, everybody. Great to be on. And I guess I need a little AI to help me with the unmuting here.

I just wanted to first comment, Dr. Matheny, on some things you talked about regarding semiconductors. I have an area, Batavia, New York, in my district where they have been working for a number of years in developing an advanced manufacturing park. One of their hopes would be to lure a semiconductor facility there because of the inherent assets we have in terms of low-cost power due to the proximity of the Niagra Falls Power Plant and also abundant water.

And in talking with them, they discussed this issue of the loss of our semiconductor industry nationally, and one statistic I just wanted to echo why this is so important what you are talking about, in the year 2000, the United States had 24 percent of the semiconductor production in the world. Now we are at 12 percent. In the year 2000, China had zero percent of the production, and now they have 16 percent, and they are investing another trillion dollars in this sector in the next decade.

So, you know, this is a major issue and look forward to pushing for policy nationally that will help level the playing field so that we can make sure that we maintain and grow this sector for the important reasons that are mentioned here.

I wanted to ask a question of Dr. West. My district, as we talk about inequalities, would be geographic. My district is rather rural and definitely have concern—we have major issues with lack of high-speed internet access, and it is being more pronounced right now with the needs for distance learning and telehealth, but in an effort to be economically competitive in the future.

And I was just curious—so, clearly, I am all in for any additional money and programs to push for rural broadband because it is important as any other piece of infrastructure right now for our area. But in terms of you mentioned innovation districts as the model of something to try to allow areas that are not on the coast to be competitive in the new day era, and I was wondering if there is examples of success that you have of innovation districts? Thank you.

Dr. WEST. Well, it is funny you should ask that—and the Chairman will love this because Louisville is actually an example. Louisville is an example where they have developed a pretty successful regional innovation district. Brookings actually is helping advise some of the organizations there. It is a public-private partnership. So you can talk to the Chair about how they did that.

On the rural part of your question, I can really appreciate this because I grew up on a dairy farm in rural Ohio many years ago, and rural areas are really being left behind right now. So we really need to address the infrastructure part and especially the broadband part because, as I mentioned earlier, like there are opportunities for remote work, like you don't have to live in San Francisco, you could live in your district and still work for any of these tech companies, but you need high-speed broadband.

Just this week my Brookings' colleague, Tom Wheeler, had a short report where he gave a couple of very specific ideas for the Federal Communications Commission, which he used to head. One is a reform of the E-Rate program, which was set up to connect classrooms. It turns out there is a $2 billion surplus in that fund, meaning there is unspent money that was designed to connect classrooms. Now that so many people are engaged in home schooling, you know, we could actually redirect some of that $2 billion to improve rural broadband in order to facilitate home schooling. It is very consistent with the purpose of that program, so you should talk to the people at the FCC about that.

And then, second, with the Lifeline program, which the FCC also runs, including cable companies, not just phone companies, in rolling out digital services and broadband, just because today people are almost as likely to get their broadband via a cable company as a phone company. So if we could broaden the Lifeline program to basically address the ways people are ordering broadband, that would help, and also making—including companies that offer prepaid services.

So in the Tom Wheeler post, he talked about all of these ideas. But I think they are particularly relevant for your district and other rural areas across America.

Mr. JACOBS. Great. Thank you very much. I yield back the rest of my time.

Chairman YARMUTH. The gentleman yields back.

I now recognize the gentleman from California, Mr. Khanna, for five minutes.

Mr. KHANNA. Thank you, Mr. Chairman. And thank you, Dr. West. I highly recommend Mark Moro's paper, and it is not just in Chairman's Louisville district, but even in Paintsville, Kentucky, they have had quite a lot of success in bringing technology to rural communities, and I appreciate your work and Brookings' work on that.

I had a question for Professor Acemoglu, whose work I admire very much. I was struck by this idea of excessive automation, and I understand the tax incentives that may be off, but bracketing that aside, what explains the move toward excessive automation? Is it a sense that there is some kind of market failure where companies are actually making irrational decisions to automate in ways that aren't profitable, or is it that it is marginally profitable but it is not having aggregate productivity gains for society?

Dr. ACEMOGLU. Thank you very much, Congressman Khanna. I think that is a great question. And it is a variety of factors.

First of all, it is indeed the tax incentives, so we cannot ignore that. You know, there is no natural rate at which capital and labor are going to be taxed, so it is a policy choice, and that policy choice is going to have consequences.

A second important factor is that labor and capital use may have social consequences and economic consequences that go beyond what companies calculate.

So, for example, if people are better citizens or they contribute more to their community or to their families when they are employed, that is not going to be part of the calculation of companies, and it is part of policymakers to actually decide that.

So do we, for the same GDP, would we be happy when that is produced by humans partly versus when a lot of it is produced by capital? I think a lot of policymakers would say actually for the same GDP, we would like it quite a bit if humans are part of that equation, which means that we actually value as a community, as a society, humans being part of that calculation.

And technology has gone in a way that makes it possible for greater substitution of machines and algorithms, so some of those external effects that were less relevant now become more relevant. And the third factor is that it is not necessarily irrational, but different companies have different business models. So if you look at the periods in which the American economy has done very well while it was also automating, this diversity of perspective, diversity of approaches was very important.

Let me give you one example. Mechanization of agriculture. That is an even more transformative automation event than the ones that we are talking about right now. More than half of the U.S. economy was agriculture, and there was a huge, tremendous decline in labor share in agriculture as machines started performing tasks that were previously done by humans.

But during that period, American growth didn't just come from agriculture. It also came from other sectors that picked up labor that was displaced or the children of the labor that were displaced often because some greater human capital was necessary. So the manufacturing sector introduced a lot of both production and non- production jobs, a lot of the non-manufacturing sector expanded.

So it is sort of diversity of approaches, diversity of technologies was quite critical. So one of the things that may be less active today is that we are not using the enormous technological platform that AI presents us in ways that can create jobs, tasks, opportunities for labor in other sectors of the economy.

So, for example, when earlier on there was a discussion of robots and what was going on in Flint, Michigan, you know, that is absolutely central that there were a lot of production jobs that were eliminated.

The same has happened everywhere. If you look at South Korea, if you look at Germany, other countries that have introduced a lot of robots, production jobs were eliminated in more or less the same number as in the United States. But in many of these cases, there were also non-production jobs that were created more or less simultaneously, sometimes in the same companies, sometimes in the same markets, and that is what we haven't seen in the United States.

When you look at Flint, when you look at Saginaw or other parts of the industrial heartland, you have these production jobs disappearing, but we are not using the technology to create other jobs to compensate for this.

Mr. KHANNA. Very briefly, how would you create other jobs? What would be one or two bullets points of what we could have done in Flint to create those other jobs?

Dr. ACEMOGLU. Well, I think in Flint, you know, it is a little bit hard for me to say from here what exactly the skills that would be easily transferable. But when you look at broadly, you know, there are many applications of AI in education, in healthcare, in manufacturing that are completely capable of creating jobs.

For instance, automation in manufacturing also enables job creation because it reduces offshoring, so there is mounting evidence that, you know, not the jobs that were destroyed to trade with China or to the first wave of automation are not going to come back. But there are certainly opportunities for many jobs to come back, offshore jobs to come back as the automation process continues because it is a cost-saving possibility.

So many of those are not in the production line. They are in the supporting capacities. But they are very, very important and potentially high wage jobs. And, again, evidence from Germany suggests that many of the jobs that were created, even in the same companies that were automating at the same time, were paying higher wages or comparable wages to the production jobs that were destroyed.

Mr. KHANNA. Thank you.

Chairman YARMUTH. The gentleman's time has expired.

I now recognize the gentleman from Virginia, Mr. Scott, for five minutes.

Mr. SCOTT. Thank you, Mr. Chairman. I had to find it.

I am sorry, I came on a little late, so let me just ask a couple of general questions.

First, to any of the panelists, how real is the threat to laid off workers that their employers might decide to increase artificial intelligence rather than rehire their workers?

Chairman YARMUTH. Any takers?

Dr. ACEMOGLU. I can give a quick answer to that.

We don't know. We don't know for sure, but in recent surveys, about 75 percent of companies are saying that they are either taking steps to increase automation or they are planning to do so. So there is a real possibility that some of those jobs will not come back even if the economy picks up.

The other issue that we need to think about is that the sectoral composition of the economy is going to change in a post COVID–19 world. The hospitality sector will probably be much slower to come back, so there will be a natural reallocation.

Some of that reallocation is, obviously, healthy and efficient, but it will still have great costs on some of the poorer communities and some of the poorer segments of U.S. society.

So I think those are, as some of the earlier comments indicated, questions related to the social safety net; but broadly—and this has been one of the main themes that I have tried to emphasize—it is not just a social safety net issue. If we think that displacement is just a social safety net issue, that would mean that we would be happy to have a lot of workers being displaced and find ways of providing good social services and a decent standard of living to them.

But, again, I don't think that would be a healthy economy or a healthy society. That is why it is important for us to find ways of using our existing and technology know-how and our technological capabilities in order to find ways of deploying our enormously productive, our very well skilled workforce in other activities.

Thank you.

Mr. SCOTT. Let me ask you a followup question to that. If there are going to be fewer workers, does that have budget implications on your people having taxes and, therefore, lower revenues?

Dr. ACEMOGLU. Oh, I am glad you asked that. That is a very, very important question as well.

So if you—one of the themes that I emphasize is that our tax system is asymmetric. It taxes capital less than labor, and it has become more so. That has major budgetary implications because if you look at the U.S. distribution of income, the share of labor has gone down from around 67 percent of national income to less than 58 percent.

So that means that income is shifting away from the more heavily taxed factor to the more lightly taxed factor, and it will have budgetary implications.

And another theme that I have tried to emphasize, but it was very quick so this gives me an opportunity to underscore it one more time, is that part of the reason is because our capital tax base is very narrow.

It is not just a question of jacking tax rates on capital and introducing huge wealth taxes or anything like that. There is just a big chunk of capital income that we don't tax, and that means it is costly, it is asymmetric, it may distort the allocation of capital and labor in work places, but increasingly has major budgetary implications.

Thank you.

Mr. SCOTT. Does that include—you know, we have tax credits for investments in machines but not in education. Is that something we ought to address?

Dr. ACEMOGLU. Absolutely. Absolutely, 100 percent. If you look at decline in the tax rates basing capital that went from over 15 percent to less than 5 percent in the last 20 years, about half of that is because of the very generous investment tax credits, which are so generous that if you have debt financed capital investment in software or S corporations, you may actually be getting a small net subsidy. We have nothing similar to that for education or training.

Thank you.

Mr. SCOTT. Well, talking about education and training, to get into an AI job, you don't sign up for an education for AI. I heard math is important, but what should the Committee on Education and Labor be doing for higher education?

Dr. MATHENY. I can take a piece of this.

One thing that I think would be especially useful is a tithe, a 10 percent allocation for public research grants to go toward teaching because otherwise we are eating our seed corn. We are spending all of our Federal R&D on the research rather than on the teaching. And in most of the major universities where AI is being taught, there is a natural tension for the professors to focus on research as opposed to allocating time to teaching.

We need to make sure that we are training the next generation, and a tithe, particularly on NSF grants, could help with that, turning it over to others.

Mr. SCOTT. Well, thank you, Mr. Chairman. My time has expired.

Thank you so much.

Chairman YARMUTH. The gentleman's time has expired.

I now recognize the gentlewoman from Texas, Ms. Jackson Lee, for five minutes.

Ms. JACKSON LEE. Thank you very much, Mr. Chairman, and thank you very much for the hearing both with you and the Ranking Member, and thank you to the panelists.

Let me just add a description that should not be taken as an offense, but we are all speaking now to the have's because the have-not's are not in the room. And I think this is a very important basis upon which we are responding because that is the focus that I will have, along with maybe a more definitive question about a tax scheme that would work to help AI.

I am going to start with Dr. West, who early in his testimony mentioned the question of income inequality and worker dislocation. Those people today are not in the room. We, as Members of Congress, represent a wide landscape of individuals.

Can you pointedly, Dr. West, talk about what should be our response on the apparent and existing income inequality and the potential worker dislocation?

Dr. WEST. That is a great question, Congresswoman, and you are exactly right. There are income disparities. There are racial disparities. This is a huge problem. We are almost in a situation where technology is helping to fuel the inequality in the sense that the have's are doing better and getting tax breaks and have programs that support them, and people at the lower end aren't even in the game. They don't have access to the digital economy. There are 18 million Americans who do not have broadband. A larger number doesn't have a high-speed broadband.

So the way that we need to address these issues, certainly infrastructure investment, the things we have talked about earlier, a rural broadband, in underserved urban areas as well, putting more money into education, and especially opportunities for online education, because that would be a way to help overcome the disparities; but you need the broadband in order to be able to access that.

The same thing applies in terms of telemedicine. One of the features of COVID is it has jump started what already was in existence, a trend toward telemedicine, and has really accelerated it, but not everybody is able to share in the benefits of that. And given the racial disparities in the incidents and fatality rates of COVID, like that is a scandal that people who need it the most are not getting access.

So there are a lot of different things we need to do, and we certainly need to address the inequities in the tax system.

Ms. JACKSON LEE. Well, clearly, it means that out of the Budget Committee we should be focusing on just the infrastructure that you mentioned. It is a shame that in 2020 we are still fighting to get broadband everywhere, and for those of us who are watching our schools open and they are hybrid or virtual, to see people standing in line trying to simply get laptops because they don't even have that and as well hot spots or the hot boxes so they can have the opportunity to have access.

Let me do a round robin question dealing with COVID–19. We have heard a very stark admission of the knowledge of how deadly COVID–19 was as early as February 7, 2020, if I might. Let me ask all of you to comment how COVID–19 could have been attacked, if I might, starting with Dr. Athey and going to Dr. Matheny, with artificial intelligence in terms of treatment, in terms of outreach, in terms of saving lives.

Doctor—is it pronounced correctly, Dr. Athey?

Dr. ATHEY. Yes, Dr. Athey. Thank you very much for the question.

And I think the telemedicine point is super important. We were a little slow getting started in trying to get information to people, getting people in touch with their doctors without broadband access and without good access to medicine. We weren't always making good decisions for patients early.

Another thing is that actually using AI machine learning to understand what treatments work best was actually very limited in the United States by our disjointed medical system and the inability to do analysis that incorporates data from multiple sources because, as the epidemic happened, patients were being treated in hospitals. The insurance companies only get the data later once bills have gone out, and that is not fast enough.

So it turned out that we were just unprepared to be able to do analysis that spanned multiple medical centers and give real-time intelligence. We also missed opportunities to have a more coordinated approach to clinical trials and R&D that was really focused on getting the most information and the best treatment decisions possible given the patient flow that we had. There was just a lack of coordination.

And I really hope that if anything like this ever happens again, we are prepared to be able to do the right analysis and coordinate the studies and the research, and that just requires really advanced preparedness and a lot of kind of air traffic control from the federal government. And AI machine learning can only do their work if they are given the opportunity to access data and really influence decisions.

Thank you.

Chairman YARMUTH. OK. The gentlewoman's time has expired.

I now recognize the gentleman from New Jersey, Mr. Sires, for five minutes.

Mr. SIRES. Thank you, Mr. Chairman. Can you hear me? Chairman YARMUTH. I can hear you fine, yes.

Mr. SIRES. I want to thank the panelists for being here today. You know, I always think of a job as something that creates self-worth in a person, and we seem to be obsessed with this productivity word and, obviously, artificial intelligence creates a lot of productivity. But you have countries like China and you have countries like India who have such large populations, and as artificial intelligence is more productive, more and more people are left behind.

Do you think that these countries with such large population will ever come to a point and they say, OK, artificial intelligence is great, but we have passed beyond the ability to provide jobs for the people of my country. Maybe we should slow down this artificial intelligence that is creating so much automation and leaving, so many people behind because, as you know, if there is no work in a country, it leads to unrest.

I just wonder if any of the panelists would want to address that where a country would say, hey, let's put a little brakes on this because our population is staying behind, is being left behind.

Can anybody talk to that a little bit?

Dr. ACEMOGLU. I would be happy to. I would be happy to comment on that.

Mr. SIRES. OK.

Dr. ACEMOGLU. You know, I think, first of all, I completely agree a job is much more than just productivity. I think self-worth is important for the community, important for society. I think these are critical. But the tragedy in some sense is that, at least on the current measurements, we are not even doing that well on productivity. Despite the bewildering array of technologies all around us and all of this excitement that goes on, we are actually enduring one of the eras in our history where productivity growth is lowest. This goes to underscore what I was trying to emphasize, that it is not a question of AI versus not AI. It is a question of how we are using AI technology. And if we are not using it well, we would destroy jobs and all of the self-worth and community contributions that we are talking about and also not reap all of the benefits in terms of productivity.

I think that is exactly the sort of situation that we are in right now, so a lot of AI goes into marginal activities, such as self-check- out kiosks or things that humans can do very well, then it will not bring the productivity gain. I don't think that China is ever going to turn back from AI, partly because they have made a huge investment in that, but also because part of the AI's appeal to authoritarian regimes is that it actually provides a much better monitoring system, facial recognition, snooping on communications, control of the internet. But those are exactly the sorts of things that are not going to bring huge productivity gains and they are not going to contribute to making jobs more meaningful.

But if you look at what American companies invest in, it is not that different. We pour a lot of money into facial recognition andmonitoring aspects of AI as well. So that, again, goes to my broader point, that I think there are ways of making use of the AI platforms in a manner that is going to bring much better social benefits and jobs and productivity than we are doing currently.

Mr. SIRES. So the productivity to work ratio for the United States is 6:1, as somebody mentioned before, and in China it is 1:1. So I was just wondering, if China does not want a 6:1 or an 8:1 productivity ratio.

Dr. ACEMOGLU. I would say China definitely wants that and has made huge progress——

Mr. SIRES. But doesn't that leave a lot of people behind? I mean——

Dr. ACEMOGLU. Right. So——

Mr. SIRES. If you reach that kind of productivity like in the United States?

Dr. ACEMOGLU. Well, it may or may not. If consumption keeps up with it and that productivity gain is broadly distributed in society, it may not. In China, it hasn't taken that form. The inequality has actually increased a lot, the gap between cities and rural areas and even within cities between migrant workers and non-migrant workers have opened up hugely.

But, sure, I think there is a huge drive in China toward increasing labor productivity, but they are also willing to invest an enormous amount of resources in order to monitor these workers better, in order to monitor their communications, the civil society participation, and other social activities, even if those things aren't proactive because they do need to maintain the current political system.

Thank you.

Mr. SIRES. Thank you. Thank you, Chairman.

Chairman YARMUTH. The gentlemen's time has expired.

I now recognize the Ranking Member, Mr. Womack, from Arkansas for 10 minutes.

Mr. WOMACK. Thank you, Mr. Chairman, and thanks to all of my colleagues who have participated, and to the witnesses, thank you very much. A very interesting discussion.

I am going to start where I kind of left off in my opening remarks, and that was about matters of fiscal accountability at the federal level, and I don't need to tell anybody engaged in this forum this afternoon that we are in some very difficult circumstances right now.

COVID has exacerbated it three times more so than what we would have otherwise had in terms of a deficit goes.

And to my colleagues on this call today, I will sound a bit like a broken record. I am an appropriator by nature. I just happen to be the Ranking Member of the Committee and formally Chaired the Committee.

But as an appropriator, I am very concerned about the escalating cost associated with mandatory spending, how much of the federal budget it is commanding and the squeeze, as I call it, that crowding out effect that it is having on the matters of the discretionary budget that we appropriators are in charge of, should be in charge of—the last few years is an exception, but that is a whole other story.

Mr. WOMACK. But the fact is, that if we are going to invest in anything in our country, if we are going to ask the federal government to have a role in resourcing a lot of this R&D, then it is going to face continued and escalating pressure from the mandatory outlays that continue to consume a larger and larger share of federal resources.

So here is my question and I am going to pose this to Dr. Matheny, and that is, with that in mind, if we can all agree that there is this crowding out effect, how would the federal government prioritize spending on matters of research and development and so forth in the AI spectrum?

And what have you seen from your federal government, if anything, that is worked? So help me understand how we would prioritize the spending that goes toward a more robust AI circumstance in our country?

Dr. MATHENY. Thank you. It is a great question.

I think that the federal government can most cost effectively focus on basic research, on testing and evaluation, and on safety and security, areas that suffer market failures so that the commercial sector is likely to under invest.

Much of the current wave of AI research that we see right now is due to federal investments in basic research, particularly by the National Science Foundation and by the Office of Naval Research, and DARPA, dating back to the mid–1980's, which funded early work on deep learning, provided training grants to much of the current generation of AI researchers.

And that work in basic research really does need to continue so that we fund the next generation of breakthroughs that will fuel future AI systems. Equally important is the work of the National Institute of Standards and Technology in its bench marking and its testing and evaluation that has been critical for actors in both the private sector and the public sector to be able to bring their tools to have them tested on a level playing field, understand where they work and where they break. And just as important also has been the federal government's investments in microelectronics.

In the 1960's, NASA effectively started our microelectronics industry, but we also have examples of less successful programs, very large projects, overly broad goals. I think the Strategic Computing Initiative which ran from the mid–1980's to the mid–1990's is an example of that.

So where the government can help is really on the cases where the commercial sector isn't going to invest on its own, where the goals, though, can be clearly defined, and where we can lift up and address those market failures.

Thank you.

Mr. WOMACK. You bet.

Dr. Acemoglu, am I even close on the name? OK. Good. Thanks for the thumbs up.

And Mr. Sires reiterated the point you made—I think it was you that made the point early on in your testimony—that China had 11 times as many people in the workforce, but they were only two times as productive. If the American worker has proven to be the most productive worker, I guess, on the planet says a lot about our ability and about our capacity.

One of my concerns has been is that the pace of the private sector in virtually every area is a lot faster than our education system seems to be trying to deliver.

Is that a fair statement?

Dr. ACEMOGLU. Yes, I believe so. I think it is definitely true that our education system has lagged behind. AI, for all the reasons that we have discussed today, has already started changing the labor market and it will change it even more, but our education system, both at the university level but also at middle school and high school level, is very backward looking.

We continue to teach in the way that we used to, you know, for the most part, 30, 40, 50, 60 years ago. AI actually provides—I think Susan mentioned this already—provides tremendous opportunities for revolutionizing many of the key sectors such as healthcare and education.

AI can be used for taking over some of the tasks that educators do that are quite boring, such as grading, but even more importantly, it can create a much more interactive classroom, enable teachers to understand the specific challenges and needs of students and cater their teaching and curriculum to their needs in real-time. It can enrich what we teach and how we teach it. There are already companies that have completely transformed their training systems using AI.

So I think there are a lot of opportunities, but sure, we are lagging behind. And it is absolutely critical, as you have pointed out, for our success that the American worker maintains their productivity edge over other nations, but we have not done very well in that regard either.

If you look at an inclusive measure of productivity growth, what the economists called total factor productivity growth, in the three or so decades following World War II that was growing over 2 and a half percent a year and it is around 1 percent for the last 20 years.

So we are not really doing enough to keep our productivity edge relative to other nations, many of whom have faster productivity growth rates.

Mr. WOMACK. Mr. Chairman, my final question—and I am going to throw this on the table. I don't know really who to direct it to, but we have seen some challenges in recent years of building government industry partnerships in what is to me even more disconcerting is a lot of the companies that we are talking about are now not only not building those partnerships, but they are just unwilling to work with the federal government or work with, you know, partner nations or you can pick from the spectrum of issues. Just last year, Google pulled out of a major AI project called Project Maven with the Department of Defense. It is my strong opinion that we need to see some change in this area.

Why is this occurring and what are the long-term consequences of not having the proper relationships between government and industry? And is it the slow pace of government in general because we all know that we don't operate with a lot of speed?

Dr. WEST. And Congressman, I would be happy to jump in on that question. And I agree, it is important for a government to work with industry. I think the Google thing, there was some idiosyncrasies to that decision. Other tech companies are embracing the role of working with the federal government, but I do think, as part of your concern about debt and deficit issues, we do need to think about agency modernization just because we have to get the federal government acting much more efficiently than it is right now just in terms of the administration of services.

And the way to cut some of the program costs without hurting the beneficiaries is to make the organization more effective. And so the public sector still lags the private sector in using AI.

Just one quick example, every federal agency should be using AI for fraud detection. It is something that is very common in private companies. We know there is waste and fraud in the federal government. The AI looks for outliers, it looks for unusual activities. Like, this is one tool the federal government agencies should be using to try and get a better handle on the spending side. I think that is an example of where technology can be part of the solution. Mr. WOMACK. Yes. And in the budget when I was Chairman that we prepared for Fiscal Year 2019, a key component of trying to do the deficit reduction was the fact that we had billions and billions of dollars of improper payments and there has to be a way that we can get after those without unnecessarily burdening ourselves.

Anyway, my time is expired. Thanks, again, to all the panelists. Thanks to my colleagues. Chris, welcome, again, to the Budget Committee.

And Mr. Chairman, as always, I am going to yield back my time and with regrets that you didn't get to see Authentic win the race there on your home track, but nonetheless a good derby.

Chairman YARMUTH. I thank the Ranking Member. I did watch it on television. Fortunately, I tried to set up a betting account and they were so swamped with people trying to do that I couldn't get on, so I didn't lose anything. That was a plus.

Mr. WOMACK. Well, AI, if we had a little better AI platform, we could have probably fixed that early on.

Chairman YARMUTH. Probably so. Thank you for that. And I yield myself 10 minutes for my questions.

Once again, thanks to all the witnesses. It has been an extremely enlightening conversation and I think a very valuable one.

I am going to kind of segue off where the Ranking Member was because we spend most of the hearing talking about impact on jobs and I think that is kind of the natural topic and how that might impact tax revenues and so forth, but we really didn't focus much on how AI might help reduce expenses for the government.

And I can see—I think Dr. Athey you mentioned telemedicine and I think there is a lot of potential as you mentioned for reducing costs in Medicaid, transportation costs, as well as probably getting better diagnoses and drug interactions and so forth. I think there is a lot of possibilities there.

Where might be some other areas in which there actually could be a positive impact of AI on expenses for the government?

Dr. ATHEY. Thank you for that question, Chairman, and I think that really does pick up from the Ranking Member's comments as well that government can be much more efficient than it is.

Now, I would have actually been pretty scared 10 or 15 years ago to suggest governments invest more in IT because IT's projects are—often fail in private sector, frankly, and when governments take them out, we have a lot of problems with procurement of large IT projects, but one of the things that I think has been really impactful in how AI and machine learning have been diffusing through the economy in the last few years is the way in which IT services delivers has changed.

We are having more software as a service, we are having more cloud computing, so that you don't have to say take on this huge project which has huge risk and then you are kind of locked into a software for the next

20 years, but rather you are getting services that meet your needs that are updated automatically and where a lot of R&D can be centralized and focused on use cases.

So I do believe that it is a good time to start thinking about modernizing the federal government infrastructure. And then alongside of that, in these very common AI applications like fraud detection was mentioned, also security. Cybersecurity is a huge problem and, again, because of its antiquated infrastructure, the federal government and all of its employees are vulnerable.

And so if we can start modernizing and we can put in best practices, we can deliver services more efficiently and effectively.

Now, I also want to pick up on another comment that you made, which we really didn't talk enough about today, I think, which is that, you know, when labor is used as an input, then that is affecting the cost of a product.

Daron and I have both mentioned that there are some cases where the worker and the machine are sort of creating similar cost structures, but there are other settings where investments can really lower the marginal costs of providing services, as well as the marginal costs of receiving services.

And actually, especially for state and local governments, that is very true. We—people are standing in line and wasting their time and taking off of work to get needs met and a person is sitting behind the counter doing something where all of this would just be so much faster and better if you could just get—do it electronically and get your needs met.

And so while that loses a piece of employment for the worker sitting behind the counter, maybe there is other things that your government could be doing—more childcare, more elder care, you know. There are other services that are under provided where those human workers could be better deployed if we use technology to do things where the human time is getting wasted on both sides of the table.

Chairman YARMUTH. I appreciate that.

And I think, even though, we are focused—we are the U.S. Congress, we are focused on the federal budget, we also need to think about impacts on state and local budgets. These are all tax dollars and we do have a federal system.

As I said before the hearing started off the air that this is something I have been planning to do for about a year and a half now.

And when people would come to my office, different groups would come to my office when they were still doing that, I would invariably ask them at the end of the meeting, what impact artificial intelligence is having on their profession or their activity?

And I never forget, I had the Kentucky CPAs in the office and they were there to lobby about tax policy, which is understandable. At the end of the meeting I asked them, in your professional meetings, do you ever talk about artificial intelligence? And their eyes all opened wide and they said, that is the number one topic at all of our meetings because they see a dramatic reduction in the need for accountants because of artificial intelligence.

I had the War College—people from the War College in my office. I asked them that, and one high-ranking soldier said, we don't think that there will ever be a battlefield decision made by a human being again. And I am sure he was exaggerating somewhat, but the idea was that AI can consider all the hundreds, if not more, variables that would go into a decision as to when or where to stage a military action.

And so particularly, you know, I talked to IBM people and they say Watson, at least in their analysis, can now do 70 percent of what lawyers do with greater accuracy. They can read MRIs. Watson can read MRIs and CT scans more accurately than radiologists can.

All of these things—meaning to say, the impact is not necessarily just going to be on the routine type of jobs; that there are going to be some very high level jobs that are going to be changed or eliminated, many cases, which connects me back to the education issue, that when you look at professional jobs that require years and years and years of education and hundreds of thousand dollars' worth of tuition and you are seeing the possibility that those jobs might be eliminated, how do you think this is going to change the future of even professional education?

Dr. West, you want to try that one.

Dr. WEST. I think you are right. It certainly is not just entry level jobs that are going to be affected by AI and automation, but higher level jobs, including the example you gave of radiologists. Accountants should be worried. They are exactly right because there is a lot of really good finance AI that is out there. Financial advisers, the same thing.

So I do think that we need to keep our eye on the education process. When I talk to young people today, I tell them one of the most important skills they need to develop is adaptability because they are going to face such a changing economy, a changing workforce, and changing job needs and job skill needs that whatever knowledge and skill they have at age 21 when they are graduating from college, it is probably going to be completely inadequate 10 years later. It is certainly going to be inadequate 20 and 30 years later. So they are going to need to constantly upgrade their job skills. It is the reason, in my testimony I talked about lifelong learning.

I think the adult education aspect is going to end up being as big as higher education today, so the education component is very important.

Chairman YARMUTH. I am glad you said that. It is exactly what I tell students when I talk to them, too. You are going to have to be adaptable. It is the number one talent.

I promised Mr. Woodall, Dr. Acemoglu, that I would let you answer—he asked about companies, corporations that are doing the right thing. So in the time I have left, do you want to expand on those that are good examples for us?

Dr. ACEMOGLU. Sure. I think—let me say two things.

One is in answer to Congressman Woodall's question, but before I do that, I want to sort of build on what Dr. West has said. I think adaptability is extremely important and it is going to become more important.

But I also think that there is a lot of uncertainty about which types of jobs AI is going to be more threatening to and there is some disagreement, but if you look at the current users of AI, which are still sort of limited, they are still more geared toward more low-paying jobs.

And part of the reason for that is because when you look at higher paying jobs, they involve a variety of tasks and only some subset of those tasks can be automated. And when the rest aren't, then the adaptable workers especially benefit a lot.

So I expect AI technology in whatever direction it goes to add to our concerns about inequality. So that I think is a very important thing.

When it comes to which companies are using AI—I think, you know, there are many companies in Silicon Valley that are using AI in extremely creative ways. I think the problem is that some of those are not very, very good when they look—when you take their social implications into account.

So, for instance, I think you can use AI as a sort of, niche industry right now, but there are a couple of companies that are working on using AI for doing test grading. That is going to be a growth industry, and I think it is going to be very, very useful. But there are many fewer of them that are using AI technology for creating more adaptable classrooms.

There are a few, but I would say that is one area that is actually very promising, but because of the complexity of the question, I think one of the concerns is that, when I have talked to some of those companies, they think that their technology would not get a hold in many school districts because it would involve hiring more skilled teachers and school districts are not going to have the resources or the interest in doing that.

So I think there is sort of a chicken and egg problem. There is a lot of creativity that could be put to use AI in very new and inspiring ways, but we may not have the infrastructure to support that completely yet.

Thank you.

Chairman YARMUTH. All right. Well, thank you very much, and my time is expired.

So as we close, let me, once again, thank all of you witnesses for your time and your wisdom and knowledge, and all the Members for participating.

And if there is no further business, this meeting is adjourned. [Whereupon, at 3:25 p.m., the Committee was adjourned.]

SHEILA JACKSON LEE

WASHINGTON OFFICE:

Congress of the United States
House of Representatives
Washington, DC 20515

JUDICIARY

HOMELAND SECURITY

FOREIGN AFFAIRS

DEMOCRATIC CAUCUS

CONGRESSWOMAN SHEILA JACKSON LEE OF TEXAS

HEARING STATEMENT:

"MACHINES, ARTIFICIAL INTELLIGENCE, & THE WORKFORCE: RECOVERING & READYING OUR ECONOMY FOR THE FUTURE"

COMMITTEE ON THE BUDGET
WEBEX
SEPTEMBER 10, 2020
1:00 P.M. EDT

- Thank you Chairman Yarmuth and Ranking Member Womack for convening this critical hearing on the subject of artificial intelligence and its effects on the economy, labor markets, income inequality, as well as implications for federal policy and the budget.

- Let me welcome our witnesses:
    - Susan Athey, Ph.D.
      Economics of Technology Professor, Stanford Graduate School of Business;

Associate Director, Stanford Institute for Human-Centered Artificial Intelligence

- Daron Acemoglu, Ph.D.
  Institute Professor of Economics, Massachusetts Institute of Technology

- Darrell West, Ph.D.
  Vice President and Director of Governance Studies, Brookings Institution

- Jason Matheny, Ph.D.
  Founding Director, Center for Security and Emerging Technology, Georgetown University;
  Commissioner, National Security Commission on AI

- Mr. Chairman, it has been over six months since the United States diagnosed its first case of the coronavirus, and, yet, we are still struggling to contain this virus.

- As more and more cities and states across the country are labeled as hotspots for the virus, the American people are losing confidence in our ability to guide the country's return to normalcy.

- As of this morning, there were 6,363,437 cases of coronavirus and over 190,885 related deaths in the United States alone.

- In the state of Texas, there are over 675,000 cases and the death toll is over 13,980 individuals.

- Harris County, which encompasses my district, has reported over 113,000 cases and 2,363 deaths.

- Throughout this pandemic, artificial intelligence has become an essential tool in understanding, treating, and facilitating recovery from the coronavirus through vaccine development, patient screening, and outbreak detection and surveillance.

- Although the term "artificial intelligence" may conjure images of sentient, self-aware machines, current AI technologies are systems that learn from data to identify patterns, improve predictive capability, and guide decisions.

- This incredible feat of modern innovation has the potential to not only help us get control over this pandemic but also boost the economy by driving productivity growth in the long run.

- In fact, in 2020, worldwide revenues for the AI market are expected to total more than $150 billion, but AI could generate up to $13 trillion in economic activity by 2030, which is equivalent to 1.2 percent additional GDP growth per year.

- While these figures are encouraging, it is imperative that we always look at both sides to an issue.

- Like previous disruptors, increased implementation of AI technology is likely to cause significant workforce changes, especially to low- and middle-wage jobs in sectors like manufacturing, accounting, transportation, retailing, and food services.

- As a result, Black and Latino Americans, who fill a large share of these positions, are disproportionately at risk of job and wage losses.

- Even before the COVID-19 pandemic slowed our economy, many workers had already struggled to compete against automation and technological advancement to find stable, well-paying jobs or advance their careers.

- And now, as companies accelerate their investments in AI-enabled automation during the pandemic, many Americans fear that the jobs they left in March could be eliminated permanently.

- The American people are looking to Congress for guidance in this time of chaos and uncertainty.

- It is imperative that we find a way forward that leverages the benefits of AI innovation while also protecting the American workforce, especially the marginalized communities that face the largest risk of job replacement.

- This pandemic and current economic crisis have already highlighted the stark disparities and barriers that low-income and people of color face every day.

- It has also shown us that income security and related programs are crucial for supporting low-income Americans and others in times of need.

- Without federal action, the continuation of AI reliance will exacerbate the trends of declining job security and labor force participation, and growing income inequality.

- Congress must commit to federal policies that focus on reskilling and upskilling our workforce in addition to requiring new approaches and federal support for training, education, apprenticeship, and credential partnerships, especially for mid-career workers who will still need to provide for themselves and their families as they learn new skills in this transition period.

- And so, I urge my fellow Members of this Committee as well as other Members of Congress to come together and create a dynamic, strategic plan of federal support that not only encourages technological innovation but also creates educational and training initiatives as well as opportunities for job creation so that no workers are left behind.

- We must act now.

- The world is changing rapidly, but we cannot let fear and uncertainty of the future keep us from moving forward.

- The American people have endured challenge after challenge, and we have always prevailed.

- This will be no different.

- As we seek to revitalize the economy in the aftermath of the pandemic, we must ensure that the implementation of AI and new technologies lead to inclusive economic growth and broad societal benefit.

- Thank you, Mr. Chairman, for convening this important hearing, and I look forward to hearing from our witnesses.

INDEX

A

B

C

I

J

L

P

Q

R

U

V

W

Y